Stating the Sacred

Stating the Sacred

Religion, China, and
the Formation of
the Nation-State

Michael J. Walsh

Columbia University Press   *New York*

Columbia University Press
Publishers Since 1893
New York   Chichester, West Sussex
cup.columbia.edu
Copyright © 2020 Columbia University Press

Library of Congress Cataloging-in-Publication Data

Names: Walsh, Michael J. (Michael John), 1968– author.
Title: Stating the sacred : religion, China, and the formation of the nation-state /
Michael J. Walsh.
Description: New York : Columbia University Press, 2020. |
Includes bibliographical references and index.
Identifiers: LCCN 2019023904 (print) | LCCN 2019023905 (ebook) |
ISBN 9780231193566 (cloth) | ISBN 9780231193573 (paperback) |
ISBN 9780231550390 (ebook)
Subjects: LCSH: Civil religion—China. | Religion and state—China. |
Citizenship—China. | National characteristics, Chinese. | Nation-state
Classification: LCC BL1803 .W25 2020 (print) | LCC BL1803 (ebook) |
DDC 322/.10951—dc23
LC record available at https://lccn.loc.gov/2019023904
LC ebook record available at https://lccn.loc.gov/2019023905

Cover image: plainpicture/bobsairport

Cover design: Lisa Hamm

For Lioba

Contents

Preface

In 1989 the campus at the University of Cape Town was a space of violence. As students protesting the apartheid regime, we faced regular clashes with the police, our ears and bodies threatened by the sound of bullhorns, shotguns, tear gas, and *sjamboks*.[1] On the streets, in the cities, the police began using a special purple dye fired through water cannons. It stained the skin for days. They could then arrest and detain at will. South Africa's own purple rain.

No amount of purple could erase the black, brown, and white skins on their return to campus. The state was dying, and we wanted a fiery revolution that could eradicate a history. Nelson Mandela had a different plan. "You have five minutes to disperse!" yelled the policeman through his megaphone. And we did feel dispersed. We would read in the newspapers the number of people killed in the townships the day before, then go to our next class. At first the dead numbered in the hundreds and then the thousands. Black smoke from burning tires filled the township horizons. Time to picket the main freeway that snaked below the university campus, making its way into downtown Cape Town.

We would attend a political rally, then attend to our studies. Yet we did not know at the time that apartheid was falling apart;

that the violence we were witnessing was the final crescendo at the end of a fireworks display. A state was coming to an end, and a new nation was going to have to be imagined. *"Amandla!"* (power) was the call for resistance. *"Awethu!"* (power to us) was always the reply.

I took a seminar and an independent study that year that helped me think about the state we were in, about politics and the sacred, violence and Christianity. (The apartheid government spoke with a God on its side. The rhetoric of a "chosen" white race and divinely bestowed sacred land went hand in hand.) The seminar was with David Chidester, who introduced me to the interdisciplinary endeavor of religious studies. I sat in his office one afternoon, pointed at his bookshelves, and asked him what my students now ask me: "Have you really read all these books?" He said he had and then grabbed one book—Mary Douglas's *Purity and Danger*—and told me to read it immediately.

What a remarkable study! It clarified for me the role of ritual in demarcating boundaries between what an individual or a group of people might consider pure and what they consider polluted. It gave me a sense of how social space could be purified through ritual, constructed, and fought over. It offered me a methodological lens to help focus the way I think about apartheid South Africa, the United States, and now China. It allowed me to think about how a state needed to produce itself and the violence required to do so. It helped me better understand the "purification process," or better yet, the sanctification process that the South African apartheid state undertook for decades, all predicated, however irrationally, on a covenant with a biblical God at a battle called Blood River on the morning of December 16, 1838.[2] The Afrikaners won that battle, having killed thousands of Zulu warriors, and understood that in their victory their God had awarded them the land on which they fought.[3] This was to be their sacred territory, cleansed of those less than human, or later, in apartheid government language, cleansed of those who were "nonwhite." Douglas also helped me understand a singular, extreme reenactment of this event.

Exactly 150 years after the battle, Barend Hendrik Strydom walked around downtown Pretoria in November 1988 shooting any black person he could see. By the time he was apprehended he had killed eight people and wounded fifteen others.[4] Strydom understood his actions to be a "type of war."[5] In 1992 he said: "It is only by expanding the white race that we can counter the numerical dominance of blacks. I did not murder out of hate for the enemy but out of love for my people. My victims were not necessarily innocent people. These are the people who today are trying to take over my country."[6] In Douglesian language, Strydom was sacrificing his victims to ritually purify what he understood to be a polluted space—a territorial (land) and imagined (nation) space of whiteness that was incoherently inhabited by blackness. Strydom understood himself in his own words to be a white freedom fighter protecting his race and religion, his people and fatherland (*volk en vaderland*), the territory he believed was God-given.[7] That way territory can be claimed, its inhabitants can be named, and control of its people and resources can be maintained. Only then can it be called sovereign space.

This logic forms part of an inviolate, cruel core of nationstatism. It is a *theos* that allows, and indeed compels, Strydom to walk through Pretoria shooting black South Africans. He felt he had the right to reclaim what he understood to be his territory, his God-given right to the land.

The apartheid regime always understood that its territory was awarded to it by God. It was sacred land to do with as the regime pleased. It was part of the mythological narrative, the same narrative that explained the regime's purported racial superiority. Strydom, citizen of a proclaimed white race, had sought to defend the purity of the state's territory. Race, territory, religion, and citizenship—signatures of the nation-state—were at the heart of his identity and actions.

◼◼◼◼

My independent study was with Jan Hofmeyr. He introduced me to the readings of Confucius, Mencius, and Laozi. Jannie had recently returned from a trip to the United States, and one of the books he brought back with him was Benjamin Schwartz's *The World of Thought in Ancient China*. Nothing could have been farther from the reality we were living in at the time, and yet that's the book we read together, along with primary texts in translation.

As we read that June about ancient China, we watched a contemporary China with more than a million of its students pouring into Tian'anmen Square. A man stood alone in front of a tank. No one will tell us how many died.[8] Three Junes later I stood in Tian'anmen Square trying to imagine the parallels between two repressive regimes.[9] In Tian'anmen, citizens tried to reclaim the public space to express their imaginings of a new democracy. Theirs was to be a new social formation, the opposite of the ones imposed on them by the state. The state cleared that space with tanks and guns, reinserting itself into the heart of Han Chinese identity construction. A citizen of China was supposed to serve the state, and the state was to protect the nation and the Han ideas that formed it. Little did I know that the politics of violence is the way of the world, and that the nation-state is both a producer and product of this: thank you, Max Weber.[10] Tracing a line back to 1839 with the first Opium War, the Tian'anmen Square protests in 1989 became a pivotal moment in China's historical narrative that marked the start of its current form of maximalist nationalism. A new state came into being.

Years later, sitting in my living room in the United States at 8 pm on August 8, 2008, I watched on television a countdown in Beijing led by 2,008 drummers who welcomed and presented China to the world.[11] The twenty-ninth Olympiad had begun. It was as if China was born anew, declaring to the world's nation-states that its nation-state had definitively arrived at the center of the world's stage. The center—China's literal name is Zhong-guo, the central territory—was where China had been for millennia, but two nineteenth-century Opium Wars, various rebellions, and the colonization of the east coast interrupted that.

But back in 2008, for many Chinese, especially Han, the Beijing Olympics were a clear sign to the rest of the world that their country had come full circle, from once the world's most powerful imperium, to more than a century of subjugation, back to being one of the strongest economies and global players on the planet. The Chinese Communist Party (CCP) offered the world's citizens and, more important, its own citizenry a new modernity and in so doing generated a nationalistic self-awareness that China is a world power. With almost two centuries of second-class status erased—a perennial narrative deployed by the CCP—China had seemingly restructured the order of things and was nearing the Confucian goal of a harmonious (*he*) state (*guo*).[12] The Beijing Olympics showcased this new modernity with Chinese characteristics.

To be "modern" is a statement of self-affirmation. It is the ultimate claim of victory made by the nation-state. China showed us this in 2008. What type of "modern" was presented at the Beijing Olympics? What ultimately makes China modern? Is China's modernity now self-evident?[13] Historian Peter Zarrow points out that scholars since the 1920s have usually focused on the May Fourth period (1919) as the beginning of a Chinese modernity.[14] This time period, however, is not self-evident. Arjun Appadurai helps us with his statement: "Whatever else the project of the Enlightenment may have created, it aspired to create persons who would, after the fact, have wished to become modern."[15] With modernity, whenever and however we posit its origins, comes nation-state building, and within that violent process we see existential questions being addressed: What does it mean to be a human being? Are we simply political creatures seeking power and sustenance in equal force? Are we just cultural products that require constant nurturing? What role should the state have in our daily lives? To what extent should the state govern our daily lives? These are universal questions that play out differently in different contexts. Consequently, we might wish to speak of Chinese modernities, in plural form. The 2008 Beijing Olympics were one of these.

The Beijing Olympics were a spectacular affair and a meticulously constructed narrative.[16] Throughout we witnessed the greatness of Chinese culture and history without rupture, as history can never actually be. The events of 1989 were erased once again. We saw a sustained expression of nationalistic pride when fifty-six children entered the stadium representing the so-called fifty-six ethnic groups of China. They were smiling. They carried an enormous Chinese flag, which they handed over to eight soldiers. The children of China ("the people") gave themselves over to the state, that formless entity that claims to protect and care for all forms. This entity, this social formation, is a state that stunts the imagination and produces biopolitical citizens.

At the 2008 Olympics, games without frontiers, the message was clear: only the state, the "motherland" (*zuguo*), can guarantee the future of those fifty-six children and those fifty-six ethnic groups.[17] The state is Han Chinese, the largest of those ethnic groups and the first among equals. The flag was raised with soldiers standing all around the flagpole, the totemic signifier of sovereignty and the *axis mundi* connecting Heaven (*tian*) and all affairs "under" it (*tianxia*).[18] All joined in to sing the national anthem, "March of the Volunteers."

Those fifty-six ethnic groups were forged into a single social body, and a nationalistic ideology was openly expressed. This ideology became a cultural production, an aesthetic in the hands of filmmaker and overall artistic director of the opening ceremony Zhang Yimou. At the ceremony a grand mythological narrative was deployed. Yet another new state came into being. Like all successful mythologies, the narrative was saturated with quasi-historical data, creation stories, strategic ideologies, psychical signifiers, and selective memory.[19] If the games were a celebration of Chinese citizenry and their newfound place in the world, they were also a celebration of China's territory, what the Chinese constitution refers to as "sacred territory."[20] The Beijing Olympics, as a microcosm of China and China's history, were a sacralization of space and time, a mythological production narrated to the world.[21]

The Argument

The central tenet of this book is that nation-states, with their claims to modernity, are the results of mythos and sanctified violence. For all their positive attributes, nation-statism perpetuates a systemic form of terror. Why do nation-states of all types defend their borders through a violence that is seen as sacred? What is common to apartheid and China's postcoloniality is the sacredness of the violence, notwithstanding their different imaginations (better and worse) of community. Nation-states are always religious states, and their territory is sacred and exclusively inclusive. The nation-state demands and expects always to be sacrificed to, celebrated, consecrated, worshipped, and sanctified.[22] By religious I mean that nation-states inhabit *relegere*, the attention paid to the meticulousness of ritual activity and the precision of sacrifice.[23] Apartheid South Africa was a religious state. China, despite the Communist Party's claims to the contrary, is a religious state. It is a religious state because it is a nation-state, that birth-child (*nascere*) of modernity which took its gods and moved them elsewhere, only to leave their shadows behind.

I am reminded of Hans Christian Andersen's tale about a learned scholar who loses his shadow in Africa. After going back to Europe, he awakens one morning to discover his shadow has returned. Over time he comes to realize the treacheries that his shadow will commit. He, the scholar, will eventually be executed. His shadow is not exactly what it appears to be, and morality is up for grabs. For me the nation-state is like that shadow. It is never exactly what it appears to be, it is morally suspect, and its inherent treachery is hallowed in sanctified violence and terror. As Andersen writes, "The shadow was master now, and the master became the shadow."

Of course, nation, state, and sovereignty have been considered and reconsidered by Hobbes, Schmitt, Anderson, Arendt, Spivak, Butler, Gellner, Agamben, and many more. The nation-state is the social formation within which we all live, and yet the nation-state as idea and form has not solved many of the problems for which it was ostensibly the panacea. Why, then, is it still the dominant mode of human organization? Has it no expiration date? Do its citizens cling to it because of the soteriological promise it holds out to them? The paradox, unfortunately, is that this social formation, looked toward expectantly for solutions, is itself part of the problem. To create nations and states, to produce, maintain, and sustain a nation-state, requires a stunning degree of systemic violence and blood sacrifice. Thus morality is always questionable when it comes to the imperatives of the state. The shadows need to be exposed. I fear I cannot expose them all in this short book, but a few can be drawn out.

Within the mechanics of the nation-state there is a structural connection between texts (constitutions, legal codes, national histories), ostensibly universal and normative categories (race, religion, citizen, freedom, human rights), and territoriality (the integrity of sovereignty and the claim and control over resources and people). These are three foundational components of the nation-state, but a fourth, I argue, binds them together: the sacred. Or, more accurately, a process of sacralization. In apartheid South Africa, God was said to justify the violent sacralization of space. In imperial China, the gods inhabited territory that humans needed to sacralize in order to reside in it. In Mao Zedong's China, the gods had to be eliminated (though the sacred remained). They have since returned, forcing the Chinese Communist Party to navigate what today it still calls "the religious question."

When territory, a text, bare life, or an idea is rendered as sacred, it becomes inviolate, and it is the inviolate that frames and sustains the nation-state. The inviolate references the ineffable, as in a claimed legitimacy beyond the scope of discourse. It is the inviolate that is used to justify territorial integrity and state sovereignty. It is also the inviolate that shapes citizens of the state and makes them members of the nation. The inviolate stipulates that there will be horrific consequences if trifled with. The inviolate is part of the sacred wrath the nation-state can bestow on its own citizenry and other states. Better understanding the production of the inviolate is at the core of *Stating the Sacred*.

To claim sacrality, or to label something as sacred, something that nation-states do all the time, is to render that thing or phenomenon as inviolate and to tie oneself to the gods.[24] Modern states, much like ancient Rome, must have the shadows of their old gods front and center—even if they are to be invisible to the public eye—for it is only by so doing that the real work of the state can take place, which is the sacralizing of space so as to produce a space within which the nation cannot be unimagined. It is the setting aside and the setting apart that forms the simultaneous exclusivity and inclusivity of the state. It is this process of sacralization that creates the state; it is the state in turn that sacralizes the nation. Without sovereign territory—established through a process of sacralization, the rendering of space as inviolate, and backed up by military force—there is no state. Without control of citizenry, there is no nation, and that process of "making citizens" requires a form of systemic violence deeply rooted, often unconsciously at least from the citizen's perspective, within the educational system.[25] In South Africa, apartheid was a form of state sacralization, which resulted in a production of institutionalized racism. In China, the identity of the citizen, and the idea of "the people" (*renmin*), both embraced and pushed back against state sacralization, like when the state reclaimed its territory in Tian'anmen Square in 1989.[26] In "the People's" Square, the location of sacrality was shifted from the space (the square) to the people (to whom it "belonged"). But when the people (in this scenario, mostly students) were the *wrong* people—incorrect in their morals, motives, and location—then the square became the sine qua non, no longer the people, who are now capable of violating the sacrality of the space. For a moment that square was the inviolate, the students an intrusion into the inviolate that had to be neutralized.

China's constitution refers explicitly to its sovereign domain as "sacred territory." To claim constitutionally that one's territory is sacred means that territorialization has become a form of sacralization. This claim has deep implications for juridical constructions, the containment of populace, the so-called freedom of religion, and human rights in general. In other words, territorialization is in fact a form of sacralization bolstered by mythos and sovereign violence, themselves prominent signatures of the nation-state. Thus to territorialize is also to sacralize, in the sense of setting apart, appropriating through division, sanctifying, and apportioning inclusivity through exclusivity. Sacrality, therefore, is deeply productive of what China is and how it engages the world: the sacred is a constitutive part of modern China, manifested in its constitution and its self-fashioning.

If we are to further the claim that inviolate sacrality is at the heart of nation-state making—a claim made only to deepen our understanding of our political formations on the broadest possible level—then to a greater or lesser extent we can follow Harald Wydra's argument that "an enquiry into the sources of power must go beyond the juridico-institutional models of sovereignty, or conceptions that ground power in individual or collective volition."[27] In other words, we can easily identify the obvious juridico-institutional models—the executive branch, the courts, the educational system, and so forth. What is not so easy to recognize is the need to and the ways in which we humans connect our imaginings of power to the types of meaning-production that result from those imaginaries. These connections require the liminal, a threshold, a certain kind of transgression that is constitutive of modern politics.

Categories

This book is also about conceptual categories implemented by the nation-state. I argue that territory, religion, and citizenship (along with race), and the way in which they are mythologized and sacralized are the imagined infrastructure of the modern nation-state.[28] I suggest that the nation is not simply imagined, but that, more crucially, the state sacralizes the nation. Stating the sacred is a structural principle. Sacralizing the nation makes it inviolate and results in a legitimized state.

Throughout we encounter the sacred. Sacrality is about the political. Sacrality is political and is constantly being negotiated and renegotiated and produced through ritualization.[29] Historian of religion David Chidester reminds us of this when he writes: "The sacred is not a stable lexicon . . . it is produced through intensive, ongoing, and extraordinary attention, through processes of interpretation, attending to minute detail, which are always overdetermined in their proliferation of meanings."[30] That overdetermination contributes to the sacred as the inviolate.

Let us begin, however, with the sacred as a spatial phenomenon. It is the spatialized territory of the state that is designated as sacred and thus inviolate. States and citizens within those states will demonize or indeed kill those that infringe on this inviolate. Additionally, there is also the deification of geographic territory that takes place quite literally.[31] (More on this in chapter 1.) There is a long history in China of territory being deified. The northeastern part of China during the Qing Empire, for example, was understood to be the land of dragons and the ancestral home of the Manchus. This understanding was in part depicted on the stunning dragon robes that were a mainstay of the emperor's wardrobe. All dynastic emperors were understood to be the Son of Heaven (*tianzi*), acting in accordance with the heavens. As such, they could inflict a form of sacred violence for the purposes of stabilizing and expanding all under the heavens (*tianxia*).[32] For instance, when the empire reached out to establish its hold in Central Asia during the 1750s under the leadership of Qianlong, the emperor undertook genocide to wipe out the Zunghar.[33] Today much of this area is now part of Xinjiang province (literally, new frontier or new territory). Tibet and Taiwan are also part of this process of imagining new maps and extending territorial claims.

In addition to the mythos production required to construct a national narrative and its accompanying systemic violence, a foundational building-block of a nation-state is territorialization, that is, the categorization and control over citizens and resources. This requires a defining and blurring of boundaries, ideas, ethnicities, and borders, what Ode Arne Westad calls "mental maps," and is a critical component of nation-state building.[34] As the state extends its reach, probing and testing its boundaries vis-à-vis its own citizenry and that of other states, a necessary and violent form of internal colonization takes place.[35] We see this in Xinjiang, where Uighurs are constantly persecuted for their differences with Han citizenry. In Mary Douglas's terms, they are "matter out of place," ostensibly citizens of China but forever outsiders.

In a different context (Britain and India)—but I think apt vis-à-vis Han/Uighur-Beijing/Xinjiang relations—Peter van der Veer writes that "the crucial difference between the modern state in the metropole and in the colony is that in the former its project of political legitimacy is in 'the nation,' citizenship, and national identity, whereas in the latter 'the subjects' are excluded from citizenship and their national identity is either denied or denigrated."[36] Does this not describe Han Beijing's (ostensibly Han and atheistic) relationship with Uighur Xinjiang (non-Han and Muslim)? Does this not describe the white apartheid government in Pretoria's relationship with the estranged black population? The "citizens" are excluded within the inclusivity of the nation-state, their national identity denigrated. The metropole and the colony are contemporaneous in the modern state. This, in part, enables the state to sacralize, to make the exclusive part of the inclusive, by defining its territory as inviolate.[37] This inviolate is where its sovereignty can be found. But it is a constructed sovereignty, again based on the prevalence of Han identity, and the idea that for thousands of years this identity held steady even in times of external threat.

None of the above can be reckoned with unless we acknowledge what Wang Hui of Qinghua University calls "the construction of modern Chinese identity, ideas of geography, and senses of sovereignty."[38] To this end I explore the links I believe exist between territorialization and sacralization by focusing on territory, religion, and citizenship, categories that have been deployed strategically in China as instruments of power and form part of the complex narrative of China's modernity. All this has implications for the structuring of international relations between China and its Asian neighbors, as well as for other nation-states.

Now, the nation-state with all its accompanying categories was a product of European mentalités. What happened when these ideas and categories were exported with colonialism in the nineteenth century to other parts of the world?[39] What happened in Asia, in China in particular, when it encountered—either through force or by willing appropriation—European categories of nation and state, along with their attendant formulations concerning science, rationality, politics, and economics, and their derivative categories such as religion, the secular, the sacred, human rights, and freedom (which itself bifurcates into "freedom from" or "freedom of")? How did an imperium become a nation?

Trying to answer these questions provides an opportunity for inquiry into the nature of the shaky superstructure of modernity and the coalescence of the nation (as imagined community[40]) and the state (the use and distribution of power via governmentality[41]). A primary focus here will be on the constitution, a document drawn up by most nation-states, which offers a blueprint for citizens of juridical protection and containment. It is, I will argue, a patently religious document and indelibly mythological, even when formulated by so-called secularized states, preserving in the Chinese example the master narrative of China's history and nation-state mythology.

Constitutionally Speaking

As an example of Chinese constitutional language, we can think of the case for and against religion, a Western imagining imposed on China during the colonial period that then shows up in bizarre fashion in China's constitution. In one sense China is unique in that it is a one-party state, and that party ardently advocates atheism; on the other hand, China uses religion as a normative category constructed and deployed during the turbulent nineteenth century and deeply politicized today. China, like many nation-states, embodies a paradox: religion is antithetical to the secular state yet central to its constitution and legal system. For the Chinese Communist Party, religion is decried as an anachronism that needs to be politically controlled and consequently is pushed as far out of the public sphere as possible. At the same time, however, religion is protected as an inalienable human right and invaluable to individual privacy. Consequently, despite officially being an atheist state, China has produced religion, figuratively, and in the process produces itself. The category becomes crucial to nation-statehood.

The contradiction between the so-called secular and religious is hardly unique to China, as demonstrated by the same nebulous divide in countries like the United States and Europe. By the mid-twentieth century, religion, whatever is meant by the term, is embedded in various international human rights conventions as well as most nation-state constitutions. Religion becomes a critical building block of the nation-state.

China's constitution, like most nation-state constitutions, presents religion as a universal, sui generis, self-explanatory term, and as a protected right for its citizenry offering ostensive freedoms. Yet, at the same time, the category is used juridically as a form of social containment. Looking at China's constitution and a variety of other official documents serves to illustrate the dynamic interrelationship between Western imperialism and nation-state making, how religion as a colonial-inspired category has become embedded in nation-state ways of seeing and being, and, in the process, helps to facilitate imperial-like territorial practices by nation-states, ones justified by "religious-like" forms of nationalism.

If China is my exemplum, and the place in which I spend most time in this book, then South Africa is my muse. Both countries provide historical and textual moments to better understand the scaffolding of the nation-state more broadly. South Africa is the metaphorical telescope and microscope that allows me to zoom in and out to generate a more philosophically complex picture of China, the nation-state, and its categories, especially religion and the sacred.[42] It also allows me the double-vision about which Roland Barthes writes—the experience of looking out a car window and simultaneously seeing the glass right in front of me and the landscape behind it farther away.[43] Looking up close, we will examine constitutional and other state documents; gazing from afar, we will grapple with existential questions surrounding the nation-state. This dual vision will enable us to raise questions about religion as a discursive, disciplining technique at work in nation-state building.

Structure

This book is not a chronological history. Instead, in view of a methodological framework, key historical moments are used in the book that come from a wide timespan, from the end of the eighteenth century up until the present. While the bulk of the book is about the modern nation-state, I use key historical moments to understand the birth of the nation-state and particular instances in which the latter sacralizes the former.

Chapter 1, "Territory," explores territorialization as a form of sacralization. Sacralization is undertaken by nation-states to legitimate their violent measures in establishing their sovereignty. "Constitution," chapter 2, is not only about constituting a state of being but also about constitutionalizing it in a document that lists the duties and freedoms ostensibly guaranteed to citizens. One of these is religion, the focus of chapter 3. It is construed as a human right and, along with a list of human rights, is at the core of sacralizing the nation even when it is disavowed. Chapter 4, "Reincarnation," tests the case of religion as a human right as articulated in the Chinese constitution. In it I look at a series of what I call theopolitical moves undertaken by the Chinese government to better control its populace, Tibetans especially. The fifth chapter, "Contact," is about colonial encounters, some of the resulting social outcomes, in many ways the foundation of nation-statism and the formation of the Other. Finally, chapter 6, "Nativity," is about the birth of nation-statism and the recategorization of human beings from subjects to citizens. This chapter also serves as the conclusion.

Throughout, the category of religion is at stake. Whether through constructing mythological narratives (chapters 1 through 6), construing the category of religion as a human right (chapter 3), using religious discourse in its constitution and using religion as a juridical category (chapter 4), to linking aggressive territorialization to the sacredness of the nation (chapter 1 and 6), China is in the "religion game." In doing so, China has unwittingly bound itself to a European Protestant narrative.

Acknowledgments

When I first started graduate school in religious studies in the early 1990s, I thought of religion the way many people do—basically, sui generis—in all places at all times, albeit in different forms, as something we recognize when we see it, and not as something critical to nation-state building. What I now think of—nostalgically but not uncritically—as the "University of Chicago/University of California, Santa Barbara (UC/UCSB) school" changed all that: Jonathon Z. Smith, Bruce Lincoln, Charles Long, Tomoko Masuzawa, Bill Powell, Allan Grapard, Richard Hecht, Wendy Doniger, Juan Campo, Tom Carlson, David White, and David Chidester, among others, taught me to think about the study of that object we call religion in deeply creative ways.[44] I am grateful to them all. Chidester's extraordinary body of work, in particular, has long kept me struggling with categories. Religion is one of these; so too is space; so too is territory; and so too is the sacred. Thus this book is an undoing, redoing, and reimagining of these terms.

If our wounds can be salvational, so are our debts of gratitude. We are nothing if not creatures of indebtedness to all who surround us and love us. I received help from many people during the course of writing this book. I thank my colleagues in my home department at Vassar College—Marc Michael Epstein, E. H. Rick Jarow, Jonathon S. Kahn, Wendy Post, Ági Veto, Kirsten Wesselhoeft, Christopher White, and Klaus Yoder. I also wish to thank the Lucy Maynard Salmon Research Fund of Vassar College for its generous financial support of this project.

Other colleagues and friends I wish to thank are Connie Ndonye and Sam Opondo, who taught me not to run away from my past; Himadeep Muppidi, who, during our early morning walks, helped me think through many of the ideas in this book; Joe Nevins, who insisted this book was more about South Africa than China; Eric Reinders, ever generous with his time and critical eye for detail; Song Nianshen, who helped me think more deeply about territoriality; as well my colleagues in the Asian Studies Program, several of whom spent a delightful afternoon with me discussing the main ideas of the book.

Thanks to all the Vassar students over the years who asked me what I was working on; specifically, Becca Endicott, Lisa

Nakashima, Shen Leyao, Seth Ullman, Sean Xu, and Wang Yifan, all of whom helped with research at one time or another.

Many thanks to the reviewers who read a draft of this book. Thanks also to my editor at Columbia University Press, Wendy Lochner, for fighting so hard to make this project come to life. Thanks also to Lowell Frye, Leslie Kriesel, Zachary Friedman, and the rest of the team at Columbia University Press. Special thanks to Anita O'Brien for her skillful copyediting and to Do Mi Stauber for the index.

Finally, love and thanks go to my family, to my daughter Brooklyn Elspeth Walsh, to my father Jack Wreford Walsh, and to Lioba Anne Gerhardi, for our life. This small book is dedicated to her.

Stating the Sacred

1

Territory

Article 12. Socialist public property is sacred and inviolable. The state protects socialist public property.

Article 55. It is the sacred obligation of every citizen of the People's Republic of China to defend the motherland and resist aggression.

     —Constitution of the People's Republic of China

Rupert Wingfield-Hayes of the BBC flew in a civilian, six-seat Cessna aircraft to Mischief Reef in the South China Sea in 2015. He went to report on what might happen were the plane to fly close to the reef.[1] As it reached within twelve nautical miles of the "island," the Chinese Navy stated in a threatening tone in English and Mandarin that this "unidentified military aircraft" must leave immediately. In early September 2018 a U.S. Navy reconnaissance plane flew close to the same reef and received a similar response: "U.S. military aircraft, you have violated our China sovereignty and infringed on our security and our rights. You need to leave immediately and keep far out."[2] In recent congressional testimony, Admiral Philip S. Davidson, head of the United States Indo-Pacific

Command, issued a stark warning: "In short, China is now capable of controlling the South China Sea in all scenarios short of war with the United States."[3]

China claims Mischief Reef among several other islands in the South China Sea. Subi Reef, Mischief Reef, and Fiery Cross Reef, previously submerged atolls, have been turned into islands with airports. These are just three out of seven massive military construction projects China built in less than eighteen months. At least 30 percent of all annual international sea trade passes through these waters. Almost all nations, including the United States, Vietnam, Australia, the Philippines, and Taiwan, regard this area in the South China Sea as international waters. As recently as June 2018, referring to the islands, President Xi Jinping emphatically told U.S. defense secretary Jim Mattis, "We cannot lose even one inch of the territory left behind by our ancestors."[4]

The Permanent Court of Arbitration in The Hague ruled in the summer of 2016, in a case brought by the Philippines, that China does not have territorial jurisdiction over the South China Sea following its nine-dash principle.[5] China rejected the ruling, arguing in an earlier "position paper" published on December 7, 2014, that the "Notification and Statement of Claim" presented by the Philippines was unfounded, and that neither the Philippines nor the Permanent Court of Arbitration has jurisdiction over the territory encompassed by the nine-dash line. The position paper stipulated the official government position on the South China Sea islands and expressed a tone common to all of China's territorial claims:

> China has indisputable sovereignty over the South China Sea Islands (the Dongsha Islands, the Xisha Islands, the Zhongsha Islands and the Nansha Islands) and the adjacent waters. Chinese activities in the South China Sea date back to over 2,000 years

ago. China was the first country to discover, name, explore and exploit the resources of the South China Sea Islands and the first to continuously exercise sovereign powers over them. From the 1930s to 1940s, Japan illegally seized some parts of the South China Sea Islands during its war of aggression against China. At the end of the Second World War, the Chinese Government resumed exercise of sovereignty over the South China Sea Islands. Military personnel and government officials were sent via naval vessels to hold resumption of authority ceremonies. Commemorative stone markers were erected, garrisons stationed, and geographical surveys conducted. In 1947, China renamed the maritime features of the South China Sea Islands and, in 1948, published an official map which displayed a dotted line in the South China Sea. Since the founding of the People's Republic of China on 1 October 1949, the Chinese Government has been consistently and actively maintaining its sovereignty over the South China Sea Islands. Both the Declaration of the Government of the People's Republic of China on the Territorial Sea of 1958 and the Law of the People's Republic of China on the Territorial Sea and the Contiguous Zone of 1992 expressly provide that the territory of the People's Republic of China includes, among others, the Dongsha Islands, the Xisha Islands, the Zhongsha Islands and the Nansha Islands. All those acts affirm China's territorial sovereignty and relevant maritime rights and interests in the South China Sea.[6]

Four themes are apparent here: indisputable sovereignty, a temporal claim, a historical marker (Japan's aggression against China), and stone markers.

Sovereignty is always indisputable until it isn't; in other words, until it is challenged, making it then disputable. This is a circular statement meant to strengthen the sovereignty that already exists. In the case above, China's sovereignty is being disputed by the Permanent Court of Arbitration. Nevertheless, here we can couple the indisputable to the inviolate, as in a claimed legitimacy beyond the scope of discourse. China is adamant: the South China Sea is its sovereign and sacred territory.

The temporal claim of two thousand years has all the dressings of historical fact but is in all likelihood a time span cited to impress. There may be some archaeological evidence to back it up, but I bet neighboring states could provide this as well.

The historical marker is Japan's aggression against China in the 1930s and 1940s. This was true, but the claim to the islands is far murkier.

It's not clear how many or if any commemorative stone markers exist. If they do, however, this would be consistent with a long-standing practice in Chinese history of erecting steles in places (sites and institutions) of importance. An example of this practice can be seen where a Buddhist temple would commission a stele to be produced and placed in front of the temple. Often the stele would refer to the temple land as Buddha land. In other words, Buddha territory is sacred territory. The territory separates a sacred "us" (Buddhist monks) from a generic "them."[7]

Are all these claims and purported historical timelines spurious, especially if all nation-states involved in the territorial claims—Malaysia, Japan, the Philippines, Vietnam, Brunei, and Taiwan—reject them? Taiwan, for instance, has its own take on sovereignty regarding the islands. In a government position paper issued March 21, 2016, the language used is strikingly similar to that in the PRC's paper. It begins as follows:

> The Nansha (Spratly) Islands, Shisha (Paracel) Islands, Chungsha (Macclesfield Bank) Islands, and Tungsha (Pratas) Islands (together known as the South China Sea Islands) were first discovered, named, and used by the ancient Chinese, and incorporated into national territory and administered by imperial Chinese governments. Whether from the perspective of history, geography,

or international law, the South China Sea Islands and their surrounding waters are an inherent part of ROC territory and waters. The ROC enjoys all rights over them in accordance with international law. This is indisputable. Any claim to sovereignty over, or occupation of, these areas by other countries is illegal, irrespective of the reasons put forward or methods used, and the ROC government recognizes no such claim or occupation.[8]

Again, we see a link between sovereignty and the inviolate with the emphatic phrase, "This is indisputable." The refusal to dispute territory is a signifier of the sacred, that which is set apart, that which is exclusive. The islands, according to both the PRC and the ROC, are sacred space. The sacred, therefore, becomes a category of separation. There is no negotiation, discussion, or disputation to be had.

In the PRC's position paper, it is not clear what China means by "Chinese activities" taking place in the South China Sea over the past two thousand years; neither is it clear that that justifies their claim. Typically, countries have sovereignty over waters that extend twelve nautical miles off their shoreline and some degree of control, specifically with regard to economic activities, over waters that extend up to two hundred miles off the shoreline. The United Nations Convention on the Law of the Sea, signed by 167 states, including China, on December 10, 1982, specifies that "every State has the right to establish the breadth of its territorial sea up to a limit not exceeding 12 nautical miles, measured from baselines determined in accordance with this Convention."[9] Territory encompassed by the nine-dash line extends far beyond this limit and includes about 90 percent of the South China Sea, an area roughly the size of Mexico.

In the U.S. presidential debate in 2016, then New Jersey governor and Republican candidate Chris Christie announced that, should he become president of the United States, he would fly Air Force One over the islands being constructed in the South

China Sea. "They'll know we mean business," he asserted.[10] A couple of weeks before, a U.S. Navy destroyer, the USS *Lassen*, sailed within twelve nautical miles of the Spratly Islands, also territory that China claims. As the *New York Times* explained: "American officials did not inform their Chinese counterparts as they planned the provocative maneuver, saying that to do so would have undercut their message."[11] The point was to establish that U.S. naval vessels were sailing in international waters.

China rejects this claim, continues to build islands, several of them with landing strips capable of handling war planes. Beijing claims that Chinese fishermen used islands throughout the South China Sea for centuries, and consequently the land and surrounding waters are considered de facto part of its sacred territory. Sacred, and therefore sovereign and inviolate. China has yet to defend that inviolate land, as that would put it in direct confrontation with at least half a dozen countries. On the other hand, it seems likely that that day will come, because China continues to fortify these islands and threaten approaching vessels. Sacred territory always involves ambiguity and tension.

The nine-dash line functions as a spatial mode of existence; that is, it functions on the level of representation and the level of actualization. These two levels operate simultaneously and can also be understood by what Henri Lefebvre called "representations of space" and "representational spaces."[12] The former is space as conceptualized (Beijing drawing nine lines on a map of the South China Sea); the latter, space as directly lived (Beijing constructing islands on top of atolls).

Lines in the Sand

With the longest land borders in the world, China shares its territorial marker with sixteen other nation-states. Along its southern border with India, China controls one tract of land,

Aksai Chin (some 14,000-plus square miles), and India controls Arunachal Pradesh. Both states claim these territories, which led to the brief Sino-Indian conflict of 1962. An agreement to stop fighting was signed in the early 1990s, but the issue is far from resolved.

Matters only worsened in the summer of 2017 when Beijing authorized the expansion of a road into a disputed area between China and Bhutan, an area claimed by both countries and a territory in which India has deep geopolitical interest. Bhutan reported to India that it had seen Chinese construction workers entering its territory. India immediately sent troops to the area. Soldiers from India's army and China's People's Liberation Army (PLA) faced each other, dug in, with just a few hundred feet separating them. The standoff lasted more than fifty days.[13] With the inviolate at stake—sacred territory—it's not impossible to imagine these two powerful nation-states sliding into a war.[14] (It would be a war sanctioned by the inviolate, the sacred violence justified by claims of sovereignty.) China has also had brief conflicts with Russia and Vietnam. In 1979 severe border clashes with Vietnam left thousands dead.[15] Nation-state borders mark the inviolate. They mark sacred territory and express sovereignty.

When the motherland, China, is threatened, article 55 of China's constitution, quoted in the epigraph above, dictates that it is the sacred obligation of the Chinese people to defend the inviolate. The citizen on the street, the soldier in the People's Liberation Army, must be willing to sacrifice—here, the destruction of the enemy and of oneself—for the sanctity of the motherland.[16]

Sacrifice

The principles of sacrifice are well established but far from settled.[17] Sacrifice is in part an act of sanctification, but a violent one. It both externalizes and internalizes, thereby resulting in a process of sacralization that produces the sacred as a category of separation. This always requires the threat of violence, over which the state holds the monopoly. Often this form of the sacred is understood to be a secularized *theos*; or, as Carl Schmitt put it in his now perhaps well-worn statement: "All significant concepts of the modern theory of the state are secularized theological concepts."[18] This statement can be supplemented to extend well beyond the political power of the state. In fact, the secular remains in the *theos* in much the same way as the medieval monk who leaves the monastery to live in the world of men. He becomes a secular monk but is still devoted to God. Christian theological constructs now are directed not to God but to the state.

In the seventeenth century the monarch was identified with God; by the early nineteenth century the sovereign had become the primary identifier. The *theos*, which is to say, the social constructs formally derived from the order of the cosmos and emplaced on the order of the government, not erasing anything but supplementing, takes on a radically different meaning in the twenty-first century. But the *theos* is still a disciplinary category couched in the language of religion. In this regard, China and South Africa are religious states. They are sovereign states and therefore, knowingly or not, employ theological tactics to manage their citizenry. As David Chidester argues, for instance, during the apartheid era "no church was necessary, therefore, to lend its religious support to the state; the state itself assumed the sacred aura of an armed religion."[19]

For Georges Bataille, the primary principle of sacrifice is destruction. It is to remove the victim out of the world of usefulness and the order of things: "What is sacrificed is *what serves*."[20] We saw in the preface how Barend Hendrik Strydom destroyed in order to preserve his space, his God-given territory. Within Strydom's worldview, his victims were a sacrifice, to be destroyed to purify his world. He, too, was a sacrifice: he was willing to be arrested, sent to jail, and condemned to death by the same state he saw himself as saving. A citizen of a proclaimed white race had sought to defend the purity of the state's territory.

American presidents routinely say that the greatest sacrifice American soldiers can make is that of dying for their country. To give one's life for the land on which one lives is the ultimate sacrifice from the military's perspective. Bataille suggests that the principle of military order is to externalize violence; it is to divert violence to the outside. Why is this? It is so that the "inside," the territory that requires blood sacrifice, can be maintained. Sacrifice in China has a history stretching back more than three thousand years. The deities change, but the sacrifice continues. The empire—and we can speak of an American empire, a Chinese empire—posits itself as a thing, Bataille warns. It can "never allow another empire to exist at its frontier as an equal."[21] China's sovereignty is at stake. Its borders are either to be expanded (South China Sea) or to be protected, whatever the cost may be. In this sense the sovereignty of the Chinese state is unequaled. China's "frontiers" are now simultaneously transnational and intensely nationalistic. China has brought the frontier to its center. From this perspective there can only be one Beijing, one capital, one China; hence the urgency of bringing Hong Kong, Macao, Taiwan, Xinjiang, Tibet, and now the South China Sea into that center.

Sacred Space

As I have argued, when territorialization becomes a form of sacralization, the sacred is then a spatial designation. It is the spatialized territory of the state that is designated as sacred and thus inviolate. It is this inviolate, so intimately connected to territory, that is at the heart of the nation-state.

In an essay entitled "In Praise of Profanation," Giorgio Agamben explains that Roman jurists knew precisely what constituted the sacred. He writes: "Sacred or religious were the things that in some way belonged to the gods."[22] If these things were then returned to the common use of men, they became free of sacred names and, strictly speaking, were profane. The territory of the state is sacred because it belongs to the state. The state has replaced the gods. Bataille, on the other hand, argues that "the sacred is that prodigious effervescence of life that, for the sake of duration, the order of things holds in check, and that this holding changes into a breaking loose, that is, into violence."[23] The life bestowed on us by the gods, the life allowed to us by the state, is held in check by these entities only to break loose. Violence is the inevitable consequence. When the state defines and categorizes, the populace, especially fringe populace, pushes back. The state reacts. These reactionary back-and-forths are internal to the nation. Externality takes hold when borders are threatened or transgressed. The territory of the nation-state is sacred and must be defended at all costs.

As we have seen, China's constitution refers to its territory as "sacred territory," in other words, inviolate, or, to borrow from Roman jurists on the cheap, belonging not so much to the gods as to the state. Perhaps some would say that the state is a godless, abstract entity devoid of soulful substance. That may be so from a Eurocentric Christian viewpoint, but it is nonetheless an entity that requires blood sacrifice to survive, and generally, loyalty from its citizens, and even more broadly, under the notion of/for the "common use of men." China's constitution states that power is in the hands of the people. Article 2 reads: "All power in the People's Republic of China belongs to the people." But for territory to be designated sacred by the state means in fact that the citizens have no direct access to that power or territory, for it is sacred space, space to be separated out and from the generic citizenry. In China the state controls all territory. The citizen may lease land, borrow land, work on land but can never own it. There is, therefore, a connection between ownership and sacrality, and it has everything to do with who the owner is—not gods in the heavens but the state here on earth. What other steps do nation-states take to sacralize their space and then protect the borders that encompass it?

In the early 1950s the General Assembly of the United Nations began condemning apartheid. As decolonization led to the formation of more Asian and African states, the UN took a tougher stance toward South Africa. By 1967 the General Assembly established a Special Committee on Apartheid.[24] It also declared that South Africa's mandate over South West Africa (Namibia) was illegal. Resistance was slow in the making. Ten years later, after the murder of Steve Biko while he was in police custody, the General Assembly declared apartheid to be a "crime against humanity."[25] The apartheid government came under intense international scrutiny.

Anxious to protect its territory, including its hold over South West Africa, the apartheid government sought to create "buffer zones" between its inviolate space and its neighbors. To this end, between 1981 and 1983 South African troops raided every one of South Africa's neighbors—Namibia, Angola, Botswana, Lesotho, Zambia, Zimbabwe, and Mozambique.[26] South Africa continued to maintain control over Namibia (then called South West Africa) and had a significant military presence in the Caprivi Strip, a sliver of land between Angola and Namibia.

After the Portuguese left Angola in 1975, the Soviet Union sponsored the transport of Cuban troops to help the Popular

Movement for the Liberation of Angola (MPLA) consolidate its power over other local factions. (This was the limited extent of communism in that part of the continent, contrary to the propaganda put out by the South African government.) Thus began a complicated asymmetric conflict that involved multiple states and actors.[27] The narrative spun by the apartheid government was that the South African Defense Force (SADF) was protecting South African citizenry from communism and black nationalism. The goal was to prevent spatial intrusion into South Africa's sacred territory by what was then called *die swart gevaar* (the black danger) and *die rooi gevaar* (the red danger). The former referred to neighboring black states and their citizenry over which South Africa's institutionalized racism had little control; the latter loosely referred to the imagined influence of the Soviet Union and communism on South Africans.

Borders even beyond South African borders were routinely deified in order to preserve the mythological narrative of a quasi-historical timeline that God had given that territory to the South African nation-state. The violence perpetuated by the apartheid state was a sanctified violence. It was a violence understood to be sacred in order to protect the sacred. It was a spatialized mythos that extended out from the center of Pretoria. For historian of religion Charles Long, we see this form of imperial outreach as the tendency to "expand the power of the center over the wider spatial areas, thereby bringing these spaces under the reign of the center."[28] For Pretoria, that reality was not unlike Barend Hendrik Strydom's. It was an imaginary—a territorial (land) and imagined (nation) space of whiteness that was incoherently inhabited by blackness. Similar to the actions of the citizen, Strydom and the apartheid state, a proclaimed white state, sought to defend the purity of the state's territory even if that meant going way beyond its own borders.

But Gilles Deleuze and Félix Guattari have shown that the state is sovereignty, and that "sovereignty only reigns over what it is capable of internalizing, of appropriating locally."[29] Apartheid South Africa ultimately failed at this local appropriation when it collapsed in 1990, but not through lack of trying during the previous decades. Beijing, today, succeeds spectacularly as it brings the frontier—Xinjiang, Tibet, Hong Kong, the South China Sea, and its hope of "getting back" Taiwan—into its center of power, internalizing and making all these spaces local spaces.

It is essential for the Chinese government in Beijing to convince its own citizens (and the rest of the world) of its legitimacy in its territorial claims and its attempts to internalize and make all space local. The most effective method of succeeding at this is to establish a link between territory and sacredness, thereby invoking the inviolate. To define something as sacred is to render it inviolate. The military-industrial complex in the nation-state is called on to prevent any violations of that which is deemed to be sacred. For nation-states, sovereign claimed territorial space is exclusively beholden to the state; thus its sacrality resides in its inclusivity, and the territorialization thereof is akin to state sacralization, a space to be set apart precisely so as to be able to control it through a politicized inclusivity. Sacralizing space is how Beijing can lay claim to the South China Sea, for example.

Consider the "one country, two systems" principle: Hong Kong falls under this category.[30] In 1997, after 156 years of British rule, this collection of islands off China's southern coast, once a frontier of sorts, came back under Beijing's control—the "centrifugal/centripetal power of the cited tradition(s)," as Charles Long puts it in the epigraph to chapter 5.[31] We witnessed the power of the center (Beijing) expanding over the wider spatial areas, and bringing those spaces (Hong Kong) under the reign of the center and its ideology, and thereby "assuring them a place in the legitimate and authentic structure of that reality designated and symbolized at this center."[32] This was the first stage of a return to the center for Hong Kong. The second will take place in 2047, when Hong Kong is scheduled to fully revert back to mainland China and become completely subordinate to Beijing.

The same "one country, two systems" principle was offered to Taiwan, but the Taiwanese government and the people of Taiwan have rejected it. In his annual speech at the opening ceremony of the Nineteenth Communist Party Congress, President Xi Jinping stated emphatically to the applause of his army generals that "We will never allow anyone, any organization, or any political party, at any time or in any form, to separate any part of Chinese territory from China."[33] He was referring to Taiwan, but also to all claimed sacred territory of the People's Republic of China. On January 2, 2019, Xi gave a speech once again emphasizing the goal of reunification with Taiwan. While no timetable was set, he did declare that the task of reunification should not be passed down from generation to generation.[34] Xi's message was clear: China must never be divided.

Other examples include Beijing's claims to Xinjiang and Tibet. Conquered in the eighteenth century, Xinjiang is home to Uighurs, Kyrghyz, and Kazakhs, who make up about half the region's population. The remaining half are predominantly Han, who began populating this new province only in the mid-twentieth century. Beijing's claims that this region was also part of its sacred territory meant that a form of neocolonialism could occur and be justified.[35] In the same way that the Chinese government has sent hundreds of thousands of Han to live in Tibet and thus begin a cultural transformation (or degradation) of Tibetan culture, a form of social control, this process has also taken place in Xinjiang. There is much resentment, and since early 2017, when the region's new leader, Chen Quanguo, took office, he has employed the same extreme surveillance tactics in Xinjiang that he used in Tibet.[36]

Since taking office, Chen has advertised for over ninety thousand new police and security personnel positions.[37] Xinjiang is effectively a police state, Agamben's state of exception, where the rule of law is lifted and replaced with x-rays, iris scans, GPS tracking systems in all vehicles, collection of DNA from medical checkups, banning of all communication software, and sporadic arrests. One estimate puts past and current detainments at more than 500,000.[38] All these actions are predicated on what Beijing calls the "three evil forces"—separatism, extremism, and terrorism—even though the number of Uighurs engaged in such activities is a mere fraction of the population.[39]

What is the Chinese lexicon of the sacred state? Xinjiang is claimed as part of China's territory. China's constitution refers explicitly to its sovereign domain as "sacred territory" (*shensheng lingtu*) and the self-referential "motherland" (*zuguo*). (The official English translation of the constitution uses the term "motherland," though a more accurate translation is "ancestral state," one that requires blood sacrifice as it always has.) Other historical categories include *shenzhou*, "sacred land," or as John Lagerwey elegantly translates it, "continent of the spirits."[40] Another term is *tianchao*, "celestial dynasty," as well as *huaxia*, literally, "glorious grand." The *xia* also refers to the Xia dynasty—the earliest dynasty of Chinese history. *Huaxia* represented a sense of cultural superiority. All these categories connect back to the concept of *tianxia*, "all under the heavens," as defined by *hua*, "culture/China," in contradistinction to *yi*, barbarian/uncultured. The *hua* are sovereign and boundless. This *hua-yi* divide meant definitively that outsiders were culturally ignorant, but should they adopt Hua customs and language, they too could become part of Hua territory.[41] All such terms had to be reinterpreted with the new idea of a bounded nation-state (*guojia*) in the nineteenth century and when a chairman replaced an emperor.

Tianxia (all under the heavens) and *tian* (Heaven) are ancient categories that still have resonance in contemporary Chinese politics, the sense that all under the heavens, that is, all on earth, must be ordered and harmonious. This duty fell to emperors, the *tianzi*, the Sons of Heaven. Several thousand years ago it was Yu the Great who was said to have drained the flood waters to reveal nine regions that needed to be governed with the help of Heaven, but also with good leadership. That duty now falls to the Chinese Communist Party and its leader, Xi Jinping.

In the Book of Documents (*Shujing*), Yu had these words of warning and hope for the emperor:

> Yu said, "Oh! Be careful, O emperor, of the manner in which you occupy the throne." The emperor said, "Yes." Yu said, "Find your rest in your resting-point.[42] Attend to the springs of things, study stability; and let your assistants be upright:—then will your every movement be greatly responded to, as if the people only waited for your will, and you will brightly receive gifts from Shangdi.[43] Will not Heaven renew its favouring appointment, and give you blessing?[44]

There are many passages in the *Shujing* that speak of the calamities that will be brought down on the ruler and the people unless the ruler rules well. For instance, we are told of the king of Shang who was favored by Heaven, and later by the king of Xia.[45] "When for oppression he substituted his generous gentleness, the millions of people gave him their hearts. Now your Majesty is entering on the inheritance of his virtue;—every thing depends on how you commence your reign. To set up love, it is for you to love your elders; to set up respect, it is for you to respect your relatives. The commencement is in the family and State; the consummation is in the Empire." These sentiments are later echoed in the Confucian classic the Great Learning (*daxue*). For the Son of Heaven, the emperor, to succeed he must first get his own affairs in order. If done correctly and meticulously (*relegere*), the empire will be stable. If not, the heavens will not "give you blessing." Sacralizing of the domain involved the sacralization of the ruler, whether explicitly in dynastic times, or more ambiguously since then. Today we still witness the implicit feeling of *tianming*, the mandate of Heaven established during the Zhou dynasty (c.1046–256 BCE). Heaven bestowed the mandate to rule should the ruler rule well. If not, disasters would happen, and indeed the dynasty could fall. We don't see such explicit claims today, but the people can still hold the ruler accountable for natural disasters that might indicate a failure to rule. When the Tangshan earthquake on July 28, 1976, killed at least 242,000 people, had Mao Zedong implicitly lost the "mandate"? He died a few months later. After the devastating Sichuan earthquake of 2008, questions of morality and ability to rule were raised.[46] Disaster in the domain still points directly to the ruler.

Deifying Space

Historically, part of understanding Chinese territory as spatialized sacrality had to do with the deification of geographic territory. The result was a social formation of concentricity, a deification of territory based on a cosmological imaginary that goes all the way back to at least the fourth century BCE. From then until the first century BCE, a remarkable text was compiled called the Classic of Mountains and Seas (*Shanhai jing*). It is an extraordinary record of the ancient Chinese world, a cosmography containing details about mountains, rivers, medicine, geography, gods, and strange creatures that inhabit the earth.[47] It is the first account of the "sacred territory" of *shenzhou*, the "continent of the spirits," the "sacred land" that is today's China.[48]

China was understood to be divided into five concentric zones. The first three were ruled by the emperor; the remaining two contained "barbarians." Likely, as John Lagerwey explains, this concentricity can be traced to the *Shanhai jing*. Lagerwey suggests that China can best be understood as a series of concentric spaces within which lived the gods.[49] The first circle contains the gods recognized by the Son of Heaven, namely, the emperor and his imperium. Territorial organization is demarcated by five mountains, marking the four directions and the center. Mountains "anchor" (*zhen*) the land. Imperial sacrifices are made on an annual basis to the gods. (They are recorded in the "register of sacrifices" [*sidian*] kept by every dynasty since the Zhou.) Every emperor had to make sacrifices to the gods resident in the concentric space. This was political control over the gods. The exercise of power was founded on this form of territorialization. Deities reigned in specific geographical space; the imperium sacrificed to those deities to have access to that space. In turn the gods could reside there; again, the *shenzhou*, the territory of spirits—China. This was an exchange process, a transformative form of religiosity.

The logic of this concentricity can also be seen in the "plan of the five dependencies," later canonized into the Confucian scholar-official tradition that marked much imperial rule since the third century BCE. At the center is the capital, the site of the emperor's body. The first two outer realms are controlled by the emperor and his princes.[50] The third zone is where *wen* (culture) and *wu* (martial/military) are disseminated as need be to pacify these regions. Inhabitants of these territories can then pay tribute to the center zone where the emperor presides. We find the *yi* ("barbarians") in this zone. (This is the same ideograph outlawed by the British in the Treaty of Tianjin; see chapter 5.) Beyond this zone is the realm of "the wilds."

The *Shanhai jing* describes the heavens as a rounded cover supported at strategic points (*xue*) by sacred mountains.[51] At Cleft Mountain in the west, the god Gonggong was said to have bumped into one of the pillars, damaging the mountain and snapping the axial cord that connected earth to the heavens.[52] Heaven tilted toward the northwest (the sun, moon, and stars all appear to move toward this direction), and a gap was the result in the southeast, the direction in which so many of China's rivers flow. The text also tells of a primordial connection that allowed the gods and humans to interact, which was severed a long time ago. Political order between humans and the gods was to be established through sacrifices by the emperor, the Son of Heaven, the one who could, and indeed must, create a balance between the rounded heavens and the square earth.

The ancient god-king Yu, founder of the Xia dynasty (trad. c. 20th cent.–c. 16th cent. BCE) and traditionally touted as the compiler of the *Shanhai jing*, established this balanced cosmography when he saved/created China by draining the waters of the Great Deluge to reveal nine provinces.[53] This imagined geography came to reflect the ideology of power and centrality that remains in effect in China to this day.

On his throne, the emperor always faced south as he gazed over his sacred territory. Throughout China's history, all important cities, tombs, temples, and houses faced south to reflect a cosmological understanding of the heavens and earth.[54] This understanding was inscribed as a map on the back of a turtle that emerged from the Luo River. We first read of this map, the *luoshu*, in the Book of Changes (*Yijing*): "Therefore: Heaven creates divine things; the holy sage takes them as models. Heaven and earth change and transform; the holy sage imitates them. In the heavens hang images that reveal good fortune and misfortune; the holy sage reproduces these. The Yellow River brought forth a map and the Lo River brought forth a writing; the holy men took these as models."[55] Beijing was built on the principle of "heaven is round, earth is square." An axis—the dividing line through the ideograph *zhong* (center)—runs through the city, through the imperial palace, through Tian'anmen Square and Mao's tomb. The most important structures in the city are along that axis, including all government offices. This axis is where President Xi rules over the sacred territory of China. He rules from the center.[56]

From past to present, imperial China and now the contemporary nation-state, cultural and political concentricity was always the mainstay of the emperor/president. The farther from the center one went, the less control was to be had. To bring those far-flung peripheral territories under control required a tributary sense of understanding. This has always been the way of China, then and now. Later this mythologization and sacralization of landscape becomes constitutionalized—all China and Chinese territory is sacred (*shensheng lingtu*).[57] The mountains may have moved, but their "anchoring" remains the same.

In the Case of Taiwan

What is usually referred to as the "Taiwan question" (*Taiwan wenti*) is a strange turn of phrase if one thinks what it means or what it might take to "solve" what is a sovereign state in all but name. China does not consider Taiwan to be sovereign; Beijing understands it to be part of the sacred territory (*shensheng lingtu*)[58] of the ancestral land (*zuguo*). In two published white papers, Beijing makes the case as to how and why Taiwan is "an inalienable part of China."[59] The first tells a dramatic tale. It begins: "Taiwan has belonged to China since ancient times." It moves quickly through 1,700 years of history to conclude that,

> like the other parts of China, [Taiwan] came to be opened up and settled by the Chinese people of various nationalities. From the

very beginning the Taiwan society derived from the source of the Chinese cultural tradition. This basic fact had not changed even during the half century of Japanese occupation. The history of Taiwan's development is imbued with the blood, sweat, and ingenuity of the Chinese people including the local ethnic minorities.

"Came to be opened up" makes it sound as if there was no one or nothing there before. We see how the document takes great pains in constantly referring to the "Chinese people," presumably Han, and to "people of various nationalities" though it's not clear at all what "Chinese people of various nationalities" means. Can everyone be Han Chinese? So ethnicity is at stake in the mythological claims above. Regardless, the conclusion is always the same. According to the document, 157 countries "recognize that there is only one China and that the Government of the People's Republic of China is the sole legal government of China and Taiwan is part of China."

The pushback from across the Straits is relentless, with a consistent stream of rebuttals as to why Taiwan is not part of China.[60] It's a back-and-forth that has gone on for decades. In 1998, when I was living in Taipei, I was interviewed on a radio station and asked to share my thoughts about the diplomatic switch that President Nelson Mandela had made from recognizing Taiwan to the PRC. It was an uncomfortable moment. Who was I to speak on behalf of a nation-state I had left so long ago? I pointed out the obvious inevitabilities and the power of pragmatism. It all felt a bit empty.

Like Tibet, China's (PRC) claim to Taiwan (ROC) is unclear, though China's constitution is unequivocal and the official English translation is as follows: "The Chinese people must fight against those forces and elements, both at home and abroad, that are hostile to China's socialist system and try to undermine it. Taiwan is part of the sacred territory of the People's Republic of

China. It is the lofty duty of the entire Chinese people, including our compatriots in Taiwan, to accomplish the great task of reunifying the motherland."[61] An alternative translation might be: "The people of China must resist both internal and external hostile and destructive forces undermining our socialist system. Taiwan is part of the sacred territory of the People's Republic of China. It is the sacred duty of all the Chinese people to complete the unification of our ancestral territory, which includes our Taiwanese compatriots [*tongbao*—literally, "those born from the same womb]." The official Chinese government translation translates the four characters *shensheng zhize* as "lofty duty," when a more accurate translation would be "sacred duty." Again, the sacred is always invoked when the inviolate is needed.

I recall vividly in 1995 and 1996, when I was living in Taipei, China firing DF-15 missiles toward Taiwan. They landed fewer than fifty miles from Taiwan's busiest ports. At least one was said to fly over Taipei. The missiles were fired in response to a speech given by Taiwan's then president, Lee Teng-hui, on June 9–10, 1995, at his alma mater, Cornell University. Beijing was furious. Live-fire exercises were organized. More missiles were fired in early 1996, just as Taiwan was gearing up for presidential elections. The message to Washington was that China would not hesitate to use force to reunite the motherland. President Bill Clinton responded by sending two aircraft carrier battle groups into the area and possibly even through the Taiwan Strait. Tensions have eased considerably over the past decade, with the establishment of direct flights between Taiwan and the mainland and even some high-level talks being held between Taiwanese and Chinese delegations.

There are some notable exceptions to the easing of tensions, such as when newly elected U.S. president Donald Trump spoke directly on the phone with Taiwan's president, Tsai Ing-wen. Beijing went ballistic, verbally, that is. Things were once again smoothed over by Trump reaffirming the one-China policy. As the well-worn phrase goes that I often heard and read during the 1990s when I was living in Taiwan, "There is only one China in the world, and that includes Taiwan" (*Shijie shang zhiyou yige Zhongguo, baokuo Taiwan*).

In a white paper published in 2000, Beijing stated categorically that "Taiwan is an inalienable part of China." The inviolate is invoked. Taiwan is part of China's sacred territory. The document goes on to state:

> On October 1, 1949, the Central People's Government of the PRC was proclaimed, replacing the government of the Republic of China to become the only legal government of the whole of China and its sole legal representative in the international arena, thereby bringing the historical status of the Republic of China to an end. This is a replacement of the old regime by a new one in a situation where the main bodies of the same international laws have not changed and China's sovereignty and inherent territory have not changed therefrom, and so the government of the PRC naturally should fully enjoy and exercise China's sovereignty, including its sovereignty over Taiwan.

And, finally, "Chinese territory and sovereignty has not been split, and the two sides of the Straits are not two states." Taiwan, however, which still calls itself the Republic of China, has a well-armed military supported by the United States, an independent government, a president, a democratic electoral system, and a constitution. The first article in its constitution states that "The Republic of China, founded on the Three Principles of the People, shall be a democratic republic of the people, to be governed by the people and for the people."[62] No mention is made of the then civil war between the Guomindang (the Nationalists) and Mao's Communist army.

Today Beijing continues to use the language of reunification and the "one country, two systems" phrase. Taipei continues to watch nervously as Hong Kong democracy erodes under pressure from Beijing. There is no solution in sight. When two territories define their space and borders as inviolate, there is no compromise to be found—an unfortunate but obvious hallmark of nation-statism.

Colonial Loose Ends

We have seen above some of the ways in which territorialization invokes the sacred to enforce the inviolate. My question now is whether colonialism plays a role in contemporary territorialization. When, for example, the government in Beijing authorizes the movement of Han populations from one part of China to, say, Xinjiang or Tibet, modes of placement and displacement both occur. The migration of Han into ethnically different spaces but within the same held territory can be construed as a form of ethnic colonialism. (This echoes Hannah Arendt's condemnation of the nation-state as a social formation that can and often does disenfranchise national minorities.)

I would suggest that territorialization as a form of sacralization is intimately connected to colonialism. This is especially true if we think of ethnic colonization, economic colonization, and religious colonization, both historically and in the current time. Might we then talk of a type of territorialization that, while ostensibly insular in function, is far-reaching in the imaginary? Chinese leaders will consistently argue for noninterference in other states' affairs, yet is this not just a deflection from its own?[63] For the state simultaneously contains and expels, protects and colonizes.

To be clear, this is not the same phenomenon as Eurocolonialism, which was a different type of migration and occupation beginning with the Spanish and Portuguese and later the British, French, and Dutch. By ethnic colonialism I mean the mass movement of people of one self-identified ethnic group (Han) into a space historically dominated by another self-identified ethnic group (Uighur or Tibetan), a space that is claimed territorially as part of a nation-state's sovereignty. On the one hand, the state is seeking to monopolize the natural resources of that differentiated space. On the other, as Arjun Appadurai puts it: "States . . . are everywhere seeking to monopolize the moral resources of community, either by flatly claiming perfect coevality between nation and state, or by systematically museumizing and representing all the groups within them in a variety of heritage politics that seems remarkably uniform throughout the world."[64] Museumizing is common in China when it comes to representing and marketing its so-called fifty-six ethnic groups.[65] Museum villages are established and exoticized by state media, careful control of the taxonomies of difference are put into effect along with the domestication of those differences, television commercials employ non-Han tropes to validate the diversity yet unity of all Chinese, and again I mention the Olympic Games narrative—and all this in the name of a unified nation and state.[66]

Ethnic colonization comes in many forms. All ethnic groups in China are referred to as being "Chinese," but not all are Han. There is slippage with the term "Chinese"—its definition wavers among racial, cultural, and national meanings according to the need. The term often translated as "Chinese" is *Zhongguoren*, literally, a "person of the central state." Are all fifty-six ethnic groups automatically *Zhongguoren*, or do they have to be incorporated or colonized to become so?

The historian James Hevia has shown how nineteenth-century empire building differed from other forms of imperialism, specifically when it came to China.[67] The production of knowledge about indigenous peoples blossomed in a way never seen before in world history. That knowledge could then be used to both territorialize and deterritorialize. Twenty-first-century strategies of neocolonialism are not the same but do share similarities. Recoding the social logic of an indigenous population with an infusion of a different ethnicity so as to be able to control them and their resources becomes paramount. Han vis-à-vis Tibetan and Uighur populations, all being territorialized and deterritorialized at the same time. Control over *tianxia* (all under the heavens) becomes layers of culture, often suffocating. A form of that requires a rejection of state individuation (see chapter 6). Doing so, however, subjects the recipient to state sanctified violence. (How much force, capital, energy, resources does it take to control a fractured, dispossessed population, in China, in apartheid South Africa?)

Nostalgia and Space

The politics of nostalgia is also at work in the sacralizing of territory. To recall, however vaguely, the wonders of what your state once was and then to project what it could become is a powerful tool in the hands of the ruling leader.[68] Beijing is exceptionally good at doing this; that is, reinfusing a mythology with credibility. The narrative: China, once the greatest empire on earth, then reduced by Eurocolonial forces to "backward" status and simultaneously being dragged onto the world stage, is now poised to become the largest economy in the world, already has the largest population, and has risen from the historical ashes of the century of "national humiliation."[69] China has risen like the phoenix, a bird so paramount in Chinese mythology so as to be recognized instantly in the collective unconsciousness of the nation.

Beijing's territorialization goes beyond just territory: its vision as an alternate political system to places like the United States and the European Union is heavily promoted in the country and abroad. One propaganda video that went viral in 2013 talks about the United States being a system where leaders are chosen based on money; China presents itself as a meritocracy where leaders are groomed for decades and tested in many ways. We are told this is one of the secrets of the "China miracle" (*Zhongguo qiji*). Xi Jinping is then shown, and we are told these many years of testing have much in common with "the long-term making of a kung fu master" (*Zhongguo gongfu shide changqi duanlian xuanxian renneng*). At the end of the day, according to the video, "as long as the people are satisfied and the country develops and progresses as a result, it's working!"[70] No subtle message here. Beijing offers a different style of leadership, one that other countries ought to consider.

All propaganda is a form of territorialization of the mind, at least at the beginning. Real political and financial results are always expected. Take, for instance, Xi Jinping's "one belt, one road initiative," ostensibly a way to reconnect territories (many once controlled by imperial China), connect much of Eurasia, and generate billions of dollars of cash.[71] China claims it is the largest infrastructure project in history. One dramatic government video promotes it as "Bold and visionary, it brings together Asia, Europe, and Africa."[72] One key player that China would like to have onboard is India. India's refusal thus far to participate has heightened tensions with China, with the former referring to the initiative as "little more than a colonial enterprise, leaving debt and broken communities in its wake."[73]

Other examples of China's bid to expand its vision and influence global politics include trying to buy magazines like

Newsweek in 2010, Xinhua broadcasting agency running ads in
New York City's Times Square, and the establishment of some
five hundred or more Confucian Institutes around the globe,
with plans to double these to a thousand by 2020.[74] Also illustra-
tive are China's extensive investments in countries throughout
Africa and South America. Recently we saw China pumping
half a billion euros into cash-strapped Greece's port of Piraeus,
making it the busiest port in the Mediterranean and giving
Beijing a major foothold in European markets.[75] One Chinese
group, front and center on helping Beijing to spread its vision
even though it is not a state-owned enterprise, is the HNA
group. Beginning in 1993 as Hainan Airlines, the group has
since expanded to become a major global investor.[76] Since 2016 it
has purchased, among others, Ingram Micro (a technology dis-
tributor based in Irvine, California), a $6.5 billion stake (25 per-
cent) of Hilton Worldwide holdings, and Gategroup (a Swiss
airline catering business), and it is now the biggest shareholder
in Deutsche Bank.

Another example is the now jailed Patrick Ho from Hong
Kong. Ho was arrested in New York City for money laundering
and millions of dollars of bribes.[77] Prior to his arrest, Ho ran a
think-tank, likely funded by the Chinese government, which he
called a "do-tank." Ho could make things happen. He called for
Globalization 2.0, with China leading the way. Ho gave $500,000
to Uganda's president. Previously, Chinese construction companies had built Uganda's presidential palace and the Ministry of
Foreign Affairs. Ho, in an email, requested from the Ugandan
president a list of all major infrastructure projects. There would
be an "open" bid for these projects, and each time a Chinese
company would win the bid. Uganda has oil, not a lot, but it's
there. Uganda would then borrow money from state-owned
Chinese banks to pay the Chinese construction companies. With
these companies come their workers and families. There are now

Chinese barbershops in Kampala. Ho is alleged to have bribed the president of Chad as well. Chad also has oil. A new form of "energy-imperialism"?

In 2015 a previously unknown Chinese company called CEFC, ostensibly a "private" company, came to Prague. Led by Chairman Ye Jianming, the company bought a media group, a football team, a brewery, real estate, a share in a bank, and an airline—$1.5 billion dollars of purchased assets in just one week.[78] It had hired Patrick Ho, the same person the FBI now accuses of also bribing the foreign minister of Uganda. Why Prague? The Czech Republic is an important part of the "one belt, one road initiative," the new "Silk Roads" connecting all of Eurasia. CEFC had subsequently also signed agreements for oil rights with Kazakhstan, Qatar, Russia, Chad, Angola, and Abu Dhabi—Globalization 2.0, or a new type of territorialization contributing to China's sacred territory. In March 2018 Ye Jianming was detained by the Chinese authorities for questioning. His fate is uncertain.[79]

Beijing's global reach is extraordinary—a new form of neo-imperialistic territorialization, and a conscious effort on that nation-state's part to offer the world an alternative to liberal democracy. In the old world order, the choice seemed to be between the Soviet Union and the United States as a model. Beijing now says there is a third choice.[80]

><

Finally, if we think back to those fifty-six ethnic groups of China presented to us at the Beijing Olympics, there is no doubt in my mind that the Chinese nation-state is engaged in what Appadurai will call culturalism, "the conscious mobilization of cultural differences in the service of a larger national or transnational politics."[81] The "master narrative" referred to earlier is constantly being rethought and reimagined by China's political elite but will, I think, be challenged by ordinary citizens as the growing disparity between rich and poor fuels their imaginations and more and more citizens seek out self-determination and social justice, which most of the time elude them. Alternate scenarios, some violent, some unremarkable, will no doubt transform China's mindscapes, and one hopes its landscapes apropos the ecological disaster happening with its current pollution challenges. (What about the human right to clean air?)

So where to now? Are there alternatives to China's current nation-statism? This question takes us well beyond China. I agree with Appadurai's contention that in our present time the imagination has become "a collective, social fact" and that this, "in turn, is the basis of the plurality of imagined worlds."[82] He is not saying that imagination is new; far from it. Appadurai is making the compelling argument that the role of the imagination has shifted from special expressive spaces—art, myth, ritual—to more everyday spaces of ordinary people. Our postindustrialized and overdigitalized age has allowed the work of the imagination to shift from more discrete venues to—and here I'll use Michel de Certeau's words on the cheap—the practice of everyday life. This shift makes for a truly globalized world where the nation-state struggles to contain its citizenry, who now reach out to all corners of the earth to communicate, interact, dream, and imagine alternative realities to the crushing force of the state and the drudgery of capitalist consumption. Lest I overstate this point (and I think Appadurai does), we are still confronted with the stark reality of more than a billion people around the globe without access to basic needs—enough food, clean drinking water, shelter. Human Rights with a capitalized H and R does little to help. Many are invisible within their own nations, and the state flounders helplessly in its attempts to see. In Appadurai's words, their "modernity is elsewhere."[83] In the next chapter we will see if constitutional rights can solve some of the challenges.

Thus far we have looked at some of the underlying structures of the nation-state using China—sometimes correlated with apartheid South Africa—as our primary exemplum. This chapter focused on the relationship between territorialization and sacralization in the formation of the Chinese nation-state. Sacred territory invokes the inviolate, and, as I suggested in the preface, it is the inviolate that frames and sustains the nation-state. It is the inviolate that is used violently to justify territorial integrity and state sovereignty. The next chapter will explore constitutionalism and religion as a human right as additional building blocks of nation-statism and contributors to the inviolate.

2

Constitution

China is one of the countries with the longest histories in the world. The people of all nationalities in China have jointly created a splendid culture and have a glorious revolutionary tradition. Feudal China was gradually reduced after 1840 to a semicolonial and semifeudal country. The Chinese people waged wave upon wave of heroic struggles for national independence and liberation and for democracy and freedom. Great and earth-shaking historical changes have taken place in China in the twentieth century. The Revolution of 1911, led by Dr. Sun Yat-sen, abolished the feudal monarchy and gave birth to the Republic of China. But the Chinese people had yet to fulfil their historical task of overthrowing imperialism and feudalism. After waging hard, protracted, and tortuous struggles, armed and otherwise, the Chinese people of all nationalities led by the Communist Party of China with Chairman Mao Zedong as its leader ultimately, in 1949, overthrew the rule of imperialism, feudalism, and bureaucrat capitalism, won the great victory of the new-democratic revolution, and founded the People's Republic of China. Thereupon the Chinese people took state power into their own hands and became masters of the country.

—Preamble to Constitution of the People's Republic of China

On April 27, 1994, South Africans of all racial and ethnic backgrounds went to the voting booths for the first time in that nation's history.[1] Nelson Mandela's long walk to freedom resulted in long lines of first-time voters casting their ballots into a new future. South Africa offered citizens of the world along with its own citizenry a new state of being that had been long in coming. Decades of international isolation and rebuke instantly eased, and the institutionalized racism that terrorized the country for decades began to crumble. South Africa's previous apartheid master narrative had to be replaced. A new mythos for a new South Africa had to be constructed. New identities had to be established in space and time. A top priority was writing a new constitution, one that eventually was drawn up in eleven official languages in an effort to recognize people of all ethnic backgrounds.[2]

The final draft was adopted on May 8, 1996.[3] The preamble begins with these remarkable words: "We the people of South Africa, recognize the injustices of our past." It's a stunning contrast to the opening sentences in the preamble to China's constitution as seen in the epigraph, even as both the Chinese Communist Party (CCP) and the African National Congress (ANC) will present themselves as the savior figure, that entity that can redress the past and save the citizenry. Regardless, in both texts, what follows are lists of rights for the citizenry, duties to be performed by each citizen, who counts as a citizen, along with a structural breakdown of how the government works. China's constitutional list has 138 articles; South Africa's, 243.

Umberto Eco once said that to stave off death we make lists. In an interview with *Der Spiegel* he stated: "We like lists because we don't want to die." He also said: "The list is the origin of culture. It's part of the history of art and literature. What does culture want? To make infinity comprehensible. It also wants to create order—not always, but often. And how, as a human being, does one face infinity? How does one attempt to grasp the incomprehensible? Through lists."[4] Eco goes on to list other types of lists, such as catalogs, museum collections, and dictionaries. To make a list is also to order things, to categorize, to prioritize, to classify. Categorizing becomes a form of control. If we can categorize the ten thousand things in the universe, then perhaps we can control our fate, or at least this appears to be a form of wishful thinking that prevails.

Governments make lists—rules, laws, inventories, definitions, budgets, a census. A constitution is a list. It is a list of articles that tries to articulate the ideas of the nation-state and to narrate the birth of a nation so as to prevent the "death" of the state. In the process of reconstructing society—post-apartheid South Africa, the new China—myth, ritual, and classification are modes of discourse that through violence and governmentality help establish social boundaries and territory.[5] Nation-states mythologize their history to better create a national consciousness that all citizens can participate in and be loyal to.[6] The national consciousness is always textualized.

Consequently, to make nation-states requires texts. A constitution provides the rhetorical framework that assures its defined citizens a variety of freedoms and rights while simultaneously serving as a juridical means of containment and social control. It is also a text that presents a certain type of history—a mythologized type. Constitutions are a mythical narrative: myth, as Roland Barthes writes, is a type of meta-language. As Barthes explains, "Myth has in fact a double function: it points out and it notifies, it makes us understand something and it imposes it on us."[7] Constitutions project an imagined reality, the ideals of an imagined community, to borrow Benedict Anderson's terms. But, like all mythological narratives, their double function both preserves and imposes.

Constitutions composed by political powers to maintain, legitimate, and reproduce their power represent an imaginary that, were we to be terribly cynical, we might say is mere words, just ideals; but we ought not to be so. Instead we should take these words seriously because again, like all mythological narratives, the reality is both simultaneously presented and hidden by those words. The words have power: for the citizen, for the government, and for the legal system. The language in a constitution is in the culture. The language in the constitution is political. It is a working politics that expresses the nation, the state, and its citizens. But equally important is what it does not say. It cannot be neutral. It must take explicit positions on a range of topics. Its implicitness also rests behind the chosen words, or in China's constitution, ideographs. The characters themselves have nuanced characteristics. Much of their meaning is beyond the citizen's control. The authors of a constitution, not the readers, have the authority. Not that we can access their intentions, a misdirected goal at any rate. All we can do is interpret the words we see in the constitution, all the while cognizant of the multiplicity of contested meaning.[8] The constitution as a myth "is neither a lie nor a confession: it is an inflexion." And here, as Barthes tells us, we reach "the principle of myth: it transforms history into nature."[9]

China's constitution naturalizes a constructed history.[10] We see this in the opening lines of the preamble above. China's constitution is part of a master narrative that explains the founding of the People's Republic. The preamble in just a few sentences depicts a feudal past that shifts in 1840 to a "semicolonial and semifeudal" state of being. By sentence 6 we are past 1911 and Sun Yat-sen's revolution, and just characters later, we arrive in 1949 with Chairman Mao Zedong, who through revolution founds the People's Republic of China. And thus began the "socialist transformation" as the "Chinese people took state power into their own hands."

The military took power, not the Chinese people. And the people never became "masters of the country" as the constitution wants us to believe.[11] The Chinese Communist Party with its master narrative did. The People's Liberation Army—and later the vast security mechanisms of the Chinese nation-state—enacted a violence that was later sanctified, enshrined in texts, and prescribed in memorials. This made it possible for a new state to come into being.

The preamble to China's constitution goes on to outline what needs to be done to consolidate power in the coming years and how the motherland must be unified. The preamble is in part a reference to China's claimed territory that is inviolate, such as Tibet, Xinjiang, the South China Sea, some of the border territory with India, and Taiwan. What constitutes the "motherland" is an open question that the constitution tries to give closure to by referencing these territories and using the phrase "the Chinese people." What is China and who counts as Chinese? A race? A nation? Is "Chineseness" part of the inviolate? Who are the "people of all nationalities in China" that the constitution will speak of? Whatever the answers, there is a deliberate blurring here between citizenship and ethnicity. Regardless, the constitution is a critical component of the master narrative.[12]

Reform

By the late 1850s the Qing Empire was struggling with Western imperial powers that insisted on further entry into Chinese markets and that missionaries have more access to the interior. Lacking the industrial technology to fully repulse Western nations, the Chinese took an inward-looking turn to see what internal resources, cosmological or otherwise, might be able to help. There were other pressures to navigate. Land shortages, overpopulation, drought, and famine all contributed to the woes of a dynasty already severely weakened by punitive treaties and loss of major seaports. As if this weren't enough, the dynasty saw a number of major rebellions—the Taiping Rebellion (1850–1864) in the South, the contemporaneous Nian Rebellion (1851–1868) in the North, the Tongzhi Hui Rebellion or Muslim revolt (1855–1873) in central and western China, and the Boxer Uprising (1898–1901). None of these toppled the dynasty per se, but all contributed to economic devastation from which the Qing would never recover. Add to all this the chronic existential crisis that the Confucian elite were facing. A range of reformers emerged, most notably Tan Sitong, Kang Youwei, Liang Qichao, and Yan Fu.[13]

One of the major challenges faced by these constitutional reformers was how to combine Western technology (especially military technology) with a Confucian-based system of government that sought to enhance state power while debating and ideally limiting broader social participation.[14] The Chinese Navy's defeat in a single day in 1894 by Japanese forces was perhaps the clearest sign to constitutional reformers such as Kang Youwei (1858–1927) and his student Liang Qichao that China desperately needed to embrace constitutionalism and immediately begin revising its legal system.[15] For Kang and Liang, the only possible way Japan could have built up its military powers to the extent that it had by the end of the nineteenth century was that in 1889, after a protracted period of governance revisions, it had adopted the Meiji Constitution, a document based on the style and language of European constitutions. China's Guangxu emperor eventually proposed Chinese constitutional reform in the form of an edict on June 11, 1898.

The reforms in 1898 were made more complicated by Kang Youwei and Liang Qichao, who sought new ways of engaging in a parliamentary-style politics but achieved few solid results.[16] Liang's strength lay more in his writing and periodical reviews than in actual statecraft. The "Self-Strengthening" movement was a bumpy, messy affair overshadowed by Japan's military-industrial machinations in the late 1800s.[17] Kang's reforms, which were based on his Confucian sensibilities, would not pass muster, but, Liang, his student, had limited success with his journal *Shiwu bao* (literally, "reports on contemporary affairs," but called in English "Chinese Progress"). By 1897 Liang had published a book on Western government and caught the attention of some prominent political leaders and governors. Liang recognized the necessity for participatory social-political action. If China was to compete in the new world of nation-states, it had to change profoundly. If Japan had been so successful at modernizing, then surely China could be as well. Social solidarity was a much-needed first step.

Philip Kuhn convincingly identifies what he calls "the constitutional turning point" as the spring of 1895 when the draft of a letter by Kang Youwei was presented to the courts.[18] The letter called for elected representatives who could give counsel to the emperor and break down the barriers between public and private. As Kuhn states: "Here we are already in the conceptual world of the modern nation-state as mediated by the Meiji Constitution in Japan. Such ideas were only conceivable under the duress of imminent foreign conquest, or even (in the social-Darwinian vocabulary of 1890s imperialism) of racial distinction." Ideas of elected representatives, the broadening of social participation in the rule of the empire, and notions about public and private all set the foundation for China's coming constitutional reforms.

When Kang gave a speech in Beijing on March 17, 1898, under the auspices of the Baoguohui (literally, the "protect-the-country" society), his use of the term *guo* aroused concern.[19] For what, essentially, did *guo* mean?[20] Kang spoke of protecting the rights of the nation, the territory of the nation, a far cry from the use and meaning of the term in imperial language. Nonetheless, the emperor was determined that reforms be pushed through. All ended in failure. Kang and Liang fled for a period to Japan, and the Boxers established themselves in Beijing. Change was short in coming, and a constitutional nation-state nothing but a dream. Liang watched all this from afar, and even as far away as the United States, where he spent most of 1903 trying to raise funds. Not overly impressed by American-style democracy, he still felt frustrated by China's inability to form some type of effective democratic government. Matters only worsened when potential breakthroughs on the horizon of constitutional efficacy were shattered by Yuan Shikai (1859–1916), a military and government official who quickly rose through the ranks and who clearly wanted to be a new emperor.

The year 1902 saw a broad, multilayered reform initiative called the New Policies (*xincheng*) program. This was a serious attempt by the Qing imperium to embrace a series of political changes that it hoped could balance the need for new ideas of rule and technology with the desire to preserve and fortify the "old ways." Along with these new policies came a broader understanding of nationalism, a new social formation in China that shaped the shift from empire to nation-state. As Ya-pei Kuo explains, "The Xinzheng reforms can thus be understood as a historical process whereby the imperial will sought to appropriate the construct of a nation for its own reification."[21] The imperium was dying, but it wasn't dead yet. It also wasn't a nation yet, and it had yet to become an "imagined community." China really was at an existential crossroads, with reformers all over the empire scrambling for clarity.

The Wuchang uprising and the Xinhai Revolution in October 1911 were the final blows against the Qing dynasty. Calls came from a number of military commanders for a parliament to replace the throne and draw up a constitution. One conceptualization resulted in a hastily issued doctrine of Nineteen Articles (*shijiu xintiao*), barely a constitutional reform, and one that still kept the emperor firmly on the throne. This was really a British-style monarchy model.[22] (One contemporary scholar has even speculated that had those reforms taken full effect, China may have "avoided a century of revolutionary tumult" as a more gradualist approach would have been the result.[23]) Then as now, the idea of each citizen having a voice in governmental affairs was unimaginable to the ruling elite. After all, people differed in education, moral repose, and ethical understanding. With imperial China, those destined to run national affairs did so by virtue of their background and their successful completion of the imperial exams held once every three years in the capital.

In some respects little has changed. China's ruling elite espouses virtually the same authoritarianism today as it did then.[24] The difference is that power is now cloaked in party and constitutional language. Force and nationalistic discourse remain at the heart of the Chinese Communist Party. The People's Republic is in name only: the CCP is the "master of the country," and it has the documentation, the narratives, and the military to back this up. Using as much force as is necessary, it controls the inviolate. China's constitution embodies the inviolate, and that is why I think we can call it a religious text. The inviolate shuts down all debate. It is ineffable. Leaning on Émile Durkheim's definition of religion (see note 22 in the preface), the constitution is the blueprint of the nation-state, the institutional structure that sets things apart and surrounds them with prohibitions. The "moral community" would be the equivalent of the nationalized citizenry. The prohibitions and the concept and duties of the citizen are embedded in the constitution.

As a religious text, the constitution provides a form of exchange of human action and transaction. The promises in a constitution are between the state and its citizenry. They are transactional. Do these things (duties) and we will offer these protections (rights). Break the transaction and you get to experience the sanctified violence of the state. It must be sanctified; otherwise it could not be justified. Here we can understand religion as being expressive (a mode of signification), discursive, and disciplinary, and as such relying on rhetoric to communicate, mythology to shape language and value, and ideological formation to enable the exchange processes of human interaction. As the constitution is enacted or manifested, two aspects are conditional. The first, religion, is an open, discursive category, subject to debate. The second, inviolate, is not. It is meant to close all conversation. It is the exclamation mark at the end of the claim, "This territory is ours!" No discussion to be had here. Then again, there is always pushback. The inviolate allows for sanctified violence to come into play. The state, with its monopoly on the use of force, does precisely that. It uses force.

Reimaginings

The Constitution of South Africa is an extraordinary document. Ratified in 1996, it is more than twice the length of China's constitution and about four times longer than the Constitution of the United States. It tries to address just about every conceivable societal scenario in an attempt to generate social affinity and launch a different type of societal consciousness. The document calls for "nonracialism"; freedom of religion and belief; citizens that have the right to human dignity, equality, and freedom; and the fact that "no citizen may be deprived of citizenship" and "every citizen has the right to a passport." South Africa's territory is to be protected by its defense force, the "only lawful military force" in the republic. But how is it mythos? Like China's constitution, South Africa's begins with a constructed historical narrative. As mentioned above, the preamble states: "We, the people of South Africa, recognize the injustices of our past."

These words are beautiful but vague. Unlike Barthes's inflexion, the statement is a form of confession. But who is confessing what? A call is then made to heal the divisions of the past. Here we see an attempt to construct a new historical narrative. As Bruce Lincoln argues, "Among the ways in which those agitating for sociopolitical change can make use of myth. . . . They can attempt to invest a history . . . with authority and credibility, thus elevating it to the status of myth and thereby make of it an instrument with which to construct novel social forms."[25] The new ANC state had to appropriate the former authority of the apartheid state and transform it to serve its own interests. It is a truism that those in power write their own histories (China has extensive imperial histories for every dynasty going back to at least 1500 BCE). The ANC had to remythologize. It had to invest its interpretation of the past with authority and credibility. To the extent that it has succeeded—it may be too soon to tell—this means it still retains control of South Africa as a nation-state.

List as Text as Mythos

A constitution is also a religious text precisely because it is a mythos production, what Wendy Doniger would say is both real and unreal. She would also say that a myth "is a story that is sacred to and shared by a group of people who find their most important meanings in it."[26] I agree with her completely, but I want to argue that a constitution is a mythos production precisely because it presents statements that are typically believed to be true for a group of people, whether or not they are in actuality. This is what Russell McCutcheon calls "mythmaking," discourses that dehistoricize and decontextualize.[27] Constitution as myth is not so much about presenting false statements as it is about creating ambiguity in society. The text is most often markedly clear; the resulting social formation less so. Myth thrives on this tension. For example, in chapter 2, article 26, of South Africa's constitution, the text states that "everyone has the right to have access to adequate housing." Driving just a few miles out of Cape Town International Airport, one sees countless corrugated iron shanty huts.[28] This dispels article 26. Racism is also forbidden, yet one witnesses it within hours of entering Johannesburg.

China's constitution also calls for equal rights for all ethnic groups. Do Tibetans feel they are on a level playing field with their Han compatriots? Does the average Uighur feel as equally protected under the law as his or her Han counterparts? The constitution declares that "no organization or individual may enjoy the privilege of being above the Constitution and the law." Except the Chinese Communist Party and the state are just that. The constitution says that the state "prevents and controls pollution" and "protects and improves the living environment." Tell that to Beijing residents walking through smog so thick their eyes burn and nose and throat rebel, forcing them inside to catch their breath and contemplate this new Chinese modernity.

Always, though, the state projects the constitution as a story that "is sacred to and shared by a group of people who find their most important meanings in it." Again, the social consciousness referred to above. As Doniger states: "Myth is not an active force in itself but a tool in the hands of human beings."[29] While the framers of China's or South Africa's constitution might not see their document as mythological narrative, I believe it is. It is *mythos* presented as *logos* and as such demands a shift in perspective.

Finally, a constitution shares a form of religiosity (more on religion in the next two chapters). It is based on a form of exchange, a form of action and transaction between the state and the citizen. It's akin to an unsigned contract. State soteriology rests on the control of its populace, but the populace must be given its fair share of rights, protections, and promises. Salvation is to be experienced in dutiful citizenship and love and loyalty for the state. God is often invoked. We see this in the current South African constitution: "May God protect our people." The apartheid constitution of 1983 mentions God ten times. It begins as follows:

> IN HUMBLE SUBMISSION to Almighty God,
> Who controls the destinies of peoples and nations,
> Who gathered our forebears together from many lands and
> gave them this their own,
> Who has guided them from generation to generation,
> Who has wondrously delivered them from the dangers that
> beset them. . . .[30]

This passage expresses a form of exchange—an understanding that maintaining the efficacy of the constitution will result in God's protection because God controls the nation and gave its white inhabitants the territory that the state now maintains. In contemporary China, that "god" is the state itself. As for loyalty, nothing can come above the Communist Party.

Constitutional Religion

Constitutions will disavow their religiosity. A tour through the language used in nation-state constitutions demonstrates a clear pattern. Let's look at the following constitutions and their approach to religion: the Republic of China (Taiwan), the Russian Federation, France, South Africa, the United States of America, Turkey, Japan, Australia, Canada, Netherlands, Mexico, Chile, Lebanon, India, the UN Declaration of Human

Rights, Japan's Meiji Constitution of 1889, and the People's Republic of China.[31] As we will see, a pattern emerges in the language about religion.

Republic of China

Article 7
All citizens of the Republic of China, irrespective of sex, religion, race, class, or party affiliation, shall be equal before the law

Article 13
The people shall have freedom of religious belief.[32]

Russian Federation

Article 14
1. The Russian Federation is a secular state. No religion may be established as a state or obligatory one.
2. Religious associations shall be separated from the State and shall be equal before the law.

Article 19
2. The State shall guarantee the equality of rights and freedoms of man and citizen, regardless of sex, race, nationality, language, origin, property and official status, place of residence, religion, convictions, membership of public associations, and also of other circumstances. All forms of limitations of human rights on social, racial, national, linguistic or religious grounds shall be banned.

Article 28
Everyone shall be guaranteed the freedom of conscience, the freedom of religion, including the right to profess individually or

together with other any religion or to profess no religion at all, to freely choose, possess and disseminate religious and other views and act according to them.

France

France shall be an indivisible, secular, democratic and social Republic. It shall ensure the equality of all citizens before the law, without distinction of origin, race or religion. It shall respect all beliefs.

South Africa

The state may not unfairly discriminate directly or indirectly against anyone on one or more grounds, including, race, gender, sex, pregnancy, marital status, ethnic or social origin, colour, sexual orientation, age, disability, religion, conscience, belief, culture language and birth.[33]

United States of America

Congress shall make no law respecting an establishment of religion, or prohibiting the free exercise thereof; or abridging the freedom of speech, or of the press; or the right of the people peaceably to assemble, and to petition the Government for a redress of grievances.[34]

Turkey

Article 10
Everyone is equal before the law without distinction as to language, race, colour, sex, political opinion, philosophical belief, religion and sect, or any such grounds.

Article 24

Everyone has the right to freedom of conscience, religious belief and conviction.

Acts of worship, religious services, and ceremonies shall be conducted freely, provided that they do not violate the provisions of Article 14.

No one shall be compelled to worship, or to participate in religious ceremonies and rites, to reveal religious beliefs and convictions, or be blamed or accused because of his religious beliefs and convictions.

Education and instruction in religion and ethics shall be conducted under state supervision and control. Instruction in religious culture and moral education shall be compulsory in the curricula of primary and secondary schools. Other religious education and instruction shall be subject to the individual's own desire, and in the case of minors, to the request of their legal representatives.

No one shall be allowed to exploit or abuse religion or religious feelings, or things held sacred by religion, in any manner whatsoever, for the purpose of personal or political influence, or for even partially basing the fundamental, social, economic, political, and legal order of the state on religious tenets.[35]

Japan

Article 20 [Freedom of Religion, Secularity of the State]

(1) Freedom of religion is guaranteed to all. (2) No religious organization shall receive any privileges from the State, nor exercise any political authority. (3) No person shall be compelled to take part in any religious act, celebration, rite or practice. (4) The State and its organs shall refrain from religious education or any other religious activity.[36]

Australia

Article 116

Commonwealth not to legislate in respect of religion

The Commonwealth shall not make any law for establishing any religion, or for imposing any religious observance, or for prohibiting the free exercise of any religion, and no religious test shall be required as a qualification for any office or public trust under the Commonwealth.[37]

Canada

Fundamental freedoms

Article 2

Everyone has the following fundamental freedoms:

(a) freedom of conscience and religion

(b) freedom of thought, belief, opinion and expression, including freedom of the press and other media of communication;

Affirmative action programs

(2) Subsection (1) does not preclude any law, program or activity that has as its object the amelioration of conditions of disadvantaged individuals or groups including those that are disadvantaged because of race, national or ethnic origin, colour, religion, sex, age or mental or physical disability.[38]

The Netherlands

Fundamental rights

Article 1

All persons in the Netherlands shall be treated equally in equal circumstances. Discrimination on the grounds of religion, belief, political opinion, race or sex or on any other grounds whatsoever shall not be permitted.

Article 3
Education provided by public authorities shall be regulated by Act of Parliament, paying due respect to everyone's religion or belief.[39]

Mexico

Article 3
The education imparted by the Federal State shall be designed to develop harmoniously all the faculties of the human being and shall foster in him at the same time a love of country and a consciousness of international solidarity, in independence and justice.

I.

Freedom of religious beliefs being guaranteed by Article 24, the standard which shall guide such education shall be maintained entirely apart from any religious doctrine and, based on the results of scientific progress, shall strive against ignorance and its effects, servitudes, fanaticism, and prejudices.

IV.

Religious corporations, ministers of religion, stock companies which exclusively or predominantly engage in educational activities, and associations or companies devoted to propagation of any religious creed shall not in any way participate in institutions giving elementary, secondary and normal education and education for laborers or field workers.

Article 24
Everyone is free to embrace the religion of his choice and to practice all ceremonies, devotions, or observances of his respective

faith, either in places of public worship or at home, provided they do not constitute an offense punishable by law.

Every religious act of public worship must be performed strictly inside places of public worship, which shall at all times be under governmental supervision.

Article 27

II.

Religious institutions known as churches, regardless of creed, may in no case acquire, hold, or administer real property or hold mortgages thereon; such property held at present either directly or through an intermediary shall revert to the Nation, any person whosoever being authorized to denounce any property so held. Presumptive evidence shall be sufficient to declare the denunciation well founded. Places of public worship are the property of the Nation, as represented by the Federal Government, which shall determine which of them may continue to be devoted to their present purposes. Bishoprics, rectories, seminaries, asylums, and schools belonging to religious orders, convents, or any other buildings built or intended for the administration, propagation, or teaching of a religious creed shall at once become the property of the Nation by inherent right, to be used exclusively for the public services of the Federal or State Governments, within their respective jurisdictions. All places of public worship hereafter erected shall be the property of the Nation.

III.

Public or private charitable institutions for the rendering of assistance to the needy, for scientific research, the diffusion of knowledge, mutual aid to members, or for any other lawful purpose, may not acquire more real property than actually needed for their purpose and immediately and directly devoted thereto; but they may acquire, hold, or administer mortgages on real property provided the term thereof does not exceed ten years. Under no circumstances may institutions of this kind be under the patronage, direction, administration, charge, or supervision of religious orders or institutions, or of ministers of any religious sect or of their followers, even though the former or the latter may not be in active service.

Article 130

The federal powers shall exercise the supervision required by law in matters relating to religious worship and outward ecclesiastical forms. . . . Congress cannot enact laws establishing or prohibiting any religion.[40]

Chile

Article 19

The Constitution guarantees to all persons:

6. Freedom of conscience, manifestation of all creeds and the free exercise of all cults which are not opposed to morals, good customs or public order;

Religious communities may erect and maintain churches and their facilities in accordance with the conditions of safety and hygiene as established by the laws and ordinances.

With respect to assets, the churches and religious communities and institutions representing any cult shall enjoy the rights granted and acknowledged by the laws currently in force. Churches and their facilities assigned exclusively for religious activities shall be exempt from all taxes.[41]

Lebanon

Article 9 [Conscience, Belief]

Liberty of conscience is absolute. By rendering homage to the Almighty, the State respects all creeds and guarantees and protects their free exercise, on condition that they do not interfere with public order. It also guarantees to individuals, whatever their religious allegiance, the respect of their personal status and their religious interests.[42]

India

[Under Part III, under the subheading "Fundamental Rights"]

15. Prohibition of discrimination on grounds of religion, race, caste, sex or place of birth.

"Right to Freedom of Religion"

Freedom of conscience and free profession, practice and propagation of religion.

26. Freedom to manage religious affairs.

27. Freedom as to payment of taxes for promotion of any particular religion.

28. Freedom as to attendance at religious instruction or religious worship in certain educational institutions.

"Elections"

325. No person to be ineligible for inclusion in, or to claim to be included in a special, electoral roll on grounds of religion, race, caste or sex.[43]

UN Declaration of Human Rights

Article 2

Everyone is entitled to all the rights and freedoms set forth in this Declaration, without distinction of any kind, such as race, colour, sex, language, religion, political or other opinion, national or social origin, property, birth or other status.

Article 18

Everyone has the right to freedom of thought, conscience and religion; this right includes freedom to change his religion or belief, and freedom, either alone or in community with others and in public or private, to manifest his religion or belief in teaching, practice, worship and observance.

Japan's Meiji Constitution of 1889

Article 28
Japanese subjects shall, within limits not prejudicial to peace and order, and not antagonistic to their duties as subjects, enjoy freedom of religious belief.[44]

People's Republic of China

Article 36
Citizens of the People's Republic of China enjoy freedom of religious belief. No state organ, public organization or individual may compel citizens to believe in, or not to believe in, any religion; nor may they discriminate against citizens who believe in, or do not believe in, any religion. The state protects normal religious activities. No one may make use of religion to engage in activities that disrupt public order, impair the health of citizens or interfere with the educational system of the state. Religious bodies and religious affairs are not subject to any foreign domination.[45]

Religion, from the perspective of the constitutional language above, is never defined but appears to be at least six things:

1. It is said to be the opposite of the secular and indeed is usually juxtaposed against the secular.
2. It is a noun, that is, a tangible social phenomenon and projected reality that influences citizens' lives, albeit in ways never explained.
3. It is always presented as a universal phenomenon. (Even "not believing" is presented as a religious option.)

4. It is fundamentally about belief and is almost always described and defined as "belief" and "believers.'

5. It is under the control of the state, especially when it comes to the role of education.

6. It is understood to be, with regard to freedom of expression, an inalienable human right.

Jeremy Gunn, a scholar of international studies, points out that the term religion "remains undefined as a matter of international law." Gunn explains that this can cause real juridical challenges, specifically when it comes to asylum law and refugees seeking asylum because of religious persecution. A judge must then decide what constitutes religion if the asylum seeker is to be granted asylum. In the United States, the Supreme Court has made decisions on the First Amendment regarding religion dozens of times over the decades. In other words, in each case that comes before them, the justices make a call as to what counts as religion, belief, religious practice, and so forth. Gunn points out that two of the most common rulings made in international court cases are (1) protecting freedom of religion, and (2) prohibiting persecution or discriminating against religion. The resulting decisions, however, are not always positive. As Gunn explains: "Legal definitions, as a result, may contain serious deficiencies when they (perhaps unintentionally) incorporate particular social and cultural attitudes towards (preferred) religions, or when they fail to account for social and cultural attitudes against (disfavored) religions."[46] A messy business, indeed, especially when the justice system must decide what is a "real" religion. From a Durkheimian perspective, all religions are real. This doesn't make it any easier for a judge's ruling. What we see in the constitutional language about religion above is that the term is a noun—a reified sui generis phenomenon.

On the Inviolable

There is a close relationship between the terms inviolate and inviolable, and one could argue that they are synonyms. The *Oxford English Dictionary* defines each term as follows:

> Inviolate—Not violated; free from violation; unhurt, uninjured, unbroken; unprofaned, unmarred; intact. Of laws, compacts, principles, institutions, sacred or moral qualities.

> Inviolable—Not to be violated; not liable or allowed to suffer violence; to be kept sacredly free from profanation, infraction, or assault. Of laws, treaties, institutions, customs, principles, sacred or cherished feelings, etc.[47]

Not all the constitutions discussed above use the terms, but many do. (If they don't, they use descriptive language akin to the terms.) My goal is to look at how the inviolate and the inviolable are used in several constitutions and then think about other domains that a nation-state could consider inviolate. As argued thus far, sacrality and the inviolate are inextricably linked. In the preface I made the claim that it is the inviolate that frames and sustains the nation-state; that it is the inviolate, or perhaps more precisely the assertion of inviolability, that is used to justify territorial integrity and state sovereignty. The inviolate works to define citizens of the state and make them loyal members of the nation. What follows are some constitutional examples.

Turkey

Article 12

Everyone possesses inherent fundamental rights and freedoms which are inviolable and inalienable. [Later the constitution also refers to the "inviolability of the domicile."]

Netherlands

Article 11

Everyone shall have the right to inviolability of his person, without prejudice to restrictions laid down by or pursuant to Act of Parliament.

Mexico

Article 7

Freedom of writing and publishing writings on any subject is inviolable.

Article 61

Deputies and senators are inviolable for opinions expressed by them in the discharge of their offices and shall never be called to account for them. [The third use in title IX is self-referential: "The Inviolability of the Constitution." The text itself is the inviolate.]

People's Republic of China

Article 13

Citizens' lawful private property is inviolable.

Article 37

The freedom of person of citizens of the People's Republic of China is inviolable. . . .

The personal dignity of citizens of the People's Republic of China is inviolable.

Article 39

The home of citizens of the People's Republic of China is inviolable.

Japan's Meiji Constitution of 1889

Article 3
The emperor is sacred and inviolable.[48]

Article 27
The right of property of every Japanese subject shall remain inviolate.

Japan

Article 11 [Fundamental Human Rights]
(1) The people shall not be prevented from enjoying any of the fundamental human rights. (2) These fundamental human rights, guaranteed to the people by this Constitution, shall be conferred upon the people of this and future generations as irrevocable and inviolable rights.

Article 22 [Right to Move, Freedom of Profession]
(2) Freedom of all persons to move to a foreign country and to divest themselves of their nationality shall be inviolate.

Article 29 [Property]
(1) The right to own or to hold property is inviolable.

Article 97 [Inviolable Human Rights]
The fundamental human rights by this Constitution guaranteed to the people of Japan are fruits of the age-old struggle of man to be free; they have survived the many exacting tests for durability and are conferred upon this and future generations in trust, to be held for all time inviolable.

Chile

Article 19

5. Inviolability of homes and all forms of private communication. Homes may be searched and private communications and documents intercepted, opened or inspected only in the case and in the manner prescribed for by law;

Article 58

Deputies and Senators enjoy inviolability only with regard to the opinions they should express and the votes registered in performance of their duties in Congressional Sessions or in Committees.

In list form we see the inviolable as follows:

- Fundamental rights and freedoms (Turkey)
- One's home (Turkey, China, Chile)[49]
- Writing and publishing on any topic (Mexico)
- Owning or holding property (Japan, Meiji Japan, China)[50]
- Freedom to move to another country (Japan)
- Human rights (Japan)
- The emperor (Meiji Japan)[51]
- The constitution itself (Mexico)
- Freedom of person and personal dignity (China)

Here we see a broad range of domains that can constitute the inviolate, but the most powerful inviolate of all is the state itself and its territory. In all the examples above, inviolableness can be undone by the state in accordance with the law. The state, of course, writes those laws.

The structural connection, then, between constitutional normative statements such as "freedom of religion" and the inviolate contributes to a mythological narrative that the nation-state must produce and narrate to its citizenry. As suggested in this chapter, the constitution as a mythos production makes it a religious text, where religiosity can be understood as a form of exchange, a form of action and transaction between the state and its populace. State soteriology depends on control of its populace via the inviolate. Salvation is to be found in dutiful citizenship.

We saw above how constitutions use and shape another category of the inviolate—religion—as a noun. The next two chapters will explore this further.

3

Religion

Living and traveling in different parts of East Asia over the last twenty-five years, I have been told many times by people, even monks, that they are not religious, or that they don't subscribe to a religion. How can this be, and what is wrong with the term as a descriptive category of reality?[1] The answer is both simple and complicated. The simple answer is that no non-European culture that I am aware of has historically had a term for religion in its indigenous language.[2] "Religion" as a noun does not exist as a tangible phenomenon outside of Christian Europe and, later, the Americas.[3] In other words, religion as a genus with a variety of subdivisional "species" below it is no more or less real than any other human activity. For practical reasons (sometime political, sometimes cultural), we try to define religion as a distinct activity in contrast, say, to baseball.[4]

Nevertheless, why so many scholars and others, like constitution writers and government appointees, seek to isolate religion out of all other possible human activities is puzzling, at least to me.[5] Jonathan Z. Smith has frequently raised this conundrum. In one interview, he asks: "Why, we in our . . . cultural complex, have we found it necessary, out of the complexity of human activities, to say that we can find one in there that we want to call religion?"[6] When we use the term, everyone in the room nods their head in agreement that we all know what religion is; or, at the least, we think we can see a type of human activity, point to it, and say "that is religion." We don't mean the same thing at all when we use the term. It is a term of designation specific to the cultural moment as to when and how it is used.

Regardless of Smith's conundrum, what we do know is that with the export of Christianity during the colonial nineteenth century, the term "religion" was always associated with a single God, the Truth, and interior belief, just as we saw in constitutional language in the previous chapter. This meant, at the time, that if someone did not self-identify as Christian, they therefore did not have religion.[7] For good reason, many people in Asia today still consider religion to mean Christianity, or phenomena resembling Christianity. (Buddhism sometimes falls into this category, along with a list of "isms.")

The more complicated answer is precisely how religion comes to be constructed and used as a category deeply entwined with Christianity and colonialism and later as a legal category in modern nation-state making. One quick example is from, perhaps somewhat ironically, a non-European colonial power—Japan. The Japanese Empire was an imperium that sought to rapidly compete in the colonial competitions of the nineteenth century. In part inspired by European expansionism, Japan had imperial aspirations, really the only Asian nation to do so, and the first to begin to build a military-industrial complex by the late nineteenth century, soon after the Meiji period began in 1868. With Western Europe, especially Germany, as the obvious model, Japan began building an army and a navy, both entities that require specific forms of nationalism to energize, motivate, justify, and successfully deploy, as was seen with Japan's defeat of the Russian Navy at the Tsushima Strait in May 1905. All of Asia celebrated. When the state seeks to create a nation, expand what is typically termed its "sacred territory," protect its claims to sovereign borders, ones usually established through violence, and simultaneously empower and contain the polity, a military becomes a requisite entity; but how to generate nationalism as a binding social force? How to create the nation-state that the state needs to sacralize? Japan's imperial history had until then seen no such social formation.

For decades, roughly from the 1850s through the 1870s, Japan struggled with the category of religion, something that was to be identified with European Christianity. A term for "religion" had to be constructed, and it was done by combining two ideographs borrowed from China, *shū* (lit. lineage) and *kyō* (lit. teaching).[8] (In Chinese this is pronounced *zongjiao*, using the same ideographs as *shūkyō*.)

The struggle in Japan over the term religion led, in part, to what is sometimes called state Shinto, a galvanizing social force that formed the basis for a powerful nationalism that was to carry Japan through World War II.[9] As Jason Ananda Josephson explains, "Japanese officials translated pressure from Western Christians into a concept of religion that carved out a private space for belief in Christianity and certain forms of Buddhism, but also embedded Shinto in the very structure of the state and exiled various 'superstitions' beyond the sphere of tolerance."[10] In the Japanese context, state Shinto would not "count" as *shūkyō* proper, but I would suggest that we can understand it as a form of religio-nationalism. In this sense, Japan had set the precedent in East Asia for repurposing the category of religion to juxtapose and bolster its newly formed state nationalism, a social force required to develop the military-industrial complex. Or, to borrow Josephson's words, "Through the legal invention of religion, the state was able to extend its power in new ways."[11] Religion, a phenomenon so clearly central to European modernity, came to be understood as an integral building block of a modern nation-state precisely because the term was needed to create antinomies that could further facilitate social control. It is here that we have the epistemological conundrum: the term religion, a European construction with intimate ties to Christianity, was now being used in East Asia and in a manner deeply connected with nation-state building.

At the end of the nineteenth century, China borrowed back this neologism from Japan so it also could categorize and galvanize certain forms of social behavior, not so much in imitation of European nations but instead with the hopes of fending them off. Soon after the Hundred Days' reform began in 1898 under the Guangxu emperor (1871–1908)[12] and Kang Youwei (1858–1927), new discursive terms describing religion, such as *zongjiao*, began to appear mainly in newspaper articles.[13] Vincent Goossaert finds the first explicit use of the term *zongjiao* in a press article published in 1901 by Liang Qichao (1873–1929), scholar, philosopher, and journalist and a contemporary of Kang Youwei.[14] About the same time we see the category *mixin*, for "superstition," used as a counterpoint to *zongjiao*.[15] Historian Rebecca Nedostup points out that while Liang helped popularize the term *zongjiao*, he fought hard against *mixin*.[16] Mayfair Yang writes that she found no use of the latter term in the entire *Siku quanshu*, a massive Qing imperial collection of more than thirty-six thousand volumes. *Mixin* first appears in late Qing publications, circa 1901.[17] The point is that none of these are native Chinese terms, and all derive from neologisms constructed in Japan in efforts to capture Western notions of religiosity (as action) and religion (as inner piety), in both cases an unwitting appropriation of Christian theological categories. Nevertheless, as Yang points out, these terms were used more to suppress religious life in China at the turn of the century, and I would say they continue to be used to suppress Chinese religiosities today. (I am aware that the term religion is still not clear in meaning and that I run the risk of reifying it. It's a risk worth taking.)

At this stage, I want to look at the category in other contemporary circumstances before investigating how the term religion is used as a state tool in China.

Coming to Terms

Semantically, the term religion is a mess; more problematic, however, is what Timothy Fitzgerald points to: "Today 'religion' is a powerful ideological term because it combines a number of analytically separable meanings which, when merged in the flow of unanalyzed discourse and rhetoric, render the term inherently unstable." Fitzgerald goes on to say that "we cannot understand what we mean by religion unless we put it into relation with what we mean by nonreligion; but then the reverse is also true. They are semantically parasitic categories."[18] Or as Mary Douglas puts it: "Religion does not explain. Religion has to be explained."[19] What, then, does China mean today by religion? For a possible answer, I went to the Museum of World Religions in Taipei, Taiwan. (It was not lost on me that mainland China claims Taiwan as part of its territory and thus in a sense claims the museum as well.) In exploring a museum that has religion as its primary exhibit, I wanted to try to understand how an institution so advertently in the public eye explains religion. Afterward we will shift to the United States to look at a specific governmental use of the category of religion.

Museification

Plain happenstance: just before leaving my Taipei hotel in the morning to visit the Museum of World Religions, I open the bedroom drawer to find the ubiquitous Bible (though this one is in Chinese and English) and, remarkably, a copy of a text called

108 Adages of Wisdom by Master Sheng Yen, a well-known Taiwanese Buddhist monk. I also find a book with the title *The Teaching of Buddha*. All three make for interesting reading, and their proximity and drawer companionship are insightful given the morning I'm about to have.

After a subway ride and some walking, I stand on the corner of Baosheng and Zhongshan Roads in the Yonghe district of Taipei, just across from a slim, handsome, gray and black building. On the left wall as one faces the entrance is a small sign that reads *Shijie zongjiao bowuguan*. Higher up the glass face of the building, vertical from top to bottom in huge brass characters, is the same, and running alongside it is the English translation as well (Museum of World Religions). Further down the structure nine colorful banners hang, each marked with a religious symbol, a deferential nod to the construction of world religions in the nineteenth century—green (crescent moon and star; Islam), maroon (*om* in Sanskrit; Hinduism), lavender (a *khanda*; Sikhism), mustard yellow (a Dharma wheel; Buddhism), red (a *tori* gate; Shinto), black (*yinyang* sign; Daoism), purple (a cross; Christianity), yellow (unclear to me), gray (an *ankh*; ancient Egypt? Gnosticism?), and blue (Star of David; Judaism).

I pay a small entrance fee and use an elevator to get to the main entrance. There I walk down a narrow winding hall with an unlikely mix of virtual pilgrims, all headed for some unidentified salvific destiny—Hare Krishnas pounding on drums, Catholic pilgrims with hands folded in prayer. The hallway resonates, and sounds of chanting bounce back and forth as I walk down it. As my brief pilgrimage comes to an end, I run into a guide who asks me if I need help. She suggests I start in the main hall where, she tells me, all the world's religions are represented. So I do. A sign on a pillar reads, "To experience eternality and life head further down the corridor." I postpone that trip for the moment and head into what the museum calls "The Great Hall of World Religions." Eight "world religions" are listed in the following order: Christianity, Islam, Buddhism, Daoism, Hinduism, Sikhism, Judaism, and Shinto.

First stop is the multiplicity of Taiwanese deities, most with roots in mainland China, some more prevalent than others. There are the usual suspects: Lao Jun (the deified Laozi), the historical Buddha (a different display behind thick glass will house more buddhas and bodhisattvas, mostly in Indian style, a nod to the Buddha's origins), some bodhisattvas, some heavenly kings, the three pure ones of the Daoist pantheon. Behind me is the "Wall of Gratitude." The museum is celebrating its tenth anniversary, and this wall expresses gratitude to all the donors. Temples, churches, synagogues, and mosques work for the living; museums represent the dead. All, however, require substantial economic resources as well as serious cultural and economic capital.

A church to the Virgin Mary is on one side of me; directly in front of it is a replica of the Kandariya Mahadeva Temple in Madhya Pradesh, India, built in 1050, stunning in its ornateness and design and in its dedication to Siva. The replica is small but accurate. As I stand close to each replica, music drops down from speakers set into the ceiling—chants, singing, and so forth, ostensibly connected to that specific temple/mosque/church/ shrine. It's surprising, a near cacophony-like experience. The music is not that loud, but as other visitors (pilgrims?) move around the replicas, I hear different styles of music coming through hidden speakers. It feels strange and disorienting, which I suspect is not the point. In other words, this center of world religiosity is supposed to encompass all, extend to all, welcome all, and surround humanity with a sense of belongingness and well-being. I do not experience this.

I stand for a long time in front of a thirteenth-century synagogue from Prague, one of the few if not only surviving Jewish structures in this region from the Middle Ages. The sign tells me that synagogues are the centers for Jewish life and community. Nearby are a Torah scroll (a model, I'm sure), a menorah, and other odds and ends that are supposedly representative of Jewishness, though no definitional position is taken per se. That's a good thing. Posing the questions "Who is a Jew, and what is Judaism?" would throw the entire presentation into disarray. Nearby, the Dome of the Rock is impressive, as is Ise Shrine, the Shinto construction dedicated to Amaterasu-no-kami. It's an odd feeling to look to my left and then to the right. On to the Egyptians. An offering table looks authentic to me; or, if not, it is an excellent reproduction. Two other exhibits (rotating) are to represent "Ancient Religions" and "Indigenous Religions." The top of the sign reads: "The Central Hall of World Religions explores the world's religious traditions through examples of the religious impulse." This sounds like a Geertzian phrase, but no definition is given.

So, what is the purpose of all this? Who is the audience?[20] The English front page of the website reads: "The Museum of World Religions belongs to all faiths. Its founding is inspiring and encouraging interfaith dialogue so that we all work together to create peace and understanding in the world we share."[21] Who doesn't want peace and understanding (and love), but why a museum? What is the significance of having a museum of world religions? It's not the intention that is in question but instead the conceptual categories that explain, contain, and represent the museum. A museum petrifies all objects within it. These are deceased objects offering a glimpse at a reality that is carefully construed to offer the viewer the maximum visual experience. Vision indeed dominates this process. The displays with their lighting draw the viewer's eye this way and that.

Giorgio Agamben argues that the museification of the world is now well established. One by one, "art, religion, the idea of nature, even politics . . . have docilely withdrawn into the Museum." And further, any space can now become a museum as it exhibits "an impossibility of using, of dwelling, of experiencing."[22] The objects in the museum are dead culture, or at best frozen in space-time and thus barely representative of the living.[23] There is a relationship between capitalism and museums, and it lies in the desire to accumulate and possess, then to put on display as a form of cultural capital. The museum also speaks to a particular type of globalization. Religion is globalized in the displays. It is portrayed as a universal part of humanity's need for upliftment and explanation. By globalization I don't mean the obvious forms, such as the World Trade Organization, the United Nations, or trade markets, but instead a more localized form of the global. The global is brought into the local, and by participating in the exhibits, by moving through them, we hope to have a globalized experience of sacrality. The problem is, we view the objects and do not interact with them. Any possible sacrality is nullified (but this nullification is usually unrecognizable by the viewer). The living walk among the dead, and the apparatuses of power at stake are based on a unidirectional vision. The viewer looks at the objects often in wonder, then immediately wanders over to the next cultural artifact.

While the sacred is not found here, the liminal is. There is a threshold to behold. Perhaps the visitor is to a limited extent a participant-observer. The rites and rituals are not present, but the viewer can still be entranced between two worlds, a liminal space of observation. This liminality is not Rudolf Otto's *Das Heilige* (the holy), but there is a *mysterium tremendum*. There can be a feeling, a form of Victor Turner's betwixt-and-between. There is a poetic irrationality in viewing these objects. Still, the power differential is oblique as the objects being viewed are so thoroughly displaced. The Museum of World Religions has little to do with the world; it simply exoticizes.

And so, in the final analysis, the sacred is not to be found here, nor indeed is the meaning of the term religion. The irony is that all attempts at sacralization end up as precisely the opposite—desacralization and an obscene displacement of artifacts. Thus there is no real global, no territorialization other than perhaps that of the viewer's reaction to the objects on display. The museum wants to express religion in a public context, or at least what religion looks like publicly. The interior of the museum is meant to orient viewers and make them participant-observers. It has the opposite effect.

Of Particular Concern

If Taipei couldn't help me, then perhaps Washington, D.C., could. There, a group of nine commissioners display on a government website their work and judgment having to do with what they call "religious freedom." They report directly to the president of the United States. They are the United States Commission on International Religious Freedom (USCIRF).[24] My main concern here is how the nation-state handles its affairs when it comes to the complex relationship between state and religion, and between religion and human rights. The USCIRF states its clear-cut reliance on the Universal Declaration of Human Rights.[25]

The commission is, by its own account, a bipartisan and independent federal body that was created by the International Religious Freedom Act of 1998 (IRFA).[26] Commissioners are appointed by the U.S. president along with congressional leaders from both the Democratic and Republican Parties. As Robert P. George, a former chairman of the commission, tells us, "The Commission monitors the conditions of religious liberty abroad and recommends policies to the President, Secretary of State, and Congress to advance this most precious right." So religion, as we also saw in the previous chapter, is ever undefined, universal, and a human right.

China is listed in what the commission refers to as "Tier 1: for 'Countries of Particular Concern.'" The USCIRF report from 2013 (coming in at 364 pages) explains the tier as follows:

> Tier 1 countries are those that USCIRF recommends the United States designate as "countries of particular concern" (CPCs) under IRFA for their governments' engagement in or toleration of particularly severe violations of religious freedom. Tier 1 countries include countries already officially designated as CPCs by the U.S. government and additional countries USCIRF has concluded meet the CPC threshold and should be so designated.[27]

In the 2019 report, IRFA is employed to make the following case regarding CPCs: "IRFA requires the president—who has delegated this power to the secretary of state—to designate CPCs annually and take action designed to encourage improvements in those countries. CPCs are defined as countries whose governments either engage in or tolerate "particularly severe" violations of religious freedom." The USCIRF recommends that the secretary of state designate the following sixteen countries as CPCs: Burma, Central African Republic, China, Eritrea, Iran, Nigeria, North Korea, Pakistan, Saudi Arabia, Sudan, Syria, Tajikistan, Turkmenistan, Uzbekistan, and Vietnam.

How does the commission ultimately decide what counts as religious freedom and what does not? Who gives it this authority? Not the U.S. Constitution; the founding fathers' take on religion is ambiguous at best and incomprehensible at worst.[28] There are no statements in the First Amendment about "religious freedom" or any definition of religion. The "free exercise thereof," yes, but is this the same thing as "religious freedom"? One could presume that in all likelihood when the writers of the Constitution used the term "religion" they simply meant Christianity (though they would have been aware of Judaism and Islam). Nevertheless, the USCIRF stands on some shaky ground when it comes to how it decides which country should go on its watch lists. Violence is one of the indicators, to be sure, but how to distinguish between ethnic and religious violence, for example, or between political and religious violence? Then there is the danger of what one scholar calls the myth of religious violence, which can easily legitimate so-called secular powers using force against religious violence.[29] While the commission can and does make policy recommendations to the president, it is far from clear what the outcome is when this happens.

China is, not surprisingly, on the watch list and is in tier 1. So what steps does China take to signify its intentions toward religion—again, bearing in mind that neither the USCIRF, the U.S. State Department, the UN Human Rights Council, nor the Chinese government has actually defined what it means by religion.[30] The unconscious assumption that religion is universal is mistaken. The decision that it is a human right assumes that religion is the same in all places at all times for all cultures. It is not, especially when there is no "it" to begin with. Specificity, though, is rarely the mark of nation-state governments, again, a space where morality is up for grabs.

Freedom of religion and belief cannot be maintained as human rights as understood through the large institutions that heretofore have laid claim to them—the United Nations, the International Red Cross, Human Rights Watch. These claims to protect and project such rights are also deeply intertwined with the export of Euroamerican ideals; ideals that stem from Christian roots and imperialist pasts. Stephen Hopgood writes: "Human Rights are a New York-Geneva-London-centered ideology focused on international law, criminal justice, and institutions of global governance. Human Rights are a product of the

1%."[31] Their origins can be highlighted in three documents: the American Declaration of Independence, which in 1776 extolled that "all men are created equal, that they are endowed with certain unalienable Rights"; the French Declaration of the Rights of Man and Citizen in 1789; and the Universal Declaration of Human Rights in 1948. The first two were in response to kingly power, the third to a post–World War II reality. So, to New York-Geneva-London we can add Philadelphia and Paris. In reference to these documents, Lynn Hunt has an important observation. All three of them refer to human rights as being self-evident. This, she points out, gives rise to a paradox: "If equality of rights is so self-evident, then why did this assertion have to be made and why was it only made in specific times and places? How can human rights be universal it they are not universally recognized?"[32]

Thus the frequent rebuke and criticism of China as a human rights violator derives primarily from liberal, democratic powers who have lost much of their legitimacy since 1945. Or, to put this another way, as Hopgood does so well, "It is not credible to name and shame a government with which you consistently align."[33] Now, granted the degree to which the United States and European countries "align" themselves with China is a matter of debate, but I think it's enough to just point to trade pacts between China and other nations, especially the United States. (On the one hand, the current Trump administration wants to contain China; on the other, we desperately need to be a strategic partner.)

Who gives the United States the moral authority to criticize China's human rights record? I think it's an important question that, if thought through, can avoid the pitfalls of apologetics and provide a more compelling critique of how nation-states use human rights (or, as Hopgood would critically say, "Human Rights" with a capital H and R) to advance their political agendas. If Hopgood is correct, then the moral authority of the United

States derives from a particular type of secular humanism that came to replace the loss of religious authority in Europe. He writes: "In other words, bourgeois Europeans responded to the erosion of religious authority by creating authority of their own from the cultural resources that lay scattered around them. And then they globalized it via the infrastructure that the imperial civilizing project bequeathed to them."[34] He calls this new form of Human Rights—new since the early twentieth century—a type of secular religiosity. In other words, leaning heavily on the separation of church and state, moral authority depended on a new set of constructed values that needed to be universal and thoroughly Euroamerican. These universal humanist principles went hand in hand with the systemic violence that the nation-state uses to maintain its hegemony. The results are all too familiar: profound economic disparities around the globe, more wealth in the hands of the few, dramatic inequalities that worsen over time, and all this amid the multipolar, globally intertwined networks of relations that are now our modern world—the hangover of global capitalism. Irrespective of these radical social disparities, human rights as a value-system has spread rapidly around the globe.

The problem, however, is they do not work in their current form as universal values. The local and the global are now so interdependent and complex that universalism doesn't stand a chance. Let us consider the following statement by Giorgio Agamben:

> It is time to stop regarding declarations of rights as proclamations of eternal, metajuridical values binding the legislator (in fact, without much success) to respect eternal ethical principles, and to begin to consider them according to their real historical function in the modern nation-state. Declarations of rights represent the originary figure of the inscription of natural life in the juridico-political order of the nation-state.[35]

In other words, human rights are as much about categorizing and controlling human beings as they are about protecting them. For Agamben, human rights are biopolitical mechanisms of control. They are a vital component of the nation-state. Further, we worsen the possibility of a positive outcome when we use human rights as a reason for intervention in another's territory.

Let's for a moment consider the refugee. In 2008 Agamben wrote the following:

> It is also the case that, given the by now unstoppable decline of the nation-state and the general corrosion of traditional political-juridical categories, the refugee is perhaps the only thinkable figure for the people of our time and the only category in which one may see today—at least until the process of dissolution of the nation- state and of its sovereignty has achieved full completion—the forms and limits of a coming political community. It is even possible that, if we want to be equal to the absolutely new tasks ahead, we will have to abandon decidedly, without reservation, the fundamental concepts through which we have so far represented the subjects of the political (Man, the Citizen and its rights, but also the sovereign people, the worker, and so forth) and build our political philosophy anew starting from the one and only figure of the refugee.[36]

Agamben points out that the first modern appearance of refugees was after World War I, with the fall of three empires—the Russian, Austro-Hungarian, and Ottoman. Some 1.5 million White Russians were displaced along with 700,000 Armenians, 500,000 Bulgarians, a million Greeks, and hundreds of thousands of Romanians, Germans, and Hungarians.[37] Agamben rightly expresses how we are used to distinguishing between stateless people and refugees. This is rarely a clear distinction, especially when a state strips individuals of their citizenship, or when a stateless person decides not to return under any circumstances to his or her former state.[38] Perhaps more important, there is a difference between the individual citizen of rights, who for whatever reason becomes stateless, and the larger phenomenon of mass refugee groups. All the inalienable rights under the sun have little or no effect on such refugees.[39] The United Nations flails in the face of such a humanitarian crisis. Agamben points out the obvious connection, then, between the inability of the nation-state to protect precisely at the time when it is most required to do so and the sheer impossibility of solving the refugee phenomenon. Sacred, inalienable rights in that moment are incapable of being just that.

Back to Religion

If human rights are fraught, freedom of religion as a human right is even more so.[40] Categories that are in different ways connected to that of religion—politics, economics, science, the state—are typically understood to be nonreligious and implicitly as more rational. Here lies our aporia: I am not questioning the everyday material practices of human beings. I question the terms we use to categorize those practices. Or as Michel Foucault once put it, albeit in slightly different circumstances, "On what 'table,' according to what grid of identities, similitudes, analogies, have we become accustomed to sort out so many different and similar things?"[41]

There are no religions (as nouns, as tangibles) "out there." The term doesn't exist as a native term in any other language other than as a neologism. This is not to say that activities we designate as religious are not taking place; of course they are.[42] But it is to say how telling that an English term with European origins now is used to explain any action and any tradition in any culture on any part of the Earth's surface as religious, or as a religion with beliefs and practices, that stunningly useless antinomy that presents itself as a dichotomy but hides the inextricable character of the thing to which it refers. Beliefs—to the extent that we are even able to access these in different places and times, a dubious possibility—are practices. So we do face the challenge of reifying the term religion (and, subsequently, its construal as an inalienable human right).

We are not, irrespective of language, culture, or discipline, talking about the same thing when we so easily refer to religion in the public or private sphere in a social setting, be it in China or elsewhere. What, then, happens to the European category of religion when China encounters and appropriates it in the nineteenth century, adds to it a large measure of nationalism, and then constitutionalizes it? When China's constitution uses the term "religion," as we saw in the previous chapter, it means, at least in part, that the term *zongjiao*, because it is made into a constitutional category, therefore becomes a legal category and as such is subject to state enforcement. The government document the Chinese government relies on most when it comes to religion is document 19.

Document 19

Document 19 is still the guiding document for religious policy in China today.[43] Published and distributed to all provincial and municipal committees, commissions, the PLA, and a variety of state organs on March 31, 1982, the document provides a historical overview of the way the CCP understands religion vis-à-vis its own composition as an ideological apparatus.

First, religion is not a tangible phenomenon that can just be eradicated, the stated goal during the Cultural Revolution (1966–1976) and the early post-Mao period. On the contrary, it is a

fungible category of emplacement and not the sui generis phenomenon document 19 claims it to be. After the preamble we
read the following:

> Religion is a historical phenomenon pertaining to a definite
> period in the development of human society. It has its own cycle
> of emergence, development, and demise. Religious faith and reli-
> gious sentiment, along with religious ceremonies and organiza-
> tions consonant with this faith and sentiment, are all products of
> the history of society. The earliest emergence of the religious
> mentality reflected the low level of production and the sense of
> awe toward natural phenomena of primitive peoples.

Religion is initially not defined but is made into a question, the
"religious question" (*zongjiao de wenti*), and one that must be
answered. Document 19 states it this way:

> Religion will eventually disappear from human history. But it will
> disappear naturally only through the long-term development of
> Socialism and Communism, when all objective requirements are
> met. All Party members must have a sober-minded recognition
> of the protracted nature of the religious question under Socialist
> conditions. Those who think that with the establishment of the
> Socialist system and with a certain degree of economic and cul-
> tural progress, religion will die out within a short period, are not
> being realistic.

And later, toward the end of the document:

> Under Socialism, the only correct fundamental way to solve
> the religious question lies precisely in safeguarding the freedom
> of religious belief. Only after the gradual development of the

Socialist, economic, cultural, scientific, and technological enterprise and of a Socialist civilization with its own material and
spiritual values, will the type of society and level of awareness
that gave rise to the existence of religion gradually disappear.

This seems like a potential contradiction: The only way to get
rid of religion is to protect it? What I believe document 19 means
here is that the only way to solve the religious problem is to contain and control it.

This containment and control is also why document 19, in its
efforts to ease the demise of religion, sets up a precedent for the
preservation and restoration of temples and churches. Each institution can then be carefully monitored.

> We must systematically and methodically restore a number of
> temples and churches in large and mid-size cities, at famous his-
> torical sites, and in areas in which there is a concentration of reli-
> gious believers, especially ethnic minority areas. Famous tem-
> ples and churches of cultural and historical value which enjoy
> national and international prestige must be progressively restored
> as far as is possible, according to conditions in each place.

In other words, the document claims, if we protect religions, their practitioners—but only those we deem to be really
practicing/believing, and only religions that we consider to be
"normal"—restore temples and churches, ensure that "all places
of worship are under the administrative control of the Bureau
of Religious Affairs,"[44] and then wait patiently, religion will
eventually disappear. Moreover, under close administrative
supervision, "We must foster a large number of fervent patriots
in every religion who accept the leadership of the Party and
government, firmly support the socialist path, and safeguard

national and ethnic unity." Here, religion is tied to patriotism. Loyalty to the nation takes precedence over religiosity, and when the latter takes place it must do so under carefully controlled conditions.

Religion and religious belief, while ostensibly protected by the Communist Party, are not activities that CCP members themselves can participate in. Document 19 is clear about this:

> The fact that our Party proclaims and implements a policy of freedom of religious belief does not, of course, mean that Communist Party members can freely believe in religion. The policy of freedom of religious belief is directed toward the citizens of our country; it is not applicable to Party members. Unlike the average citizen, the Party member belongs to a Marxist political party, and there can be no doubt at all that s/he must be an atheist and not a theist. Our Party has clearly stated on many previous occasions: a Communist Party member cannot be a religious believer; s/he cannot take part in religious activities. Any member who persists in going against this proscription should be told to leave the Party.

This is still the official policy today, but it is well-known that many party members do participate in religious practices. Unless public visibility becomes a distracting issue, little tends to be done about this. One section of document 19 outlines the need for protection from antirevolutionary activists who hide behind the "facade of religion":

> The resolute protection of all normal religious activities suggests, at the same time, a determined crackdown on all criminal and anti-revolutionary activities which hide behind the facade of religion, which includes all superstitious practices which fall outside

the scope of religion and are injurious to the national welfare as well as to the life and property of the people. All anti-revolutionary or other criminal elements who hide behind the facade of religion will be severely punished according to the law.

The reference to "normal religious activities" is the most troubling phrase in document 19 and in article 36 of the Constitution of the PRC (to be discussed more fully in the next chapter). It gives the government sweeping juridical power to declare any organization, group, or individual as engaging in "nonnormal" activities. They can therefore be detained, put on trial, and imprisoned if need be, as we saw with Falungong members.[45] The basic position of the Party toward "normal" religion is described as follows:

The basic policy the Party has adopted toward the religious question is that of respect for and protection of the freedom of religious belief. This is a long-term policy, one which must be continually carried out until that future time when religion will itself disappear. What do we mean by freedom of religious belief? We mean that every citizen has the freedom to believe in religion and also the freedom not to believe in religion. S/he has also the freedom to believe in this religion or that religion. Within a particular religion, s/he has the freedom to believe in this sect or that sect. A person who was previously a nonbeliever has the freedom to become a religious believer, and one who has been a religious believer has the freedom to become a nonbeliever. We Communists are atheists and must unremittingly propagate atheism. Yet at the same time we must understand that it will be fruitless and extremely harmful to use simple coercion in dealing with the people's ideological and spiritual questions—and this includes religious questions.

Contrary to the claim in the final sentence above, we will see examples of coercion in the next chapter.

With document 19 as the guiding principles, it is the State Administration for Religious Affairs (SARA), an organization under the State Council, that is directly responsible for overseeing religious activity in China.[46] SARA's mandate is as follows:

> Its major responsibilities are to study and propose policies and guidelines for the work related to religious affairs, formulate and implement such policies and guidelines, investigate and study the religious situation in China and abroad to maintain grasp of the developments, study the issue of religious theories, propose policy suggestions; guide and promote religious circles to conduct their activities within the framework of law and policies and protect citizens' freedom of religious belief.[47]

All members of SARA, including all members of the local religious affairs bureaus at the county level, are typically members of the CCP; thus they are not allowed themselves to be religious. Again, how this is monitored and how at the local level one decides who is religious is virtually impossible to explain. Any enforcement of juridical determinations, however, tends to be carried out by the Ministry of Public Security, also an organization under the State Council.[48] This ministry has what are called Public Security Bureaus (PSB) at the provincial and county levels, and within these there are units whose responsibility is to investigate religious groups and their activities.[49] Again, the definitional problem never goes away. Many indigenous groups in China (for lack of a better phrase, "non-Han" Chinese) engage in a variety of practices that do not fall neatly under the five sanctioned religions; however, these activities are regarded as cultural rather than religious, an iffy distinction by any account.

Decree no. 426, which backs up what document 19 stipulates, was adopted at the fifty-seventh executive meeting of the State Council on July 7, 2004, and signed by then premier Wen Jiabao. This decree was updated in September 2017 and signed by Premier Li Keqiang.[50] It repeats much of what is already stated in document 19 but presents two categories that I haven't seen in any of the other documents, namely, the "religious citizen" (*zongjiao de gongmin*) and "nonreligious citizens" (*bu xinjiao gongmin*). They appear in article 2, which reads as follows:

> Citizens have the freedom of religious belief.[51] No organization or individual may compel citizens to believe in, or not to believe in, any religion; nor may they discriminate against citizens who believe in any religion (hereafter referred to as religious citizens) or citizens who do not believe in any religion (hereafter referred to as nonreligious citizens). Religious citizens and nonreligious citizens should mutually respect one another other and coexist in harmony. So too should citizens who believe in different religions.

The puzzling parts are the last two sentences. Presumably "religious citizens" are those who practice any of the five officially sanctioned religions (Buddhism, Daoism, Islam, Protestantism, and Catholicism), but then who are these citizens who believe in different religions?[52] It must therefore be about social control: the language of article 2 gives the state the power to decide when and which religious practitioners are not coexisting in harmony, and the state gets to decide what constitutes religion. Citizens who "believe in different religions," presumably those outside of the sanctioned five, would in effect be breaking the law. Reification of the term aside for the moment, any religious citizen not registered with the five oversight organizations is breaking the law.[53]

For instance, there is a special security office called the "610 Office" (its name comes from June 10, 1999, when the office was formed) whose primary mission is to seek out and persecute any members of the Falungong movement.[54] It also tracks and detains members of groups considered to be illegal—in constitutional language, groups that are not "normal religions." The 610 Office is likely under the purview of the Ministry of Public Security, not the State Administration for Religious Affairs, because it tracks groups that the central authorities do not consider to be real religions, whereas SARA oversees the five oversight organizations, the officially recognized religions.

Speaking Clearly

On February 19, 2001, the then head of the State Administration for Religious Affairs (called the Bureau of Religious Affairs at the time), Ye Xiaowen, gave a speech on religion in China at Chung Chi College of the Chinese University of Hong Kong.[55] Within the first few sentences Ye makes the statement that one of the key policies of the CCP is "respect for freedom of religious belief." He then recounts the humiliation China has suffered over the past century, a standard rhetorical reference made by countless politicians in China to national humiliation (*guo-chi*).[56] Ye points out the necessity of looking at the past century in China to better understand the most recent fifty years, during which, he argues, religion has undergone an "evolution."

Right from the start Ye uses the terms "religion" and "belief" as universal and reified categories, perhaps even sui generis. The categories are never in question. Instead, Ye uses the speech to assess the "merits or demerits of China's religious policies" against the backdrop of the nineteenth century. He argues that for the past thousand years, China's religions were patriotic because of the stability of Chinese civilization. China, he says, has never been "interrupted by any alien culture." This, for Ye, explains why China's religions "took pride in being patriotic." But, in the last century, because of semicolonialism, the interruption of China's stability by foreign powers, China's religions took on a "patriarchal-feudal" character. With regard to Tibet, he says that "there was for a long time a brutal theocratic system that combined Tibetan Buddhism with a feudal serfdom." The criticism is apparent, the results unambiguous. Beijing and the CCP have saved Tibet from itself.

They have also saved Xinjiang. Ye writes: "In Northwest China, there was once a hereditary Menhuan system that combined the Islamic faith with the landlord system, resulting in the emergence of a number of 'imams' who held absolute power over the life and property of the believers." Statements like these reflect an attitude toward religion seen in document 19. They are also historically dubious and require more context. In the end, Ye's speech offers no clarity either. It sheds no light on the "religious question."

━━━

Today every nation-state must negotiate what China refers to as the "religious question." This is especially true now that religion has come to be understood as a universal and, as almost all nation-state constitutions refer to the freedom of religion, an inalienable human right. But it is precisely as a human right that the term fails us and thereby calls into question the efficacy of human rights in general. As one legal-religious studies scholar puts it: "Can 'lived religion' ever be protected by laws guaranteeing religious freedom? Religion and law today speak in languages largely opaque to each other."[57] Freedom of religion as a human right is in some ways deeply flawed. It uses one set of rules administered by judges, courts, governments, and constitutions to manage everyday practices that we designate as "religious." For human rights to work, they must be comprehensive, universally accepted and respected, and have real legal teeth to them; anything else and we simply witness weak barks by the human rights watchdog hounds. You will forgive the metaphor, but the juridical nature of human rights is in a state of crisis. Just ask any Tibetan *tulku* who plans on reincarnating.[58]

4
Reincarnation

I n September 2007 order no. 5 drawn up by China's
State Administration for Religious Affairs went into
effect. The order stipulates that no living Tibetan buddhas (*tulkus*) may reincarnate without state permission.[1] On first
reading, order no. 5 seems peculiar: How can a self-proclaimed
atheist government that doesn't believe in reincarnation decide
who can or cannot reincarnate? Here, I want to think about the
mechanics of the order vis-à-vis article 36 in China's constitution, and all underscored by document 19, the state's final say on
religion. I then connect the order to the territorialization of
Tibet.

The order was passed by SARA—at the time under the direc-
torship of Ye Xiaowen—on July 13, 2007. It was implemented
fewer than two months later, on September 1. It consists of four-
teen articles, the last of which states when the order will be
implemented. Article 1 begins by indirectly referencing article
36 of the constitution and claims that the order is going into
effect "to protect the freedom of religious belief of the people,
to respect the tradition in Tibetan Buddhism of living buddhas,
and to manage and regulate the incarnation of living buddhas"
(under the auspices of SARA).

Article 2 is telling as it stipulates that reincarnating buddhas should safeguard and respect the unity of the state, protect the unity of minority ethnic groups, protect religious and social harmony, and protect the normal order of Tibetan Buddhism. The term "normal" (*zhengchang*) resonates with the third sentence of article 36 of the constitution, which says that "the state protects normal religious activities." The term "normal" is the same in this case—*zhengchang de zongjiao huodong* (normal religious activity). In almost all situations, the State Administration of Religious Affairs decides what is "normal religious activity." There is nothing subtle about this phrase. It is explicitly aimed at controlling and containing Tibetan Buddhism, the mainstay of Tibetan culture.[2] The state's method of deciding who reincarnates is in direct contradistinction to how most Tibetans understand reincarnation processes (see discussion below on article 8).

Article 3 stipulates that reincarnating living buddhas must meet certain conditions: (1) A majority of local religious practitioners (the Chinese term translates as believers) in the monastic community to which the living buddha belongs, along with monastic management, must all request the reincarnation. (2) The inheritance lineage must be authentic and have existed until the present day. (3) The monastery submitting the application must be the same one that the living buddha is registered at; the monastery must be registered as a Tibetan institution; and, the monastery must have the capability and facilities to train and support the living buddha.

Article 4 outlines two conditions under which the living buddha cannot reincarnate: if Tibetan Buddhist protocol is not followed correctly, and if those in local government above the city level deny the reincarnation.

Articles 5 through 7 explicitly state that it is the "impact" (popularity/social influence) of the living buddha that dictates which bureau or level of government the application should go to first. First, the monastery responsible for the living buddha applies for permission for his reincarnation to the county-level religious affairs department. If the living buddha's influence is relatively large, then the application goes to the regional level; if the influence is even greater, then the application goes to SARA. Only if the living buddha's status is so overwhelmingly popular (and presumably could constitute a threat to national stability) does the application go to the State Council for approval. At all levels, the Buddhist Association is involved; in other words, the Buddhist Association under which the monastery is registered oversees the application process and, should the application be approved, convenes a "search party" to look for the "reincarnate 'soul' child" (*zhuanshi lingtong*).[3]

Article 8 takes a decidedly historical turn and claims to present the legitimate method of choosing/discovering a reincarnate soul child: "Historically, those living buddhas who were discovered by drawing names from a golden urn, should use the same method in determining their soul child." Now, traditionally a reincarnate soul child would be found based on a predictive letter by the predecessor in his former life (I say "his" as there are so few female reincarnates). It is a process by which the child identifies and chooses articles from his predecessor's possessions. Sometimes in difficult cases a divination practice is performed in front of a sacred image. The method of choosing from a golden urn was used only a few times during the Qing dynasty, for the eighth and ninth Panchen Lamas, for example. The current Dalai Lama, who points out the obvious manipulation for political purposes that can and likely does occur, deems it a highly problematic practice.

An incidence of manipulation took place in 1994–1995 when the Dalai Lama and the Chadrel Rinpoche from Tashilhunpo Monastery, as head of the search team, concurred that Gendün Chögi Nyima (b. 1989) was the eleventh Panchen Lama. Beijing, however, insisted on using the golden urn method, drawing several slips from the urn and declaring Gyaincain Norbu (b. 1990) as the authentic eleventh Panchen Lama, a choice rejected by most Tibetans and by the Dalai Lama as well.[4] Gendün Chögi Nyima subsequently "disappeared" and is said to be hidden somewhere in Beijing. It was predictable that the central government would reject the Dalai Lama's choice and accuse him of disregarding tradition—predictable in the sense that the choice of high-ranking lamas is a political process and has everything to do with social control over the Tibetan region.[5] In other words, it is as much about territory as it is about incarnate lamas. The Chinese government understands Tibet to be part of the sacred territory of the motherland.

Articles 9 and 10 of order no. 5 specify which departments the recognized soul child should be registered with. The living buddha is then issued a "living Buddha" certificate by the China Buddhist Association, which is reported to the State Administration of Religious Affairs.[6]

Article 11 points out the legal consequences of not following all the proper procedures. Should this occur, a criminal case shall be opened.

Article 12 stipulates that once the living buddha is in place, the monastery must put together a formal training program, recommend a teacher, and submit all this information to the local Buddhist Association. The association in turn should submit it to the provincial level for final approval. Article 13 states that the plan must then be sent to SARA.

I want to think further, for a moment, about article 8. This article has real territorial implications for what constitutes Tibetan Buddhism and indeed who controls Tibetan territory. The historian Elliot Sperling has pointed out that the question of when and how Tibet became part of China proper is perhaps the most sensitive and political of issues pertaining to Chinese territorial expansion. Beijing's position is that Tibet has been part of China for centuries (since at least the thirteenth century); the Dalai Lama accepts Tibet as part of China but will not deny its historical independence. As Sperling clarifies, it was a gradual process of Tibet becoming integrated into the Qing Empire: "Qing expansion into Tibet followed a pattern common among empires in which unforeseen security concerns precipitate unintended expansion in response to crisis."[7] Based on dynastic histories, Tibet was likely subject to juridical claims made by Yuan dynasty (1279–1368) and Qing dynasty (1644–1911) emperors, and during these periods Tibet was not independent per se but at most could be considered a protectorate of sorts. Ming dynasty (1368–1644) emperors made no categorical claims on Tibet. Thus Tibet may have submitted to a limited degree to the Mongol and Manchu empires; neither properly considered Tibet part of China. From 1912 to 1951 the Dalai Lama's regency ruled Tibet with little or no Chinese interference. Or, as Sperling puts it: "Tibet was not 'Chinese' until Mao Zedong's armies marched in and made it so."[8]

The Dalai Lama's position today is clear: he consistently states that he does not want independence for Tibet but requests full autonomy for the Tibetan region. The problem, however, is that the Tibetan region historically covers an area that includes much of China's western territory—parts of Qinghai province to the north and Sichuan province to the east. It is impossible to imagine China giving this up. Beijing continues to declare its lack of trust in the Dalai Lama and his intentions and regularly refers to him as a "splittist" who wants to break up the sovereignty and stability of China. Government spokespersons in Beijing have also referred to him as a "wolf in a sheep's clothing" or, as one government official put it, "a wolf wrapped in robes, a monster with a human face and an animal's heart."[9]

Whenever the Dalai Lama meets with government leaders, the Chinese central government reacts strongly. In response to a recent planned meeting between then president Barack Obama and the Dalai Lama, the Chinese Foreign Ministry spokesperson Hua Chunying said: "The United States' arrangement for its leader to meet the Dalai would be a gross interference in China's internal affairs and is a serious violation of the norms of international relations. . . . It will seriously damage Sino-U.S. relations." Also, if "the U.S. president wishes to meet any person, it's his own affair, but he cannot meet the Dalai. The Dalai is definitely not a pure religious figure. He is using the cloak of religion to engage in long-term activities to separate China. He is a political exile."[10] Hua urged the White House to cancel the meeting. The president went ahead anyway and met with the Dalai Lama for about an hour on February 21, 2014. They met again, despite Beijing's anger, on June 15, 2016.[11] No real damage to China-U.S. relations occurred, but these back-and-forth word-flurries are common, telling, and important in the sense of how they reflect broader geopolitical issues.

Some more technical aspects apropos previous discussions in chapters 2–3 might include inquiring as to what China means by a "spiritual leader" and what it might mean by a "pure religious figure."[12] The larger issue is the territory of Tibet and control over the Tibetan populace, who, according to China's constitution, are Chinese subjects. The same holds true for Taiwan. Though Taiwan-China relations have improved dramatically over the past decade primarily because of billions of dollars invested in China by Taiwanese companies, it wasn't long ago when regular saber-rattling was the order of the day.

Control and Authority

Order no. 5 is a theojuridical document. It forms part of a comprehensive approach by the Chinese state to maintain total control of any aspect of its citizenry's activities that might potentially impinge on the routinized, ostensibly secular structures of the central government and thereby constitute a perceived or actual threat to its authority.[13] Religion, and religious organization, whatever the central government might mean by these terms, is capable of independent social action and thus is a potential political threat. In order no. 5, Tibetan Buddhism is considered a religion, a noun, an object of scrutiny to be forcefully controlled.[14] Further, order no. 5 is a theological, or better, a theopolitical move on the part of the government to establish a stronger protocol regarding the current Dalai Lama's reincarnation upon his death. The idea is straightforward enough: control the Dalai Lama and the formalization process following his death, and you then attain greater social and political control over Tibet, an area that China, as defined in its constitution, considers to be part of its sovereign "sacred territory" (*shensheng lingtu*).

There is a metaphysics at work when the nation-state can declare what counts as real or false reincarnation. It is an ontologically minded metaphysics, one that questions tacitly the state of being in a particular state, that is, a deceased then reincarnated state. It also raises serious questions about what constitutes authority; and, at least superficially, one that sets up a potential contrast between the religious and the secular. The metaphysics at work here is a spatial one; it is about Tibetan territory, but it operates with an authority unknown to us—unknown because we do not know how, when, or often why the Central Committee of the Chinese Communist Party, as well as the executive branch of the State Council, decides what it does—but one that has tangible effects in space and time.

In its coverage of order no. 5, *China Daily* (*Zhongguo ribao*) wrote the following: "The rule, an important move by the government to safeguard religious freedom of citizens according to law, has won staunch and extensive support from the Tibetan Buddhist circles and believers in China."[15] Hyperbole aside, this claim to safeguard religious freedom is nevertheless explicitly stated in article 36 of China's constitution. To this end, let's take a closer look at article 36. The official Chinese government English translation reads as follows:

> Citizens of the People's Republic of China enjoy freedom of religious belief. No state organ, public organization or individual may compel citizens to believe in, or not to believe in, any religion; nor may they discriminate against citizens who believe in, or do not believe in, any religion. The state protects normal religious activities. No one may make use of religion to engage in activities that disrupt public order, impair the health of citizens or interfere with the educational system of the state. Religious bodies and religious affairs are not subject to any foreign domination.[16]

There are five sentences in total. I will discuss them one at a time.

1. Citizens of the People's Republic of China enjoy freedom of religious belief.

Scholars often blithely state that after 1911 China became a "secular regime."[17] By way of contrast, as the co-editors of one recent book put it in their introduction: "An astounding revival of religion has occurred in China since the late 1970s. China has now the world's largest Buddhist population, fastest growing Catholic and Protestant congregations, expanding Muslim communities, and active Daoist temples. According to state statistics there are 100 million religious believers."[18] So which is China: secular or religious? Clearly the question is inadequate but nonetheless worth asking since it enables us to evaluate some of the meanings of the categories secular and religious. On the one hand, China seems to be both; on the other, it all depends what one means by the terms "secular" and "religious." As Peter van der Veer has argued, "It is important to understand the

secular and the religious as mutually dependent. Their definition cannot be separately reached but depends on this structural relationship."[19]

Complicating matters further, one scholar of religious studies, Timothy Fitzgerald, argues for two hegemonic views of religion still common today in contemporary rhetoric on religion.
The first is an earlier idea of religion as monotheistic Truth (in
contrast to pagan falsehood); the second is a more modern discourse that depicts religion as universal. According to Fitzgerald, both positions—what he calls "encompassing religion" and
"privatized Protestant inward piety"—have their roots in Christianity.[20] These ideologies are necessarily in conflict with each
other, and furthermore, it is from both ("encompassing religion"
and Truth) that secularism secures its political roots based on
the tacit understanding that religion is more about interiority
than exteriority. We see this in China's constitution with the use
of the word "belief." With religion internalized, a secular, public sphere can be maintained. "Not so fast," the anthropologist
Talal Asad would tell us.

Asad has shown us how secularism is not simply the separation of the religious from secular institutions in government and
state. Instead, what is distinctive about secularism is that it pre-
supposes new concepts of religion, that it is in fact a form of
Protestant discourse. Asad makes the compelling point that it's
not just any form of religion that can be allowed to depart from
the private sphere and enter into public debate. He writes that
"the legitimate entry of religion into these debates results in
the creation of modern "hybrids": the principle of structural
differentiation—according to which religion, economy, education, and science, are located in autonomous social spaces—no
longer holds."[21] The type of religion that will be allowed to enter
into public debate is supposed to be one capable of rational debate
and liberal discourse and not be coercive in any way.[22] This is

the point where it becomes easy to see the discriminatory elements of, for instance, debates over the wearing of the *hijab* in France, or the disallowing of Islamic educational institutions in Xinjiang, the banning of Falungong, and the oppressive control of Muslim Uighurs via so-called re-education centers, in reality internment camps. One consequence is that certain types of public space become exclusionary in their ostensive inclusivity. It is no wonder, then, that so many of these types of spaces become explosive and violence erupts, seemingly spontaneously, but with a strong perennial undercurrent of real social discontent simmering just below the surface of public discourse. The religious and the secular, which are critical to nation-state formation, lie at the heart of all this.

Perhaps the most common narrative of the secularization thesis is that as societies modernize, their need for religion dissipates.[23] Scholars have of course pointed out the more basic understanding of the secularization thesis—José Casanova with perhaps the greatest clarity. Three elements are understood to be essential: (1) increasing structural differentiation of social spaces, resulting in the separation of religion from politics, economy, science, and so forth; (2) the privatization of religion with its own sphere; and (3) the declining social significance of religious belief, commitment, and institutions.[24] Without belaboring the point, while the first two have indeed occurred globally, the last has not. Asad asserts that many scholars have argued the falsity of the third part of this thesis as we witness the rise of deeply politicized religious movements throughout the world; defenders of the secularization thesis argue that this is a resistance to modernity and its many failures.

The assumption is that for a society to be modern it must be secular.[25] This means that religion must be relegated to nonpolitical spaces. How many nation-states take this stance? China has, and it continues to do so. In the case of China pre-1949, Rebecca Nedostup helps us by using the term "secularism" and the phrase "the proposition of secularization" to describe the idea that political authority and numinous power ought to be clearly separated. In explaining this she references Zhang Zhenzhi, an official in the Nationalist government, who in 1929 wrote an essay in which he differentiated between religion and superstition. Nedostup goes on to point out that, for better or for worse, much of the time that the term secular is used, particularly by scholars and government officials, it entails a conscious or unconscious move toward modernity and a rationalization of everyday living. If not that, then we are in the realm of superstition.[26]

Nedostup makes it clear that whatever we might mean by these terms, secularism, nationalism, and the category of religion are inextricably linked. Furthermore, religion, so a common argument goes, is part of the private sphere, whereas politics is public, something to be kept away from religion, or specifically the belief in God. This, however, works on the assumption that because the one can influence the other, they are therefore essentially separate and different. It is precisely on these turns that the idea of modernity is bandied about in contemporary academic disciplines as well as in the media. So far so good; let's remind ourselves of what Timothy Fitzgerald has explained in his essay on religion and modern politics, namely, that the term "secular," beginning in its most frequent usage during the sixteenth and seventeenth centuries, was used to refer to the "secular clergy" as distinct from a special class of clergy within the Catholic Church who were considered the "religious clergy," monks, friars, nuns, and the like.[27] The secular clergy were those living in the commoners' world, as opposed to the religious clergy, who were sequestered in monastic seclusion. In other words, the term "secular" was always used within the space of the religious and was not understood to mean what so many moderns mean when they refer to the secular as being the opposite of the religious.

Hard to Believe

Why is belief, a foundational category in European Christianity and vital to Christian theology, the cornerstone of what China's constitution defines as freedom of religion?[28] Why is the term "belief" used as a marker of religion when every historical instance, especially in Asian contexts, but also to some extent in the monotheistic traditions, seems to default to orthoprax? All of China's documents on religion express the category as "belief" (*xinyang*),[29] a Protestant bias if ever there was one. Donald Lopez writes the following about the expression "to believe":

> The accumulated weight of this discourse has resulted in the generally unquestioned assumption that adherents of a given religion, any religion, understand that adherence in terms of belief. Indeed, belief (rather than ritual, for example) seems to have been the pivot around which Christians have told their own history. And with the dominance of Christian Europe in the nineteenth century, Christians have also described what came to be known as "world religions" from the perspective of belief.[30]

In Europe the use of the term "religion" found its highest yet most convoluted expression in the late nineteenth century with what came to be called "world religions."[31] To reach this point, one prevailing discourse of modernity with its Enlightenment roots would strip religion away from the idea of Christian Truth and have it become a universal category to be found in all cultures at all times. This played out extensively during the nineteenth century when colonialists often claimed that a "newly discovered" social group had no religion (meaning that they had no knowledge of Christian Truth), only later to decide that they did have religion, but that it was inferior to their (the civilized colonialists') religion.[32] A result of this was a new way of using the category of religion to mean a universal phenomenon, something that "everyone" has (the subnarrative being that of all the world's religions, Christianity is still the only real Truth). In other words, the phenomenon of religion was universal but hierarchical, with European Christianity being first on the list—"first among equals" (*primus inter pares*).

This universalizing discourse prevails today—particularly in the language and notion of "world religions"—but when used in supposedly discrete fields such as politics or economics, this hierarchical bias is subjugated under a different narrative that renders it ostensibly benign, thereby reifying the category of religion and thus reproducing its ideological legitimation. Subsequently, as we saw in the previous chapter, the term becomes critically linked to constitutional language and to human rights.[33] Furthermore, in modern-day discourse between politics and religion, the latter is tied in binary opposition to the "secular," a category fundamental—so we are told—to most nation-states, their constitutions, and the idea of freedom and the rights pertaining to it. Religion in this secular sphere is relegated to the private. This is essentially what China has done with the category. In other words, the writers of its constitution unwittingly employed post-Enlightenment tactics of supposedly stripping religion out from the daily course of political events and relegating it to the private sphere where the citizen can "choose to believe or not to believe." The notion of "belief" as a precondition for religiosity, and indeed the idea of religion as a universal, derives from Protestant Christian biases.[34] Are the writers and revisionists of China's constitution clear about their use of the term "belief," and to what extent were the writers aware of the term's origin? Did they even care, as the name of the game at the time was precisely to enter the global game of international politics? "Having" religion is a prerequisite for the nation-state.

The "freedom of religious belief" hinges entirely on the notion that there is also such a thing as having no religious beliefs on the part of citizens. To use phrases such as "traditional beliefs," "the people believe," or "religious belief" effectively undermines the thing the expression is trying to capture. What governments want to know are the motivations for organized social action.[35] As Qianfan Zhang so rightly points out, for now the government fears the civic ability for religious groups to form and engage in social action. He writes: "The more harshly a government cracks down on religious activities in the name of social order, the more disorder and unrest it will bring to society."[36]

Motivations, however, are impossible to ascertain most of the time. Motivations can change based on what somebody eats for lunch, or what mood one wakes up in in the morning. Belief as ostensibly a substantive category of everyday realities is no more accessible to us than evaluating someone's belief that the moon is made of green cheese simply based on its hue, or that someone believes they were kidnapped by aliens. Lest I sound flippant, my point is that the grounds on which belief rests as a cognitive category of descriptive behavior are shaky at best and nonexistent at worst. Thus for article 36 to say that Chinese citizenry "enjoy freedom of religious belief" is overly optimistic and not clear by any means.

This first sentence of article 36, for all its vagueness, is nevertheless an explicit statement made by the state; what is implicit is the ability of the state to deny that "enjoyment."[37] Even more implicit is, a *mutatis mutandis*, that in the potential denying of religious belief there is the violence that accompanies the bestowing and denying of enjoying freedom of religious belief. China's constitution is not unique in this regard: no nation-state gets off the hook. The ability of the state—the only institution that can legitimately claim the rights to violence—bestows and thus can take away.

Finally, "enjoy" is an odd word choice given the Chinese ideograph, which reads as "have," in the sense of, literally, "to have religious belief freedom." For religion to be "enjoyed" adds a frivolous dimension to an otherwise potentially more nuanced category. In either case, the statement is a relative truth. Only five "religions"—Buddhism, Daoism, Islam, Protestantism, and Catholicism—are considered legal and must submit to the state to maintain legality. Only the state can legitimate a religious institution. An irony lies in the state's own religiosity (and belief in itself).

2. **No state organ, public organization, or individual may compel citizens to believe in, or not to believe in, any religion; nor may they discriminate against citizens who believe in, or do not believe in, any religion.**

One of the oldest arguments against religion entering the public domain is that the former is irrational, faith-based, illogical, potentially just superstition, and at the least, more interested in the numinous realm than in everyday realities. This position bears on the one taken in China's constitution. (The statement about the "freedom to believe in, or not to believe in" hinges on it.) What it completely ignores is the complex diversity of the public.[38] Citizenry is remarkably diverse irrespective of the effectiveness of educational ideological formations.

It is helpful to keep in mind that the essentialized idea leading up to the eighteenth century of religion being private and interior means, then, that the state deals with violence. For thinkers such as John Locke and William Penn in the seventeenth century, religion was about inner peace, the afterlife, and a personalized accountability vis-à-vis a creator god; the state was about protecting the citizenry via force if necessary. Much later, when this protection is tied to human rights, modern nation-states must then negotiate the thorny avenues of human rights challenges, something China too must continually negotiate.[39] These are the same human rights, incidentally, advocated by human rights watch groups around the globe that, as argued by Hannah Arendt and, more recently, by Giorgio Agamben, show a profound weakness in application and improbable ability to actually protect those in their most dire moment of need. (We saw this in the previous chapter.)

It therefore becomes crucial—at least from within all nation-state mythological narratives—to separate out the rights of personhood and the rights of the citizen. In the Chinese case, the person (*ren*) is not the same legal entity as the citizen (*gongmin*); the latter juridically elevates the notion of "public" and renders any connection to the private as untenable. The "religious bodies" are state bodies with all the rights that pertain to and contain such entities. It is not clear to me at all how a "state organ, public organization or individual could compel a citizen to believe in, or not to believe in, any religion," and yet the writers of China's constitution feel compelled to say so.

3. The state protects normal religious activities.

This is the most problematic sentence in article 36. Its message is clear: the state, and only the state, gets to define what is "normal" religious activity. When, according to the state, a "not normal" religion is exposed, the term *mixin* (superstition) is used.[40] As Goosaert and Palmer explain, historically the term religion as used in a Chinese context primarily referred to Christianity.

Science was seen to possibly accompany religion to some extent, as opposed to superstition, which was seen as "unscientific."[41] It was after 1901 that the *zongjiao/mixin* dichotomy took full effect and all temples not considered to be part of a religion were by default superstitious and destined to be changed into schools. Kang Youwei had already suggested something similar in 1898 when he argued in an edict sent to the Guangxu emperor that any temple not included in the register of state sacrifices (*sidian*) ought to be destroyed. Kang still used the older dichotomy of "immoral cults" (*yinsi*) to categorize these institutions. Of course, Kang's goal was to see a Confucian revival and establish Confucianism as the state religion (*guojiao*). Kang had few supporters in this, though widespread destruction—mostly rebuilding temples into schools—did begin in 1901. Goosaert and Palmer explain some of these transitions as follows:

> The birth of the antisuperstition movement and the beginning of the destruction of the temples may be best understood as a transition between two approaches: one that implied being part of Chinese religion and trying to improve it from the inside . . . and the other in which one viewed Chinese religion critically from the outside, without (or at least attempting not to use) its vocabulary or categories. . . . In post-1898 texts, Chinese religion (but not religion in general) is constantly described as what prevents China from developing and enriching itself.[42]

By 1927 the legislature had passed reforms calling for the elimination of many of the "lesser" deities in favor of those "with redeeming social value"—Confucius, Muhammad, the Buddha, and Jesus Christ.[43] Further, campaigns to fully eradicate superstition were increased. One of the more important legislative tactic could be seen in the 1928 text, "Standards to Determine the

Temples to Be Destroyed and Those to Be Maintained" (*Shenci cunfei biaozhun*).⁴⁴ Inevitably, the Nationalist government could not eradicate "superstition," especially in the countryside.

In Max Weber's essay on politics as a vocation, the state, and only the state, has the monopoly on violence, which typically erupts when "normal" (in the case of China) is juxtaposed and imposed against "deviant" (*xie*). Goossaert has demonstrated that temples designated as immoral (*yinci*) during the Qing period, along with the notion of "immoral sacrifice" (*yinsi*), were considered transgressions of proper (moral) activity by the imperium (and, I would add, later by the state in postimperial China). He writes, "This very flexible category includes all those temples which officials (at all levels of the bureaucracy) regarded as unacceptable and which therefore had to be destroyed." Later he explains: "What is not orthodox is considered as heterodox (*xie*) or immoral (*yin*)—two notions that widely overlap, even though the term *xie* applies more specifically to texts and devotional groups, whereas the notion of *yin* refers more to the notions of interdiction, excess (in terms of money spent and emotions expressed) and immorality (mainly sexual immorality in late imperial times)." All cults not included in the Register of Sacrifices (*sidian*) were considered immoral.⁴⁵ For the Qing imperium and every other imperium prior to it, the realm of the sacred was never fully separated out from other spheres of social and political control. After 1911 the state as sovereign decided what was "normal" as opposed to deviant. Juridical institutions later backed this up. The state sustained itself only to the extent of its ability to cloak a reconstructed secular under a veil of sacredness. This is necessarily a violent process. But, as Weber has taught us, because the state has the monopoly of the legitimate use of force, it can be done on a regular basis. The state protects until the moment only it decides not to, at which point a state of exception is instituted.⁴⁶ Only five religious groups are protected in

China, but only if they are registered, demonstrate loyalty to the state, and do not engage in public demonstrations (see below). All this maintains their "normalcy."

4. **No one may make use of religion to engage in activities that disrupt public order, impair the health of citizens, or interfere with the educational system of the state.**

Of course, all this was written long before Falungong, though it reads, especially the phrase "health of citizens," as if it were composed post-1999.[47] Social harmony is the matter at hand. Further, social reproduction can ensure the continuity of mythos production precisely through the educational system. In any event, religion in this regard is seen as antithetical to state politics. The problem, however, is that a discourse that refers to either "religion" or "politics" and interconnections between the two as natural phenomena in social space is highly unstable, a social fact conveniently ignored by most nation-states, including by the Chinese central government. (Mythological narrative in nation-state constitutions maintains the fiction; the state then spends a lot of energy policing the resulting instability.) "Religion" and "politics" as categories of emplacement are in this sense circular, able to continuously essentialize and reify whenever discursively deployed. To further complicate matters, their use is often coupled with an overreliance on history as redemptive and salvational (in part because of the fetishization of the state), and with the unwitting use of post-Enlightenment secularism with its overdetermined reliance on science as the path to national salvation. Thus the instability of a discourse on religion and politics lends itself to the problematic reification of these categories as we tend to use them today—both in and outside the academy. To render these categories in this manner is to cripple them with a self-referential quality, thereby creating a false distinction of reality. Either way, the term religion now becomes connected to politics by virtue of the need to separate it out from politics. But how to avoid a circular argument? In other words, if I argue for the interconnectedness or impossibility of the separation of religion and politics, simply using the same terms for the argument leads us into circular territory by the tacit assumption that religion and politics are two separate phenomena. Fitzgerald writes: "A non-religious domain of politics, for instance, could not have been thought of unless 'religion' had been siphoned out of the totality and placed in a special essentialized category. . . . The idea that religion can under specific circumstances become political; or that religion can have an impact on politics, only makes sense under the prior assumption that they are essentially separate and different."[48] This false antinomy is clearly demonstrated in an oft-mentioned idea that religion and state in China have competed with each other. Pitman Potter begins his otherwise important essay with this assumption when he states: "The relationship between religion and state power in China has long been contested."[49] This doesn't explain anything and ignores the role of the educational system in social reproduction. From Beijing's perspective, public order and social reproduction are the primary goals.

5. **Religious bodies and religious affairs are not subject to any foreign domination.**

Here we have a clear throwback to the *guochi* (national humiliation), a narrative so carefully cultivated by the Chinese Communist Party. The final sentence of article 36 is all about the nineteenth century. With the two Opium Wars, the Sino-Japanese War (1894–1895), the invasion by eight allied forces (1900), the war with Japan (1937–1945), along with all the missionary activity, Shanghai legations, loss of Hong Kong, and millions paid in indemnities, we have a time period often described as *guochi*, national humiliation (usually expressed as *wuwang guochi*, "never forget national humiliation").[50]

The scholar Zheng Wang recently published a study exploring the notion of "historical memory" and *wuwang guochi* in which he focuses on the dissolution of the Celestial Empire, and the subsequent period of "national humiliation" during the nineteenth century. The CCP later exploited this to generate Chinese pride and promote advances in the concept of national identity. Wang writes: "Chosen traumas and glories are passed on to succeeding generations . . . increas[ing] members' self-esteem by being associated with such glories." Combined with phrases such as *gedi peikuan*, "to cede territory and pay indemnities," or *sangquan ruguo*, "to surrender sovereign rights and bring humiliation to the country," *wuwang guochi* provides a powerful additive to China's historical trauma and makes for an incendiary and pervasive nationalism.[51] Or, as historian James Hevia has argued, "resistance of the colonized produced a powerful discourse on the colonizer as victim."[52] This narrative could then be construed in mythological form that taps into the collective unconscious of the Chinese citizenry. Memorials, educational policies, textbooks, government spokespersons, national newspapers, white papers, nationalistic movies, and so forth all work discursively to disseminate these narratives.

Out of China's colonial experience comes a sense of how damaging it can be when other countries intrude on your territory. Today China also likes to claim that it never meddles in other countries' affairs, though the next chapter will show differently. Given its mythologized history, the CCP wants to make clear to external organizations (USCIRF, Human Rights Watch, the U.S. government, Christian organizations wanting to donate money to Chinese churches, the government of Taiwan) that they are not allowed to have any influence over religious bodies, actual and institutional, in the People's Republic. This last sentence is also aimed at the Vatican. For decades, Beijing has wrangled with the pope to make sure he has little or no influence over Chinese Catholics.[53] This would constitute "foreign domination" from the government's perspective. After all, Catholics owe their allegiance to the pope. The CCP wants Catholics and members of the remaining four officially recognized religious institutions to pledge their allegiance to the CCP.

In all five sentences, none of the terms are defined and no specific ramifications are laid bare. The lack of specificity is intentional. The paucity of details has meant an abundant workload for those brave Chinese human rights lawyers. To broaden our understanding of this and to further highlight the importance of sentence 5 in article 36, the next chapter will look at some of the early contacts with China, in particular missionary contacts. It is colonial encounters that come to shape China's historical trajectory up to the present day.

5
Contact

For the greater part of history, cultural contact has come about as a result of the centrifugal/centripetal power of the citied traditions—the tendency to expand the power of the center over the wider spatial areas, thereby bringing these spaces under the reign of the center and its ideology, assuring them a place in the legitimate and authentic structure of that reality designated and symbolized at this center.

—Charles Long

I
n Bernardo Bertolucci's film *The Last Emperor*, a scene unfolds in which the young emperor, Puyi, asks his English tutor where his ancestors are from. The tutor, perfectly played by Peter O'Toole, tells him, "Scotland, your Majesty." The precocious Puyi then asks him why is he not wearing a skirt, because don't all Scots wear skirts? O'Toole, enunciating every syllable, emphatically states: "Scotsmen do not wear skirts, they wear kilts . . . a matter of words, perhaps, but words are important. . . . If you cannot say what you mean, Your Majesty, you will never mean what you say, and a gentleman should always mean what he says."[1]

Overwhelmingly, the chief criticism of the Chinese by the British during the nineteenth century was their supposed inability to say what they meant, meaning simply that they were neither rational nor civilized—perhaps teachable, but not civilized. Furthermore, in the views of nineteenth-century colonialists, China was not behaving in a gentlemanly fashion. There was perpetual frustration on the part of the British that the Chinese could not understand what it meant to be an English gentleman, particularly one with God, trade, and empire on his side.[2]

An example of this frustration can be seen in Rev. William C. Milne's memoir, *Life in China*, where he writes: "Picture to yourself an Englishman 17,000 miles away from home . . . an Englishman living among a people, not only unable to sympathize with him, but totally different in language, habits, dress, religion . . . a single, solitary Englishman living there alone and companionless; and by sympathy you may be able to realize something of the position in which I found myself at the close of 1842." Milne goes on to say how often he was disparaged as he walked the streets often been called a "foreign devil." He tells us that he "took no notice of it, except with a significant look or by asking the offender if he knew the meaning of his language."[3]

A contemporary of Milne, William Dean, who spent some twenty years in China as a missionary, begins his memoir by explaining just why the Chinese could "not understand" foreigners. They could never say precisely what they meant, and when they tried, it was always the exact opposite of a civilized gentleman. Dean begins his first chapter by setting up these oppositional dichotomies. "Where do the Chinese live?" he writes. "They live on the other side of the globe." And, for Dean, they are some of the "queerest people, to be found on the globe." He goes on for pages with these opposites. What they wear is the opposite of what we wear. What they eat is the opposite of what we do. "We read horizontally; they, perpendicular. We read from left to right; they, from right to left. . . . We locate the understanding in the brain; they, in the belly. . . . We worship God; they offer incense to the devil."[4] I think you get the picture. But after several pages of this, Dean goes on to say how they "love a lie and hate the truth" and that they never spoke the truth. To borrow Puyi's tutor's words, the Chinese could not say what they meant and therefore did not mean whatever it was they said.

Many a missionary argued for the inscrutability of the Chinese and their inability to communicate effectively. And yet, as Eric Reinders writes, it was always "the foreigner who says the Chinese are inscrutable, the foreigner who couldn't understand." Reinders goes on to say that, "As the modern hermeneutic tradition has stressed, understanding lies in the interaction between native and foreign, and this just as true for *mis*understanding or the despairing failure to understand." Nineteenth-century reportage on China so often described the Chinese among other things as "babblers, speaking and listening to incoherent gibberish or 'pure noise.'" Reinders cites the French missionary Evariste Huc, who in no uncertain terms said: "This speech was completely Chinese—that is to say, a lie from one end to the other."[5]

William Edward Soothill gives us a sense of how clear the missionary's voice must be in contrast to the Chinese. In the first chapter of his book *A Mission in China*, published in 1907, somewhat later than our earlier nineteenth-century voices, he writes that for "the kind of man required abroad" (for missionary service), three qualities are essential: "True Piety, Common Sense, and Enthusiasm." Soothill goes on to say that "two more are also called for in almost equal degree, a good ear for vowel and consonant sounds and ability to express his meaning clearly."[6] Soothill could just as well have been Puyi's tutor.

Historian James Hevia, in part, explores British frustration with the Chinese ostensible inability to understand properly. He begins his study with an image of headless Boxer rebels, blood everywhere, one poor fellow about to have his head chopped off, several British officers watching the spectacle from a few feet away. In the background we see a sign on a wall behind the executioner that reads: "English language lessons available at a nearby school." As Hevia explains: "Imperialism was always more than guns and goods; it was also a cultural process involving resistance to and accommodation of forces or entities attempting to achieve hegemonic control over specific geographic spaces. To be directed from the execution ground to the language class was to trace one kind of passage along the colonial divide separating Westerners from the 'inferior' races of Africa and Asia."[7] Language and its meaning was, therefore, a critical component of that "cultural process." Language was always a political tool. Coupled with free trade and proselytizing, imperial contact was always about controlling geographic space and those who inhabited it.[8]

Barrow's Travels

China had long been that centrifugal/centripetal citied tradition power that Charles Long writes about in the epigraph above.[9] Its ability to expand its imperial power outward from Beijing was remarkable if we look at the geographic size of the Qing Empire. But it was not ready to accept any reproach to that power. London, also as a citied imperial power, sought access to most of Africa and of course India, with considerable success. Contact with China came in many different forms. An important early contact, one between the two most powerful and wealthiest empires in the world, took place at the end of the eighteenth century.

It was the autumn of 1792, and Lord George Macartney (1737–1806), newly appointed envoy to imperial China, sailed from

England with his embassy in the sixty-four-gun H.M.S. *Lion*, captained by Erasmus Gower. Accompanying them were the East Indiaman *Hindostan* and the brig *Jackal*. Dispatched by King George III to open up trade with China, Macartney's mission was to convince the Chinese that they needed the technological wonders of Britain. On board was John Barrow, secretary to the admiralty, and much excited member of Lord Macartney's entourage.

In his capacity as comptroller of the household, Barrow was in charge of the many scientific gifts—clocks, guns, barometers, telescopes, and the like—that were to be presented to the Qianlong emperor.[10] Barrow had several objectives with this mission, but one in particular stands out when he writes: "I endeavored to settle, in my own mind, the point of rank which China may be considered to have attained in the scale of civilized nations."[11] Macartney's entourage and gifts were ultimately rebuffed and forced to return home, leaving Barrow to further ponder his question about rank and scale.[12] One empire, Britain, with its market-seeking, proselytizing, and conquering aims, clashed with another type of empire, one that operated more by cultural and ritual assimilation. This was called *wanghua*, "kingly transformation," and a different type of centrifugal/centripetal power from that of London with the vast naval power at its disposal.[13]

European imperialism renders the Other as less than human The author J. M. Coetzee demonstrates this perfectly in his novel, *Dusklands*. In his story "The Narrative of Jacobus Coetzee," he tells a harrowing tale of what can happen to the human spirit when confronted by the frontier and trying to gain control over it. In this case, the frontier is an eighteenth-century frontier, the interior of South Africa (not yet sacred territory) and also the frontier of the imperialist's psyche and sanity.[14]

The story is a violent one. In many ways it is the perfect metaphor for so much of the colonial period. As the protagonist,

Jacobus Coetzee, tells us: "The one gulf that divides us from the Hottentots is our Christianity. We are Christians, a folk with a destiny." And later, "The Bushman is a different creature, a wild animal with an animal's soul."[15] How does it feel to believe deeply that you are on the right side of history, that precisely because you have a destiny, the world is ripe for the picking? What might it have felt like to claim ownership of people, place, narratives, and ideologies, and that through this claimed ownership maintain the right to kill? These Hottentots are like children for Jacobus Coetzee; in one confrontation with them he asks himself if they are even adults.

He tells us: "I am an explorer. My essence is to open what is closed, to bring light to what is dark. . . . I am a tool in the hands of history." But the world Jacobus Coetzee enters into requires a taxonomic reordering; it requires that the white, predominantly male, Christian European enter the frontier to claim it and to name things. As Jacobus points out, "The Hottentots knew nothing of penetration. For penetration you need blue eyes." Or, as the fictional report as a follow up to his explorations states: "In his way Coetzee rode like a god through a world only partly named, differentiating and bringing it into existence."[16] This is a reterritorialization of the mind; it is Aimé Césaire's "thingification."[17]

Chinese imperialism, on the other hand, rendered the other as culturally inferior. *Wanghua*, the "kingly transformation" mentioned above, is part of this. For most of its history, when contact was first made with the imperium, a tribute system was almost always the goal. It was not that the imperial Chinese felt themselves to be racially superior to the tribes that made their way into the capital of the middle empire, though surely this must have been the case sometimes; instead, it was that they considered themselves to be culturally superior. The emperor was always understood to be *tianzi*, the Son of Heaven, who balanced the heavens and earth and did so ritually and methodically from his capital that stood in the cosmogonic center of his empire. Should he lose that balance, so too would he lose the mandate to rule bestowed on him by the heavens (*tianming*) to rule over the "four quarters" (*sifang*). If foreign groups and tribes and "barbarians" could acknowledge and accept the mandate and the central role of the emperor as the custodian of the middle empire, then they too could participate in the all that he ruled under the heavens (*tianxia*) and a tributary system could be set up. Lord Macartney, along with King George, rejected this system in their bids to open up China for trade. When China (under tremendous duress) and Britain signed the Treaty of Tianjin in June 1858, Britain made sure that China should refer to it as a sovereign nation equal at least to China.[18] From China's perspective, the British were barbarians, *yi*, strange strangers.

Lydia Liu, in *The Clash of Empires*, makes a compelling argument for the extraordinary influence this character (*yi*) had on world history. In colonial terminology, it first shows up in the Treaty of Tianjin, where the document states that the term *yi* shall not be applied to the government or the subjects of her Britannic majesty. Liu goes on to connect this term to ideas of sovereignty, because whoever used the term henceforth would be breaking international law. She argues that "the discourse of *yi* names the boundaries of sovereign rule and advances a classical theory of sovereignty through the millennia-long commentarial scholarship surrounding the Confucian texts and, in particular, the *Spring and Autumn Annals*." So Puyi's tutor is correct: words do matter in saying what one means, and using *yi* was unacceptable to the British when it came to international relations. The reverse was also the case; in other words, as Liu puts it: "By calling the Native Americans and other non-European races savages and barbarians, the European empires had secured the episteme of colonial otherness as well as a universal order of civilizational superiority and inferiority based on race, culture, technology, language, proprietorship, and so on."[19] One more category needs to be added to this list: religion.

Five years later after the failed diplomatic mission to China, John Barrow was to travel to South Africa, another frontier of colonial contact where language, trade, and religion were to play critical roles in shaping the entire continent.[20] Barrow, having spent time in both geographical regions, finds the Chinese and the native South Africans fascinating. Like Jacobus Coetzee's disposition, Barrow feels they are like children, with so much potential, and yet they too have fallen from grace. His log entries describe in intimate detail virtually every aspect of what he saw, from descriptions of military hardware, to farming techniques, to similarities between different ethnic groups, and religion. In this regard, he writes: "So different are the opinions and the feelings of different nations concerning religion, and so difficult do the most civilized people find it to express their notions clearly and consistently of the 'unknown God,' that little satisfactory information can be collected on those points without a very familiar and extensive knowledge of the language of the people among whom the inquiry is made."[21] Here Barrow recognizes that language is essential. And, as Hevia points out above, the cultural process of assimilation and education was a constant challenge for both London and Beijing. Neither recognized the other, and both constantly misunderstood each other.[22]

Another instance of misrecognized cultural contact took place with Barrow when he was in conversation with a Xhosa king in South Africa. Barrow asked the king whether he believed in a supernatural power of some sort. The king said he did. Barrow then showed him his watch, and the king surmised that it was a ghost. By this time, Barrow had tired of the inquiry and apparently changed the subject, concluding that, while these people might be superstitious, they had no religion. For Barrow, religion as he understood it to not exist in China and South Africa coincided with the desire of the English gentlemen to establish a mission to both conquer and educate the rest of the world. Barrow was not the only one to criticize the religiosity, or lack thereof, of the Chinese. Trade and God went hand in hand, and, according to many nineteenth-century visitors, the Chinese lacked both.[23]

On a Mission

As part of the "the great game," colonial missions in China helped to produce and confirm an imperial sense of religiosity (i.e., militaristic, conquering, and civilizing) as well as what we might call a colonial religiosity.[24] A principal function of this colonial religiosity was the subduing of "the heathen" via a variety of pedagogical discourses, such as preaching, proselytizing, visiting temples, map making, and writing journals, processes and things that Bruno Latour will call "immutable mobiles," in many ways a clumsy expression but nevertheless one that refers to epistemological objects that do not deteriorate as they move through space and time.[25] Colonialists in China maintained domination not only through occupying territory but also through the development and categorization of certain types of knowledge about the people who came under their rule. Defining your subjects allows one, in part, to control them. Missions, missionaries, travelers, botanists, cartographers, and paper-shuffling bureaucrats all participated in this.

Sometimes these early visitors to China played multiple roles. W. A. P. Martin, the translator of Henry Wheaton's *Elements of International Law* (discussed later in this chapter), was regularly employed as an official U.S. government translator—during the Tianjin Treaty negotiations in 1858, for instance. While Martin liked to think of himself as the Protestant Matteo Ricci, as a missionary first, Liu points out how "the translator [in this case Martin], who literally and figuratively plays the 'diplomat,' is a central agent in the colonial and cultural encounters."[26] In other scenarios, missionaries were also cartographers. The Kangxi emperor employed European missionaries to draw territorial boundaries that could then be used to create treaties recognized by both China and foreign powers.[27]

Missionaries wrote prodigiously about China and nineteenth-century events, shaping and adding to what some scholars have called the "colonial modernity" of China.[28] Decades of Christian proselytizing missionaries regularly interfered in local politics. For instance, missionaries often become involved in disputes over land and water rights. Complaints were lodged with the Qing government, especially if the European party understood that Christians were involved.[29] Let us briefly consider some instances of a similar type of colonial mentality shaped by nineteenth-century Christianity.[30]

The Reverend William C. Milne, whom we met at the beginning of the chapter, was an active missionary in China for many years. Milne begins his memoir by listing pages of cultural and practical differences between the English and Chinese, not least of which is foot binding among "the fair sex," an endless source of fascination for foreigners in nineteenth-century China.[31] The differences Milne indicates naturally cause constant misunderstandings.

In early June 1841, about a month after the British held Canton to ransom during the first Opium War, Milne spent a few days visiting Tiantong Monastery, a seventeen-hundred-year-old Buddhist monastic institution located just east of the city of Ningbo in Zhejiang province in southeastern China. His first reaction on seeing the temple and its surrounding area was as follows: "When we reached the vicinity of the temple, called Tiantong, the scene was truly so fine and so grand that I dare not attempt to describe it. The site appears as if it had been designed to be a sacred spot." Milne, however, later shudders as he recalls that "we were now treading on ground desecrated by idolatry, and occupied by one of the seats of paganism, a school of prophets themselves deceived and promoters of a delusion."[32] He is simultaneously transfixed and horrified; attracted, yet repulsed by what he sees. The site, in Milne's own words, was a "sacred spot," and yet it housed wickedness, providing a nice twist to Rudolf Otto's "mysterium tremendum" and "mysterium fascinans."[33] For Milne, Buddhist space was simultaneously capacious, magnificent, and despicably idolatrous. To borrow historian of religion Mircea Eliade's words, something sacred was revealed, but the horror of its reality, its natural reality, was not to be taken lightly. This was a reality as deployed by monastics with a fetish for the wholly other. Upon his departure from the monastery and his return to the city of Ningbo, Milne wrote about his visit to the monastery, reflecting an attitude of so many missionaries in China at the time:

> Among some mournful reflections on "the idolatry in high places" which I have witnessed . . . one anticipation, suggested by the "sure word of prophecy," kindled up the bright hope that, when the glorious Gospel shall run its free course, these halls of superstition shall be consecrated to the service of the Divine Saviour, and shall be converted into colleges for Christian ministers and evangelists, who shall run to and fro as ambassadors for Christ.[34]

Missionaries like Milne and many others wrote detailed accounts of their experiences in China that provide valuable insight into how the English felt about the Chinese.

Colonial Religiosities

Thanks in part to such nineteenth-century descriptions of religions (not only in China but in India as well), we still hear and see depictions of these traditions, especially Confucianism, as being philosophy and not religion.[35] Religion, for most if not all missionaries to China, meant Christianity. Clearly a desire to Christianize, which is also to say, civilize, was well established by 1841. So it is not at all surprising for an Englishman to use this tone in his reflections as a missionary serving in a foreign region; it is also not surprising that Milne finds the landscape and architecture impressive but shudders as he recalls that "we were now treading on ground desecrated by idolatry, and occupied by one of the seats of paganism, a school of prophets themselves deceived and promoters of a delusion." Missionaries were to an extent some of the first ethnographers in China; their work, their missionizing, paved the way for later visits by foreign visitors and troops.

Missionary descriptions were detailed and often harsh. In an account by Arthur Evans Moule (1836–1918), resident missionary in China from 1861 to 1894, he describes in 1876 the "nature" of some Buddhist monks. Referring to a picture of the two monks Moule met while staying at a monastery, he writes: "One would not wish to say aught uncharitable about living and dead; but neither memory nor this photograph enable the writer to entertain a very high opinion of these ecclesiastics." Moule then tells us he had a conversation with the older of the two monks, during which the monk "grew scornful at the subject of Christianity and said: 'Come, tell me, which are there most of at Ningbo, Christians or Buddhists?' And he laughed in triumph at this hopeless exposure, as he supposed, of the false claims of Christianity. 'Come tell me,' I replied, 'which are there most of in Ningbo and in the world, good people or bad people?'" Needless to say, the monk's reaction was not a happy one. Moule writes that he cannot imagine more "helpless subjects" than these two "inmates."[36] Some years earlier, Moule had reported to the *Church Missionary Gleaner* on visiting a Buddhist monastery: "Should not Christians offer up special prayer for these strongholds of idolatry, that light may penetrate the dark, self-satisfied minds of these teachers of error, of these deluded men, whose life is spent in doing that abominable thing which God hates? The name of Jesus is not unknown in T'in Dong, but 'we natives,' is the reply of the priests, 'have a different religion from yours.'"[37] "But you don't have religion at all" might have been the reply. "Only *we* do."

At these first contacts—missionaries were often the first to arrive in China, even before the trading ships of the British Empire—we are told that we are meeting with children who are "miserably ignorant and superstitious," "hopeless subjects," and "idol-worshippers" but nonetheless "friendly and kind." Be they the Xhosa, Cape Hottentots, the Chinese at the imperial court, or Buddhist monks, these are subjects devoid of religion, thus rendered as subjects to look at but not to listen to, especially as they never said what they meant.[38]

One American missionary, Harlan Beach, wrote circa 1898 that "ancestral worship is China's bane, as well as a sin against God. It is a useless expense—$151,752,000 per annum." Putting aside the accuracy of that figure, he felt the money could be better spent elsewhere. Beach suggests that while the Chinese had religion, it was not the right religion. For instance, he recognizes Buddhism (or the "sect of Fo," as he calls it) but writes that "the Buddhist priesthood is too ignorant and inactive to merit special attention" and that the worship that takes place in monasteries "is largely liturgical and hence incomprehensible." Not surprisingly, in commenting on Catholics' presence in China, Beach writes that "Catholicism's relation to Protestant missionaries and their work is a blot on the name of the Church, from which one would gladly turn away."[39] In other words, like many nineteenth-century Protestant missionaries, he draws parallels between liturgical and monastic Catholicism and Chinese Buddhism, writing them off as equally disastrous in one sweep.

William Dean, whom we also met earlier in the chapter, established that there were three "forms of idolatry" to be found in China, namely, "Confucianists, Budhists, and Tauists." The first he dismisses as being "a system of philosophy" as opposed to real religion. The second, "Budhism" (Dean's spelling), "presents more of a religious character than any other system in the empire," though Buddhists, he tells us, "have no god to fear, no god to worship, no god to punish or protect them." He concludes that "had the messengers [the missionaries who brought Buddhist ideas and practices into China in the first century CE] gone a little further toward the west they might have encountered the religion of the Holy One. Instead of this they introduced into China a form of idolatry which is decried by the learned, laughed at by the profligate, yet followed by all." So, in the end, it too is not religion. Finally, the Tauists (his spelling) he rejects as being believers in a system "sustained by abstruse speculations of a mystic philosophy" whose founder was last seen "going westward riding on a blue cow." Dean concludes with a summary that is worth quoting in full length and speaks for itself:

> The atheistic teachings of Confucius, which ignore the doctrine of the immortality of the soul and the eternity of Jehovah, leave the heart of man uncleansed, and the sin of the world uncanceled. The superstitious dogmas of Budhism, which profess to moralize the whole animal kingdom, leave its votaries without God in the world, and lead to an extinction of all being hereafter. The mystic speculations of the Tauist end in table-turnings, the doctrines of devils and deeds of darkness. The morals of Mohammedanism are demonstrated by fire and sword, piracy and plunder;—and

even the mutilated form of Christianity presented in Roman Catholicism fails to curb the passions or control the lives of its disciples. It is left for the simple teachings of Jesus Christ alone, to remove the curse of sin, to cure the world of sorrow, and fit mankind for happiness and heaven.[40]

William Soothill, too, had much to say on the topic of religion in China, particularly Buddhism. He writes: "Buddha, 'the Light of Asia! . . . wearing a garb of fantastic grotesqueness puerile to the Western mind." He continues: "Here, pondering alone the problems that men still ponder,—Whence? How? Wither?—he found no hopeful answer, and fashioned his beliefless creed. . . . Such is the gospel of Buddha, a gospel without God, and whose only hope lies in the cessation of consciousness."[41] Not a flattering picture, but then again, Soothill's task, like all the missionaries in China, was to see Christianity prevail as the primary force of imperialism. As Hevia explained above, imperialism was always more than just "guns and goods," as important as these might also have been. Imperialism was also about religion (Christianity) or the lack thereof.

Visualizing Religion

A colorful figure and contemporary of John Barrow was the Rev. William Winterbotham (1763–1829). His memoir begins with a reference to the Macartney embassy and immediately takes us to trade. God will come later.

> From the expensive preparations made for the late Embassy to China, the British nation was certainly led to expect that a commercial intercourse would have opened between the two nations, which might have proved of the utmost importance to both. These

hopes have, however, been frustrated and disappointed for the present, but the Embassy has given rise to a laudable spirit of inquiry with respect to the Chinese empire, which we have no doubt will ultimately prove advantageous to British commerce.

Unlike some of his later missionary counterparts, Winterbotham sought to find similarities between Christianity and early Chinese ideas about the universe. In his chapter "Religion of the Chinese" he writes: "To judge properly of the religious system of the Chinese, the ancient and permanent religion of the state must not be confounded with popular superstitions introduced in latter ages." Later he continues: "We see, in these monuments of remote antiquity, the most evident traces of the patriarchal faith; and that the ancient Chinese worshipped only one Supreme God, whom they consider as a free and intelligent Being. And as an all-powerful, avenging, and rewarding Spirit."[42]

That Winterbotham is decidedly overinterpreting the ancient notion of *tian* (the heavens) is beside the point; what matters here is his determination to find a monotheistic center in early Chinese practices. Winterbotham goes on to describe erroneously, in marvelous detail, some of what he sees are the core components of Daoism ("the Tao-sse") and "the sect of the god Foe, or Fo," a sect "still more pernicious, and much wider diffused throughout China than the preceeding" (the "preceeding" being the Tao-sse, the Daoists). He refers to the Buddha as "this pretended god." Ultimately, Winterbotham does go down the same path as his later missionary compatriots. He describes Buddhism as "extravagant and absurd . . . better suited to the comprehension of the vulgar."[43]

We see in these observations a combination of the aspirations of the age of discovery, the explorer uncovering new territory and discovering, seemingly for the first time, peoples (who ultimately will be classified as subhuman), landscapes, templescapes, and, raw materials and potential labor force. As sociologist Pierre Bourdieu would say, every point of view is also a view from a point, that is, a particular perspective, an ocular positioning, so that the colonialist will see what they wish to see. [Religion, for nineteenth-century colonialists, is manifested from the perspective of the viewer and not the object being viewed. Religion comes to be defined as a serious exercise in the control of the human experience from the perspective of the viewing agent, and this process, which begins in the eighteenth-century Enlightenment period, finds its definitive voice during the nineteenth-century era of colonial engagement: that is, the interaction between the center and the periphery, the rational and the wild frontier.]

Thus the conceptualization of religion is a form of control that begins at home long before the ship arrives on colonized soil. For John Barrow, religion is produced when he takes a first step toward understanding the difference of the Other. As a result, religion is constructed via a path of what I would call "colonial authentication," that is, verifying one's own identity vis-à-vis the stereotyping of someone in your view. Vision dominates this process.

This approach to understanding and categorizing newly acquired knowledge is one dominated not just by vision but also by *a* vision, a view of the world, a worldview that demands the viewer be at the helm. The visual, at least since the Enlightenment, always took priority over the other senses.[44] Religion for these colonialists is conceptually constructed prior to departure, then reified in situ. Religion is produced, categorized, defined via visual reference to the other. It has no reality other than the textual kind, that being a colonial era mentality articulated by ambassadors, emissaries, missionaries, the first and foremost orientalists, civilized religious people with a worldview that contained within it a remarkably clear view of the world.

Law and Order

Colonial missions to the frontiers in the nineteenth century, throughout China and indeed the globe, owe their existence to many reasons, one of which is that those who transgress against civilization will be punished and then made to be civilized. Education came in many forms. China had to be taught a lesson by all the imperial powers who engaged in the hostile act of colonization beginning with the two Opium Wars (1839–1842 and 1856–1860). The Qing emperor needed to be humiliated, through physical and symbolic forms of violence, through textual means, through lessons whose purported legitimacy was the God-given right to discern the noble from the savage, the pauper from the prince. China needed to be made a prince among nations, while the king and queen of England remained just that: after all, princes owed allegiance to kings and queens. And princes behaved, or at least ought to behave, like gentlemen: all this so that China could play nicely in the growing game of geopolitical global relations.

As we have seen, a central component to these global relations was the relationship between what it meant to be civilized, to engage in trade, to be Christian, and new ideas about international law. As early as the sixteenth century ideas about what constituted a "civilization," and thus what it meant to be civilized, insisted on the freedom of trade, travel, and Christian proselytizing. This came to fruition in the nineteenth century.

In addition to all the above was the newly construed domain of international law. Henry Wheaton's book in particular, the *Elements of International Law*, published in 1836, had an extraordinary influence on East Asia in general, and especially China.[45] The text was translated into Chinese in 1863 by W. A. P. Martin, an American missionary from Indiana. The new translation was put to the test to good effect when China used an existing

treaty with Prussia to force the Prussians to release three cap-
tured Danish ships in Chinese territorial waters. The idea of "territorial waters" came right out of Wheaton's book.[46]

The *Elements of International Law* also came to set the standard by which the major players in the region would decide China's fate and the outcome and requirement for China to engage
with foreign powers on equal footing. China was to abide by and
engage in international law as defined by European and American constructs. It is worth quoting Wheaton at length:

> The progress of civilization, founded on Christianity, has gradu-
> ally conducted us to observe a law analogous to this [international
> law] in our intercourse with all the nations of the globe. . . . It may
> be remarked, in confirmation of this view, that the more recent
> intercourse between the Christian nations in Europe and Amer-
> ica and the Mohammedan and Pagan nations of Asia and Africa
> indicates a disposition, on the part of the latter, to renounce their
> peculiar usages and adopt those of Christendom. . . . The same
> remark may be applied to the recent diplomatic transactions
> between the Chinese Empire and the Christian nations of Europe
> and America, in which the former has been compelled to aban-
> don it inveterate anti-commercial and anti-social principles, and
> to acknowledge the independence and equality of other nations
> in the mutual intercourse of war and peace.[47]

Christendom, progress, civilization, and trade went hand in
hand. And in this instance, Christendom was religion; that is to
say, the true religion. Christianity was the ultimate universal,
and under this new international law, China need to "renounce
their peculiar usages," understand Christianity as the universal,
and "adopt . . . Christendom." The Chinese were understood to
lack real religion, to be uncivilized (Wheaton characterizes them
as "semi-civilized'), to be antisocial and anticommercial. All

this required European remedying. Trade and God were inextricably intertwined, and China was understood to lack both.

Finally, the depictions discussed above, whether by a missionary or a diplomat, are by no means unique in their harsh descriptions of the peoples they encounter. Nineteenth-century descriptions of China (and South Africa) are remarkably similar in tone. What is important for our purposes, however, is that their legacy has influenced the way the Chinese Communist Party has come to conceptualize what religion is. Confucianism is presented as a philosophy. Buddhism and Daoism are considered religions and tightly controlled. Protestantism is now tolerated, though the CCP worries that practitioners have more loyalty to God than they do toward the state. Catholicism is deeply troubling to the CCP because of the pope's sway over Catholics worldwide, including in China.[48] And, Islam, specifically in the Northwest, is considered real trouble. What missionaries initiated, the attempt to convert the Chinese to Christianity, on the one hand, and the attempt to disparage local forms of religiosity, on the other, set the stage for later government policies toward religious groups, policies that almost always sought to control and contain.

Change

To return to Barrow's and Macartney's first encounter with China in 1793, it was an inevitable clash of worldviews since the Qianlong emperor made it clear that China had not the slightest need for British expertise. From Qianlong's perspective, the world revolved around China, cosmologically at least, if not culturally. In many ways the mission was doomed from the start, for unbeknownst to all parties and players, this meeting between Britain and China led to perhaps the most poignant moment of

China's forced entry into modernity and nation-state building, namely, the first Opium War.[49]

With the first Opium War, China had its first substantive brush with a European modernity. This was a brutal affair that saw the British forcefully opening several ports along China's east coast for trade. The Americans, Russians, and French set sail immediately. Even the sixth president of the United States, John Quincy Adams, weighed in regarding China's so-called irrational behavior (not opening its ports to trade) prior to the war. Historian Julia Lovell points out that Adams blamed the emerging hostilities, in his own words, "on the kowtow—the arrogant and insupportable pretensions of China, that she will not hold commercial intercourse with the rest of mankind not upon terms of equal reciprocity, but upon the insulting and degrading forms of the relations between lord and vassal."[50]

The changes China went through and the changes it is still going through are hard to comprehend. Peter Zarrow puts it best in an introductory essay: "What historians label transitional is experienced as clashes, compromises, and sometimes seamless restructuring of everyday practices, values, and assumptions."[51] From Lord Macartney's court appearance in Beijing in the final years of the eighteenth century, to the first Opium War and the second, then through the Self-Strengthening movement (c. 1861–1895) and the Hundred Days' Reform (June–September 1898), not to mention the Taiping Rebellion (1850s), the Boxer Rebellion (1898–1901), the 1911 Revolution, the May Fourth movement in 1919, and, overall, the radical shift from a dynastic tradition to a nation-state with a constitution, as Zarrow puts it, few Chinese experienced all this as simply transitional. Modernity, says Zarrow rightly, "is not a moment but a process."[52]

If, as historian Philip Kuhn has argued, the main point of making a modern state in China was to resist foreign domination "by using some of the 'foreigners'' own technologies of dominance, both material and societal,"[53] then it may well have also been the case that it was a self-conscious decision by the same logic to appropriate the category of religion so as to resist the dominance of the category as a societal norm and organizing force. Irrespective of the potential outcomes, what was essential to what Zarrow calls the process of modernity were the attempts at constitutionalism, engaged nation-state building, creating new categories of containment, and, perhaps above all, territorialization.

China on its path to nation-statehood was never colonized in the same manner as, say, India, but the desire on the part of Western nations and Japan to do so was there (and one can talk about part of the east and south coast as being colonized). The imperium came crashing down for many reasons, not least of which was the influence of Western nations as they sought access to China and forced the country onto a world stage dominated by industrialization, colonialism, and trade. China had to adapt and did so through fledgling constitutionalism, a civil war, and, since 1949, the massive failures and successes of the Chinese Communist Party, which still rules the country today.

When in 1908 the first written constitution in China was finally promulgated, it marked the beginning of the end of imperial China and an entry into the global game of nation-states, a social reality expressed poignantly exactly one hundred years later with the Beijing Olympics in 2008. The irony of having come full circle from a crushed empire to a resuscitated one today is not lost on Beijing. As Edward Wong writes: "Of the global powers that dominated the 19th century, China alone is a rejuvenated empire."[54] Once again, Beijing, the "centrifugal/centripetal power of the cited traditions" that Long wrote of in the epigraph to this chapter has indeed expanded its power outward from the center to rule its massive territory, most of it acquired during the Qing dynasty, and bringing those territorial spaces "under the reign of the center and its ideology, assuring them a place in the legitimate and authentic structure of that reality designated and symbolized at this center." Beijing is that center, and just as in the old imperium, the new imperium exerts its force on the "ten thousand things" in multiple ways, one of them being the power to once again draw political leaders to that center and pay homage to the new empire.[55] Imperial contact with China—the import and importance of trade, religion, and guns—has brought about a new type of nation-state, different from, but no less dangerous than, other nation-states. It is this nativity, this new sacralized nation with the inviolate at its core, that we return to in the next chapter.

6

Nativity

S ome time ago Michel Foucault explained that in the eighteenth century, with the formation of the modern state, individuals (now citizens, not subjects) could be integrated into this new social structure. He argued, "In a way, we can see the state as a modern matrix of individualization or a new form of pastoral power."[1] Pastoral power is salvation oriented. We can see this so clearly in China. Prior to the formation of the modern Chinese nation-state, we had imperial power. China is once again somewhat unique in the development of its legal system. Euroamerican societies have their juridical roots in royal power.[2] China's juridical roots stem from imperial power: there are parallels, especially when the shift from royal/imperial to constitutional takes place; then the crisis of the distribution of power is in the forefront of reestablishing what sovereignty is. In both cases—Euroamerican and East Asian—late nineteenth- and early twentieth-century constitutionalism renegotiates juridical categories and the prerogative of power. It also negotiates the change from subject to citizen.

After 1949 the state offered salvation to all, a release from the shackles of feudalism, a salvific escape from imperial power. Even today President Xi Jinping portrays himself as a father of the nation. He embodies the state but pastorally takes care of the nation.[3] Salvation is not to be had in the life hereafter but in the here and now, the present, a state of being in which the state can ensure your well-being and, most important, your security. Pastoral/CCP power will stabilize the nation (as concept and form) and bring harmony and security to all citizens.

This is part of the mythos—state-sanctified violence is justified to bring about salvific peace. Any citizen who interferes with this sacralized process will be swiftly dealt with. We know that in China, thousands of citizens "disappear" every year for any number of reasons, but the primary one is the threat of bringing instability to the state. Pastoral power is no longer ecclesiastical rule but state power—the ability of the state to macro- and micromanage most if not all aspects of the lives of its citizenry.

Foucault references Immanuel Kant, who in a short piece written in a German newspaper, the *Berliner Monatschrift*, at the end of the eighteenth century titled his essay, "Was heisst Aufklärung?" What does enlightenment mean? Who are we in this particular moment? What are we right now? This is a stunning existential question, and Foucault recognizes what Kant is doing. When Kant asks that question in 1784, as a philosopher, he moves beyond metaphysics and brings his attention to a specific historical event, a wrinkle in troubled times. Foucault suggests that what Kant is doing is asking, "What are we?" What are we as *Aufklärer*, as part of the Enlightenment? This, in stark contrast to Descartes's "Who am I?" As Foucault explains, "I, for Descartes, is everyone, anywhere, at any moment." But Kant is asking what we are in this specific historical moment. Foucault concludes:

> Maybe the target nowadays is not to discover what we are but to refuse what we are. We have to imagine and to build up what we could be to get rid of this kind of political "double bind," which is the simultaneous individualization and totalization of modern

power structures. The conclusion would be that the political, ethical, social, philosophical problem of our days is not to try liberate the individual from the state and from the state's institutions but to liberate us both from the state and from the type of individualization which is linked to the state. We have to promote new forms of subjectivity through the refusal of this kind of individuality which has been imposed on us for several centuries.[4]

This call to reimagine our state of being, to reject state-imposed individuality, to promote new forms of subjectivity, threatens the structures of the nation-state. In many states—for example, China, Syria, Russia, Turkey, and Iran—this gets you arrested. It does too in other nation-states, but there is a little more wiggle room for the citizen to push back against the state. Still, the boundaries are always there, and to imagine too powerfully against the stability of the state will always incur the wrath of the state. That wrath is sacralized violence. It forms part of the shift from citizens sacrificing themselves for the state to the state killing its own citizens. Weber taught us this a long time ago: only the state has the monopoly on the legitimate right to violence. Only the state can legitimately kill.

Thus there is always a tension between nation-citizen-state. The nation is imagined but its citizens are tangible, and nationalism binds them to an overtly singular narrative but inherently a multitude of narratives, the proverbial "We all have our story, but we are part of a much larger story."[5] The state, on the other hand, is a territorial signifier with the claim to sovereignty as its foundation. This modern form of sovereignty was a new form developed in the eighteenth and nineteenth centuries, especially during the colonial period. It was power applied directly to bodies, a biopolitics of production. Foucault explains: "It was a mechanism of power that made it possible to extract time and labor, rather than commodities and wealth from bodies."[6]

So a shift had indeed occurred from an earlier form of sovereignty that stressed royal territory and the products of that territory to a focus on the subject's body.[7] The importance of territory never disappeared, though. It just transformed into what we can call an idea about sovereign space and the borders that mark that space.[8] The state claims sovereign space, within which its citizens must reside and without which they could not exist. (In other words, they would be stateless.) The process of negotiating power in and for the state must result in a production of space; indeed, modern sovereignty rests on the successful production, reproduction, and ideally expansion of that space, along with the control of bodies (citizens) who reside in that space. The space of the state is its territory, and states go to extraordinary lengths to justify and protect it. As we've seen, in China, the state refers to its territory as being sacred space (*shensheng lingtu*), a not uncommon classificatory scheme.

Blood and Soil

Let's decouple nation and state to be able to further reflect on these two entities.[9] We know the idea of a modern nation representative of Western sentimentalities originated in Europe.[10] The idea of the modern state is a creation of the Enlightenment, culminating in the Westphalia peace treaties in 1648 and Hobbes and *Leviathan* in 1651 (political power as modeled on God). During the first half of the eighteenth century, royalty still had precedence. In the second half of the eighteenth century we see the publication of Jean-Jacques Rousseau's *The Social Contract* (1762), an attempt to establish what a rightful political community ought to be. It was a radical critique of the monarchy and an argument for sovereignty in the hands of the populace.

Key events occurred with France's revolution (1789–1799), the Napoleonic Wars (1806–1813), and the Franco-Prussian War (1870–1871), leading into German unification, a new type of integrated nation-state combining thousands of former principalities. All these events were predicated on a newly formed general desire on the part of Europeans to form collective identities, expand and protect their territories via a constructed legitimacy regarding the use of violence, ideas about national unity, and common culture. And, as Hannah Arendt explains: "Because society becomes the substitute for the family, 'blood and soil' is supposed to rule the relationships between its members; homogeneity of population and its rootedness in the soil of a given territory become the requisites for the nation-state everywhere."[11] "Blood and soil" (*Blut und Boden*) becomes the rallying cry of Nazi ideology; yet this notion finds its way into all nation-state ideologies. In the United States, giving your life for your country, as in a soldier dying on the battlefield, is from the mouths of presidents the most sacred act a citizen can do. As politically determined as the expression "blood and soil" is, Italian philosopher Giorgio Agamben explains its innocuous roots in Roman law: *ius soli*, birth in a certain territory, and *ius sanguinis*, birth from citizen parents. Roman "citizenship" was the "primary inscription of life in the state order." Agamben makes this compelling argument: "The principle of nativity and the principle of sovereignty, which were separated in the *ancien régime* (where birth marked only the emergence of a *sujet*, a subject), are now irrevocably united in the body of the 'sovereign subject' so that the foundation of the new nation-state may be constituted." For Agamben, in conjunction with these two principles, it is sacrality that is "the originary form of the inclusion of bare life in the juridical order."[12] We are all now *homo sacer* and, with the nation-state, are all capable of being reduced to bare life (*zoe*), capable of being put into a state of exception, and capable of being killed by the state (though never sacrificed by the state; we can only sacrifice ourselves on behalf of the state). The inclusion of bare life into the juridical order takes place with the shift from king-subject to nation-state-citizen, the beginning of a new biopolitical order. The sacredness of life is now understood to be a fundamental human right, thus inserting sacrality into the political order.

It is the declaration of rights, listed in constitutions (see chapter 2), that forges the passage from divinely authorized sovereignty to nation-statism. This is the precise moment, as Agamben points out, that the subject (in the quote above) transforms into a citizen. And it is those rights that are considered by the nation-state to be sacred and inalienable. We see this first in the United States in the Declaration of Independence in 1776: "We hold these truths to be self-evident, that all men are created equal, that they are endowed by their Creator with certain unalienable Rights."[13] At this point, the "nontransferability" comes from God.

By 1789, just thirteen years later, we see the Declaration of the Rights of Man in France. Here the unalienableness of these rights are sacred, not divinely bestowed on subjects, but legislatively. The preamble reads as follows:

The representatives of the French people, organized as a National Assembly, believing that the ignorance, neglect, or contempt of the rights of man are the sole cause of public calamities and of the corruption of governments, have determined to set forth in a solemn declaration the natural, unalienable, and sacred rights of man, in order that this declaration, being constantly before all the members of the Social body, shall remind them continually of their rights and duties; in order that the acts of the legislative power, as well as those of the executive power, may be compared at any moment with the objects and purposes of all political institutions and may thus be more respected, and, lastly, in order that the grievances of the citizens, based hereafter upon simple and incontestable principles, shall tend to the maintenance of the constitution and redound to the happiness of all.[14]

The inalienable inhabits the inviolate. Article 3 is critical: "The principle of all sovereignty resides essentially in the nation. No body nor individual may exercise any authority which does not proceed directly from the nation." The inviolate, as a result of a process of sacralization (here, the bestowing of rights that are sacred), renders the sovereignty found in the nation. All then becomes constitutionalized and enshrined into law.

Nascere: Growing Citizens

A more mundane aspect of a functioning state is the following, as explained by Judith Butler: "The state signifies the legal and institutional structures that delimit a certain territory (although not all of those institutional structures belong to the apparatus of the state). Hence the state is supposed to service the matrix for the obligations and prerogatives of citizenship. It is that which forms the conditions under which we are juridically bound."[15] All good and well, except that in China the state moves beyond itself as a signifier of legal and institutional structures; the state moves toward a more contained matrix of power. Its modular mode is far more encompassing and extends beyond the containment of its own citizens to economic imperialism in the form of massive investments around the globe (see chapter 1). Its territory, while delimited to be sure, is also sought to be expanded on. But it is also "the obligations and prerogatives of citizenship" that must be negotiated for the state to sacralize the nation. A citizenry must be formulated.

In China's constitution, the term used for "citizen" is *gongmin*.[16] The first ideograph, *gong*, is made up of two components, meaning "to divide" and "private"; in other words, to divide up that which is private, meaning to make public. The second ideograph, *min*, has literal references to sprouting plants. So we have as "citizen" a public signifier of potential cultivation. The new state had been forced onto the world stage, and thus a completely new imagining of its space and a nation had to take place. This, in part, required the creation of citizens; in turn, citizens require rights under the law for the nation-state to function.[17]

Consider an individual citizen. In its earliest form, say around the beginning of the fourteenth century, the term referred to the civic rights of an inhabitant of a city or town, in a literal sense, a townsman as opposed to a countryman. By the eighteenth century it referred to a member of a state, usually enfranchised, and beholden to the laws of that state. This meaning has remained with us through the present time.

Part of how the citizenry is made depends on education and language, both of which are always political. In China's constitution, article 19 stipulates: "The state develops socialist educational undertakings and works to raise the scientific and cultural level of the whole nation. The state runs schools of various types, makes primary education compulsory and universal, develops secondary, vocational and higher education and promotes preschool education. . . . The state promotes the nationwide use of Putonghua [common speech based on Beijing pronunciation]." Add to this the civic duties required of the individuals and you then begin to see a growing citizenry.

Three articles in the constitution address this:

Article 24

The state strengthens the building of socialist spiritual civilization through spreading education in high ideals and morality,
general education and education in discipline and the legal system, and through promoting the formulation and observance of
rules of conduct and common pledges by different sections of the
people in urban and rural areas. The state advocates the civic vir-
tues of love for the motherland, for the people, for labour, for
science and for socialism; it educates the people in patriotism, col-
lectivism, internationalism and communism and in dialectical
and historical materialism; it combats the decadent ideas of capitalism and feudalism and other decadent ideas.

Article 52

It is the duty of citizens of the People's Republic of China to
safeguard the unity of the country and the unity of all its
nationalities.

Article 54

It is the duty of citizens of the People's Republic of China to safeguard the security, honour and interests of the motherland; they
must not commit acts detrimental to the security, honour and
interests of the motherland.

From the duty of loving the motherland, safeguarding unity—
that unity prioritizes Han ethnicity—and safeguarding the security, honor, and interests of the motherland, you get a sense of
what type of obedient citizenry the state desires. Article 28 backs
up all the above: "The State maintains public order and sup-
presses treasonable and other criminal activities that endanger
State security; it penalizes actions that endanger public security
and disrupt the socialist economy and other criminal activities,

and punishes and reforms criminals."[18] State security—a sprawling network of ideology, party politics, and institutions—is separate from public security; the former protects and contains the latter.

Claiming the State

The degree to which the citizen can make a claim against the state is always an important litmus test in the desire to better stabilize human rights. At its simplest, citizenship is the juridical relationship between individual and the state/polity (or the national). The relationship is perpetually unclear, which works to the advantage of the state. It is through the lens of human rights that pressure can be brought to bear on the state; in other words, in its most basic formulation, the function of human rights asks how the state is treating its citizens. More than that, however, human rights falter inevitably at the precise moment they are needed the most, for instance, with refugees.[19] The notion of citizenry, itself a product of the imagination, serves the collectivity by providing identity and potential protection. Thus when a governing body feels threatened by its social body, steps are taken to contain that citizenry, to shut down the public square (if it indeed even existed in the first place), to take refuge in the legal vagaries of constitutional documents, and to find ways to circumvent human rights.[20] All too often the same documents that claim to defend human beings in general and nation-state citizens in particular—constitutions, human rights conventions—can also be used to control and detain the entities they purport to protect.

So there is always a tension between the individual or social group engaging in the process of producing a space within which to live a meaningful existence and the state's attempts to create controllable spaces within which their citizens must reside.[21] There are many way in which states go about doing this, some more repressive than others. China is caught up with its own insecurities about its citizenry and what I see as a dangerous form of nationalism growing ever stronger by the year. (Though, to be fair, most forms of nationalism are inherently dangerous and ultimately unstable.) As scholars have pointed out, digital space becomes a serious site for citizens to negotiate and supersede national territoriality and further open up the global.[22] This was all too obvious during the Arab Spring, where social media played a formative role. Beijing's censors block almost all these sites—Twitter and Facebook, for instance. But, there are always workarounds, the Great Firewall notwithstanding. In the end, citizenship and a challenging citizenry are subject to and claimed by the state.

Comparing Citizens

Let's compare three current constitutions as they use the term "citizen": the People's Republic of China, the Republic of China (Taiwan), and South Africa In the PRC constitution, we see the first use of the term citizen in article 13: "The state protects the right of citizens to own lawfully earned income, savings, houses and other lawful property." This was later amended to the following: "Citizens' lawful private property is inviolable. The State, in accordance with law, protects the rights of citizens to private property and to its inheritance. The State may, in the public interest and in accordance with law, expropriate or requisition private property for its use and shall make compensation for the private property expropriated or requisitioned." The inviolate is brought into focus and tied to territory in the form of property. The state can lift these rights, as it often does when confiscating property from citizens. One obvious example is the razing of *hutong*, old alleyway structures in Beijing, with little or no compensation to the residents. Families are forced to move out of the inner city to the far-flung suburbs.[23]

Articles 33 through 56 delineate the various rights and duties that a citizen has and must perform. The closest the constitution gets to defining the term citizen is in article 33: "All persons holding the nationality of the People's Republic of China are citizens of the People's Republic of China. All citizens of the People's Republic of China are equal before the law. Every citizen enjoys the rights and at the same time must perform the duties prescribed by the Constitution and the law. The State respects and preserves human rights."[24] Taiwan's constitution first mentions the term citizen in article 3: "Persons possessing the nationality of the Republic of China shall be citizens of the Republic of China." This is similar to the PRC version. (The obvious difference is article 35, which states: "Citizens of the People's Republic of China enjoy freedom of speech, of the press, of assembly, of association, of procession and of demonstration." In Taiwan this would be true.)

The current South African constitution has a section (article 3) called "Citizenship." It states: "(1) There is a common South African citizenship. (2) All citizens are: (a) equally entitled to the rights, privileges and benefits of citizenship; and (b) equally subject to the duties and responsibilities of citizenship. (3) National legislation must provide for the acquisition, loss, and restoration of citizenship." These attempts to expand the notion of citizenship within the sovereign state simultaneously shrink the definition to contain the populace. The question then arises, to rephrase Agamben, "Who and what is Chinese? Who and what is South African?" (And, therefore, also "Who and what is not Chinese? Who and what is not South African?")

So where are we then? When nationalism bolstered by various forms of sacralization is used as the primary motivating force for ostensible liberation—political, economic, postcolonial—little good can come from this historically. In China, the rhetoric of a postcolonial and postrevolutionary nationalism is leading this nation-state down a slippery slope where the imagined community might just fall apart in spectacularly violent ways. The nurturing of a citizenry loyal to the state is itself a form of containment, one that in the Chinese example is necessary for that nation. Not that this is a good thing. A different type of citizenry needs to be imagined, a citizenry that, while part of the nation-state, is vigorously opposed to nationalism.

What of alternative forms of citizenry? The European Union form of citizenship is the most obvious example where citizenry becomes translocal and potentially postnational, though given cultural differences and the many nationalistic forces that seem to still prevail across Europe, it's not clear to me how that might work.[25] Dual citizenship is always a path toward a more globalized condition; however, translocal law is still a problem. Is the citizen with British and American citizenship subject to two sovereigns?

Sometimes a redefining of citizenship comes in unexpected ways, say when Crimea almost overnight voted to become part of the Russian Federation in 2014, albeit with thousands of Russian troops on the borders of Ukraine. One moment Ukrainian citizenry, the next, Russian, though it's far from clear what that means vis-à-vis the national polity.

Citizenship is always a contested category—witness the debates raging in the United States—and never more so than when it is tied to the category of race or of religion (again the United States is an example, with the Trump administration's repeated attempts to block citizens from several predominantly Muslim states coming into U.S. space). That contestation results in a proliferation of meaning that often splits the polity, thereby endangering the nation as imagined community. It also brings us dangerously close to what Agamben calls "the camp," the underbelly of the liberal, modern, nation-state. He writes: "The camp is thus the structure in which the state of exception—the possibility of deciding on which founds sovereign power—is realized *normally*. The sovereign no long limits himself . . . to deciding on the basis of recognizing a given factual situation (danger to public safety) . . . he now de facto produces the situation as a consequence of his decision on the exception." Are all nation-states already under a continual state of exception? Apartheid South Africa was so. The state inserted itself into the bare life of the citizenry and had complete control over their bodies—biopower as normalized. Contemporary China now has a sovereign who can rule indefinitely like the emperors of old. He no longer "limits himself." He has ultimate authority over his camp, and the camp is a "hybrid of law and fact in which the two terms have become indistinguishable." This is the "new normal" of the nation-state. As Agamben puts it: "The state of exception, which was essentially a temporary suspension of the juridico-political order, now becomes a new and stable spatial arrangement."[26]

Different States

Nation-statism ostensibly liberates, but is this always so? And if it is, what does it liberate us from? (Beijing state discourse, for example, will always refer to Tibetans and Uighurs as having been liberated by the state.) Scholar of religion Bruce Lincoln points out that when Europeans withdrew from their empires they left behind what we now call secular structures of power, but only in the hands of the most Westernized elite of the geographical region they were departing from. Lincoln writes:

"Whatever its benefits—and they are not negligible—the secular state remains inconsistent with precolonial conditions, and insofar as it bestows state power on the most successfully Westernized fractions of the population, it has created numerous difficulties."[27] Africa, following the colonial period, was left as a carved up continent with some fifty or so states in which each had to create a brand new form of nationalism primarily based on the British and French models. Britain just assumed that there were no African models; thus the British model was the only one to work with.

The tensions continue today.[28] We witness the gaps and vacuums that occur and that are too quickly filled with quasi-legitimate entities that claim to speak on behalf of their people yet never clarify who those people are and whether "their people" pledge allegiance in the first place. The kinds of nationalisms—ones that were supposed to liberate—tried by so many of the new African states led to a serious destruction of social ties. As Basil Davidson puts it: "Liberation thus produced its own denial. Liberation led to alienation."[29] South Africa, it seems, might be an exception, though it now is experiencing its own form of postcolonial hangover, one that in part stemmed from a postapartheid world in which the former institutions of racial hierarchy still cast their shadows over the people. Here, too, a new citizenry was needed.

In his state of the nation address on May 24, 1994, in the Houses of Parliament in Cape Town, newly elected president Nelson Mandela said: "The government I have the honour to lead and I dare say the masses who elected us to serve in this role, are inspired by the single vision of creating a people-centered society. Accordingly, the purpose that will drive this government shall be the expansion of the frontiers of human fulfilment, the continuous extension of the frontiers of the freedom." With the phrase "people-centered society," Mandela was using the state to accord more humanity to the citizen, something profoundly lacking under the apartheid regime and especially during a declared state of emergency.

One was declared after the Sharpville massacre in 1960 when 67 citizens were shot, most in the back, and 186 were wounded. Over 6,000 were arrested.[30] One I experienced was declared in July 1985 as I was finishing up high school. On June 12, 1986, the government declared a nationwide state of emergency for an indefinite period of time. Tens of thousands were detained, and torture was widespread during police custody. South Africa became a space devoid of law.

The sovereign, in this instance President P. W. Botha, extended the state of emergency, or what Giorgio Agamben calls a state of exception.[31] Violence is necessary to maintain a state of exception, and violence erupts continuously as bare life is separated out from *bios* or *polis*.[32] It is the capacity for bare life to be ended that empowers the sovereign and politicizes the act of killing.[33] Sacralization—as process and outcome—is what incorporates bare life, that is, the subjects of the state. Sacrality extends only within the ability of the sovereign's inclusive exclusivity. It is within the state's boundaries, the sovereign sphere—the exclusivity permitted by the juridical function of borders that seek to contain the sovereign's subjects, or today what we call citizens— that life is considered sacred (precisely because it can be killed).

What further complicates this social reality is the extension of sovereignty beyond territorial borders. Talal Asad makes the following observation, perhaps obvious, but no less critical: "The political interests of liberal democratic states are not confined to their sovereign territory, especially when the welfare of populations depends on changing political, economic, and cultural relations in other parts of the world." He goes on to say that "the violent freedoms of industrial capitalism can be said to have constituted political life as the space of an earthly permanence that can compensate for the death of the past—at the cost of a fatal threat to the future."[34] In other words, the nation-state has the right to defend itself, even to use nuclear weapons, the ultimate erasure of political life.

With modernity, and the foundational role of biopolitics in establishing and maintaining the nation-state, it is the sovereign who decides the value of life. And, as Agamben explains, "life—which, with the declaration of rights, had as such been invested with the principle of sovereignty—now itself becomes the place of a sovereign decision."[35] Thus, in stark contrast to the political claims of citizens' rights, and of human rights, from the sovereign's perspective only bare life is truly political.[36] This is one node where the violence perpetuated by the modern, industrialized state is a sanctified violence, as the absolute right to defend one's inviolate takes precedent over everything else.

Other Possible States of Being

Efforts to teach ourselves how to be human cannot be fully realized with coercive power hanging over our heads. Some space is needed—political, social, communal—otherwise the stifling of imagination is the inevitable result. A new imaginary is needed. This is always needed—what Appadurai calls the "constructed landscape of collective aspirations."[37] The imagination by which we construct ourselves, our social spaces, has changed markedly from the Enlightenment until the present age. This might be a truism, but while an opening up of power distribution has taken place over the past three centuries, we have also witnessed and continue to see a closing of imagination with the formation and perpetuation of the nation-state.

This is one of the reasons we have yet to see the demise of the nation-state. We struggle to imagine other possibilities. Gilles

Deleuze and Félix Guattari's assemblage is still to be found. The state is antisocial, breaking up social gatherings because they are seen as a threat to the monopoly. In China, the state of exception becomes normalized when the CCP decides to allow its leader to be in power indefinitely.

On the other hand, power is never just top down. The Communist Party with its iron grip on forging a single will for over a billion people must realize the inevitable circulatory nature of power. That is to say, the way in which power circulates in networks—the Internet, underground organizations, social gatherings, be they peaceful, legal, violent, or illegal. We can always come back to Pierre Bourdieu's notion of a field as a network of relations. Individuals occupy multiple fields and move through multiple fields.[38] Power does so in a similar manner.[39] It flows and circulates, distorts and reinforces. One of the biggest challenges for China's leaders is how to constrain that flow and circulation. No amount of censorship and political silencing can ultimately cut off the flow. Where is the sacrality in this? In the death of a state's own citizens? In the forms of systemic violence that allows the state to bind and unbind?

If it is the state that sacralizes the nation, then could it also be that the nation and its multiplicity of constructed nationalisms sacralize the state? It emboldens the state to act unilaterally in the world in a direct and often confrontational manner. This is not coincidental: the nation-state construes itself via its own ideological renderings. It is the projection of those renderings that requires a process of sacralization and indeed sanctification. Who sanctifies? Who sacralizes? Who speaks for whom and on behalf of whom?

Whatever the answers, we are dealing with what Judith Butler calls "a particular formation of power and coercion that is designed to produce and maintain the condition, the state, of the dispossessed.[40] It is this state that can simultaneously contain and dispossess. (Think Israel and the Palestinians, Uighurs in China,

Syrians in Syria, prisoners at Guantanamo—national minorities everywhere, as Arendt argues.) All states are implicated. I think this is the reason Butler will call for a reconceiving of both spatiality and location, especially, as she puts it, "once we consider the departure from within, the dispossession that demands immobility."[41]

I have never been in a state of dispossession; my experience stops at that of a kind of self-imposed exile (a self-displaced South African American with Namibian and British colonial roots). I don't know statelessness or the disenfranchised national minorities that Arendt will talk about. So what can we do when Tibetans set themselves on fire in opposition to Han citizenry, in opposition to religious containment? Is this Foucault's rejection of the type of individualization that is linked to the state? What can I do when I listen to a Syrian father on the BBC describe how his entire family—wife, children, grandparents, aunts, and uncles—was killed in an instant by one of Bashar al-Assad's bombs? He sits quietly in the street, a public space, rocking gently from side to side. He is dispossessed. He is stateless; he is disenfranchised in his own state, that is, his state of being, and his corrupted state of location. Is this what Foucault means by calling for a rejection of the way in which the state extracts time and labor from bodies? This is the state-individualization that we must reject? Like Kant, we need to ask who we are in this specific moment. Are we really *Aufklärer*? Regardless of response, it seems the nation-state is rarely capable of allowing for the answer to be fully lived out in the world.

Conclusion

China is offering the world a new blueprint of a modern nation-state, but it is doing so by too often unwittingly borrowing Eurocentric terms and ideas. Throughout this book, I have tried to uncover some of those terms and ideas and see how they are deployed in the Chinese state. Territory, religion, citizen, and race—all can be used to produce the inviolate, the foundation of the modern, nation-state saturated with mythos and violence. The inviolate conjures the sacred, and the state uses this sacrality to sacralize the nation. To come full circle back to what I wrote in the preface: stating the sacred is a structural principle. Sacralizing the nation produces the inviolate and results in a legitimate state. Whether that state can survive depends heavily on how it protects that inviolate (always a violent process) and how it maintains its conceptualizations of territory, religion, and citizenship—not just juridically but culturally and politically as well.

At the beginning and end of his book on state and religion in China, Anthony Yu quotes the Han emperor Yuandi (r. 48–32 BCE), who stated at the beginning of his reign, "We make it a point to establish personally our ancestral temple, because this is the ultimate power to build up our authority, eliminate the sprouts of rebellion, and make the people one."[42] The "ancestral state" (*zuguo*) has always been an authoritarian one. The ancestral temple at the heart of Han identity still stands, albeit not one that Yuandi would recognize. The ancestral state that is China today uses narrow categories, many, as we have seen, borrowed from European mentalités, to build up its authority and "eliminate the sprouts of rebellion." I have argued that territory and religion, citizenship and race are foundational constructs of the nation-state, bound together by the inviolate and encoded in constitutional language. This is how the state sacralizes the nation.

In a well-worn refrain, commonly heard during South Africa's apartheid era, I continue to have hope for no particular reason other than for hope itself.[43] I am utopian in my outlook. I continue to believe in possibilities other than the nation-state, with its deep-fixed belief in itself and in its complete renouncement of its origins in mythos and sanctified violence.[44] I don't pretend to have any solutions other than to say that the work of the imagination, individually and collectively, is needed all the more urgently now. As Ian Buruma reminds us: "Similar fears haunt anxious minds."[45] China and South Africa are not the same; Europe and the United States are also different. But everywhere citizens, the people, struggle with wanting a more fixed, stable identity. When nation-states breathe the inviolate into those struggles in search for a national culture, then territory, religion (or, to control what they call religion), and citizenship are always part of the mix. Invoking the sacred institutes the terror of the inviolate. A challenge for the future will be to limit the degree to which the state can sacralize the nation. Like Hans Christian Andersen's duplicitous shadow, in the end the nation-state is never what it claims to be.

Glossary

ba	八
Baoguohui	保國會
bu xinjiao gongmin	不信教公民
Chen Quanguo (1955–)	陈全国
daxue	大學
di	狄
fa	發
facai	發財
gedi peikuan	割地賠款
gong'an bu	公安部
gongmin	公民
gudai	古代
guo	國
guojia	国家
guojiao	國教
Guojia zongjiao shiwuju	国家宗教事务局
guomin	国民
Guowuyuan	国务院
Han	漢
he	和
Hsin Tao (1948–)	心道
hu	胡

hua	華
huairou yuanren	懷柔遠人
huangdi shensheng buke qinfan	皇帝神聖不可侵犯
huaxia	華夏
huofo	活佛
hutong	胡同
I	夷
Jiao tazhe zuguo de dadi, beifuzhe minzu de xiwang	脚踏着祖国的大地, 背负着民族的希望
jindai	近代
Kang Youwei (1858–1927)	康有為
ketou	磕頭
Kongzi xueyuan	孔子学院
li	禮
Liang Qichao (1873–1929)	梁啟超
Liji	禮記
ling	领／領
long de chuanren	龍的傳人
man	蠻
menhuan	门宦
mixin	迷信
Puyi (1906–1967)	溥儀
quan	權
quanguo	全国
ren	人
renmin	人民
rong	戎
sangquan ruguo	丧权辱国
Shanhai jing	山海經
shen	神
Shenci cunfei biaozhun	神祠存廢標準
sheng	圣/聖
shensheng lingtu	神聖領土

shensheng zhize	神圣职责
shenzhou	神州
shijie zongjiao bowuguan	世界宗教博物館
shijiu xintiao	十九信条
shūkyō	宗教
sidian	祀典
sifang	四方
Sun Baoqi (1867–1931)	孫寶琦
Taiwan wenti	台灣問題
tian	天
tianchao	天朝
tianming	天命
tianxia	天下
tianzi	天子
tongbao	同胞
tu	土
wanghua	王化
wei renmin fuwu	为人民服务
wen	文
wu	武
wuwang guochi	勿忘国耻
wuxing	五行
wuxu bianfa/bai ri weixin	戊戌變法/百日維新
wuyue	五嶽
xiandai	現代
xie	邪
xincheng	新政
xinyang	信仰
xue	穴
Ye Xiaowen (1950–)	叶小文
yi	夷
yin	淫
yinci	淫祠

yinsi	淫祀
yu	玉
Yuandi (r. 48–32 BCE)	元帝
Yuan Shikai (1859–1916)	袁世凱
zhanguo	戰國
Zhang Zhenzhi (1906–1931)	張振之
Zhang Zhidong (1837–1909)	張之洞
zhen	鎮
zhengchang	正常
zhengchang de zongjiao huodong	正常的宗教活动
zhong	中
Zhongguo	中国(國)
Zhongguo guochi ditu	中国国耻地图
Zhongguo qiji	中国奇迹
Zhongguoren	中国人
Zhongguo ribao	中国日報
zhongxin	中心
zhongzu	種族
zhuanshi lingtong	转世灵童
ziqiang yundong	自强运动
ziyou	自由
zongjiao	宗教
zongjiao de gongmin	宗教的公民
zongjiao de wenti	宗教的问题
zongjiao xinyang ziyou	宗教信仰自由
zuguo	祖国

Notes

Preface

1. A *sjambok* is a leather whip that is traditionally made from the hide of a rhinoceros or hippopotamus. It was the "nonlethal" weapon of choice for the South African Police (SAP) during the apartheid era.

2. Possibly as many as ten thousand strong, the Zulu army attacked at dawn. Andries Pretorius led five hundred men armed with guns and fifty-seven wagons in laager formation as they repelled the Zulus, killing at least three thousand. The Zulus were armed with spears.

3. This narrative was later mythologized in the Constitution of South Africa adopted on April 24, 1961. The preamble begins with the recognition that God gave the territory of South Africa to the Afrikaners: "In humble submission to Almighty God, who controls the destinies of nations and the history of peoples; Who gathered our forebears together from many lands and gave them this their own."

4. For a brilliant analysis of Strydom's act and his understanding of the space within which he lived, see David Chidester, *Shots in the Streets: Violence and Religion in South Africa* (Boston: Beacon Press, 1991), chap. 1.

5. Chidester, *Shots in the Streets*, 8. Strydom was sentenced to death but, after speaking before the Truth and Reconciliation Commission, was released. The official commission website is at http://www.justice.gov.za /trc/.

6. John Carlin, "'White Wolf' Ready to Murder Blacks Again," *Independent*, October 4, 1992, http://www.independent.co.uk/news/world/white -wolf-ready-to-murder-blacks-again-1555578.html.

7. A disturbing interview with Strydom can be seen at https://www .youtube.com/watch?v=C_76q9-TfdU.

8. Estimates range from 300 to 2,600 deaths or higher.

9. In a foreword to Elizabeth Dauphinee's *The Politics of Exile*, Naeem Inayatullah makes the claim that "each of us writes about one substantive theme for the duration of our lives," and that "the theme emerges from a 'trauma,' or a 'space/time' wound." Elizabeth Dauphinee, *The Politics of Exile* (New York: Routledge, 2013), ix. The nation-state of South Africa, where I spent my childhood during the apartheid era, is for me a "wound"; China, a place in which I have invested so much of my professional life, has become one too. Yet, with hope, our wounds can be salvational.

10. See Max Weber's Munich lecture of January 1919, "Politics as a Vocation," in David Owen and Tracy B. Strong, eds., *The Vocation Lectures*, trans. Rodney Livingstone (Indianapolis: Hackett, 2004).

11. The number eight in Mandarin, *ba*, sounds similar to *fa*, which is part of the expression *facai*, to attain wealth. Eight is an auspicious number. Historically, it appears in many combinations—the eight Daoist immortals, eight Buddhist emblems, eight symbols of scholars, eight trigrams, eight pillars of heaven corresponding to the eight directions described in the *Liji* (*Book of Rites*), and so forth.

12. Together with harmony is the key concept of centrality (*zhong*). The Chinese name for China, Zhongguo, reflects this. The first ideograph, *zhong*, is a line bisecting a rectangle, symbolizing territory. The line indicates the centrality and balancing poles of its position. The second ideograph, *guo*, in its simplified version is the character for jade (*yu*), symbolizing the emperor, who is located at the center of the world, surrounded by his domain. In the traditional version, the inner ideograph is a lance, emblematic of the ruler, encompassed by four borders. The emperor resides at the center of his palace; his palace is located at the center of the capital; the capital is located at the center of the empire; and the empire, Zhongguo, literally "central empire," was understood to be the cultural center of the world. China today seeks to regain its centrality. One way China exports its model of "benign authoritarianism" and its focus on harmony and culture is through the establishment of what it calls Confucius Institutes (*Kongzi xueyuan*) around the globe. They are not without their controversy and seem to be part of the state's propaganda program. (See, for example, Elizabeth Redden, "New Scrutiny for Confucius Institutes," *Inside Higher Ed*, April 26, 2017, https://www.insidehighered.com/news/2017/04/26/report-confucius -institutes-finds-no-smoking-guns-enough-concerns-recommend -closure.) The National Association of Scholars has called on universities to close down their Confucius Institutes. China's Ministry of Education began establishing these institutes in 2004. The first one

established in Europe was at Stockholm University. The university closed it down in 2014. Many people understand them to be part of a "soft power" strategy to promote Chinese Communist Party ideas; some have referred to them as a "Trojan horse." The National Association of Scholars put the number of Confucius Institutes in the United States at around a hundred.

13. One of China's most important scholars on this topic is Wang Hui. See his book *China from Empire to Nation-State* (Cambridge, Mass.: Harvard University Press, 2014). Another important work by Wang is his four-volume *Xiandai Zhongguo sixiang de xingqi* (The rise of modern Chinese thought) (Beijing: Shenghuo dushu xinzhi sanlian shudian, 2004).

14. See Peter Zarrow, ed., *Creating Chinese Modernity: Knowledge and Everyday Life, 1900–1940* (New York: Peter Lang, 2006), 7. By way of contrast, I would suggest that European modernity begins with Hegel's question: "What is the ultimate design of the world?" Georg W. F. Hegel, *The Philosophy of History*, trans. J. Sibree (Minneapolis: University of Minnesota Press, 1996), 16. One could argue that early Chinese scholars grappled with similar questions.

15. Arjun Appadurai, *Modernity at Large: Cultural Dimensions of Globalization* (Minneapolis: University of Minnesota Press, 1996), 1. Pankaj Mishra has a different spin on this when he asks: "How do peoples with traditions extending back several millennia modernize themselves?" Pankaj Mishra, *Temptations of the West: How to be Modern in India, Pakistan, Tibet, and Beyond* (New York: Picador, 2006), i. In China, constitutionalism would become a key component of modernity.

16. The narrative extends to today: President Xi Jinping has ordered China's media to "tell China's story well." See Ben Blanchard and Michael Martina, "China's Xi Urges State Media to Boost Global Influence," *Reuters*, February 19, 2016, https://www.reuters.com/article/us-china-media/chinas-xi-urges-state-media-to-boost-global-influence-idUSKCN0VS1IF.

17. The term "motherland" is misleading. It is indeed the term used in officially translated Chinese government documents. For instance, the term appears eight times in China's constitution. A more literal, and I think more accurate, translation of *zuguo* is "ancestral land," thus making it primarily male.

18. These terms are discussed in chapter 1.

19. For a more detailed discussion, see Michael J. Walsh, "States of Exception: The Violence of Territoriality, Sacrality, and Religion in China-Tibet Relations," *Journal of Religion and Violence* 1, no. 1 (Spring 2013): 62–63. Brief parts of the discussion in this chapter were drawn from this article.

162 ■ Preface

20. The term used is *shensheng lingtu*. A breakdown of the four ideographs is discussed in chapter 1.

21. The games were also an example of *relegere*, the meticulousness of ritual and attention to detail. Wang Hui suggests that the continuity between modern China and imperial China rests in part on two mythological narratives. The first is the myth of a common Chinese ancestry going all the way back to emperors Yao, Shun, and Yu, through Kings Wen and Wu of Zhou, the Duke of Zhou, and on to Confucius. The second myth focuses on a projected continuity from ancient (*gudai*) to early modern (*jindai*) to modern (*xiandai*), an unbroken dynastic flow in which all Chinese are seen to be descendants of the Yellow Emperor and "descendants of the dragon" (*long de chuanren*). Both narratives find their way into textbooks and the mass media. Wang, *China from Empire to Nation-State*, 100–101.

22. Émile Durkheim's classic definition of religion has some bearing here: "a religion is a unified system of beliefs and practices relative to sacred things, that is to say, things set apart and surrounded by prohibitions—beliefs and practices that unite its adherents in a single moral community called a church." Émile Durkheim, *The Elementary Form of Religious Life*, trans. Carol Cosman (New York: Oxford University Press, 2001), 46. For Durkheim, "a church" is the institutional structure within which the community resides. His definition also has bearing on the nation-state, that institutional structure that sets things apart and surrounds them with prohibitions. The "moral community" would be the equivalent of the nationalized citizenry.

23. I am in agreement with Giorgio Agamben, who argues that "the term *religio* does not derive, as an insipid and incorrect etymology would have it, from *religare* (that which binds and unites the human and the divine. It comes instead from *relegere*, which indicates the stance of scrupulousness and attention that must be adopted in relations with the gods." Giorgio Agamben, *Profanations*, trans. Jeff Fort (New York: Zone Books, 2007), 74–75. Agamben goes on to say that it is not *religio* that unites humans and gods; *religio*, on the contrary, is what keeps them distinct. Negligence is the gravest danger. Ritual meticulousness is paramount.

24. Harald Wydra argues that "democracies require practices of the sacred that ritually and symbolically bind the empty place of power." Harald Wydra, *Politics and the Sacred* (Cambridge: Cambridge University Press, 2015), 18. Also see chapter 4. In both apartheid South Africa and China today, that "empty place of power" became a space of centrality from which the state exercised its power. The center had to be legitimized for a citizenry that questioned it.

25. History and geography textbooks in China during the opening decades of the twentieth century always presented China as a unified, sovereign territory. What was left out was the violence required to maintain that fiction. For a classic study of citizenship during this period, see Robert Culp, *Articulating Citizenship: Civic Education and Student Politics in Southeastern China, 1912–1940* (Cambridge, Mass.: Harvard University Press, 2007). Also see Henrietta Harrison, *The Making of the Republican Citizen: Political Ceremonies and Symbols in China, 1911–1929* (New York: Oxford University Press, 1999). Harrison explores some of the new social formations that shaped identities during this period, such as calendars, sacrifices to revolutionary martyrs, and national songs. See also Peter Zarrow, "Introduction: Citizenship in China and the West," in *Imagining the People: Chinese Intellectuals and the Concept of Citizenship, 1890–1920*, ed. Joshua A. Fogel and Peter G. Zarrow (Armonk, N.Y.: M. E. Sharpe, 1997), in addition to the other essays in the same book.

26. In his powerful book *China in Ten Words*, the first term that Yu Hua begins with is *renmin*, the people. He writes that in his childhood years "the people" was just as marvelous an expression as "Chairman Mao." He could write the characters for *renmin* before he could write his own name. Today, however, according to Yu, it's only officials who use the term. It was only later in life, he writes, that he fully came to understand the meaning of "the people." It was 1989, in Beijing, when he was riding home on his bike and came to a bridge being guarded by students just as the PLA soldiers were entering the city. The students were singing the national anthem, and the heat from more than ten thousand of them poured over a shivering Yu Hua: "That night I realized . . . when the people stand as one, their voices carry farther than light and their heat is carried farther still. That, I discovered, is what 'the people' means." Yu Hua, *China in Ten Words*, trans. Allan H. Barr (New York: Anchor Books, 2011), 14.

27. Wydra, *Politics and the Sacred*, 3–4.

28. While race is an essential component in nation-state building, it is beyond the goals of this book to discuss it in any sustained manner. To the extent that I do, I link it to the category of citizenship. Toward the end of the nineteenth century, Liang Qichao (1873–1929)—whom we will meet again in the coming chapters—was instrumental in trying to locate China in the world of races and solidify Han identity (about 92 percent of the population today). Historian Peter Zarrow writes that "race knowledge" was a kind of "applied knowledge" that Qing dynasty intellectuals, Liang Qichao especially, used to promote political modernization and to argue that the Chinese race could and must be a strong one. See

Peter Zarrow, "Liang Qichao and the Conceptualization of 'Race' in Late Qing China," *Bulletin of the Institute of Modern History*, Academia Sinica, 52 (June 2006): 113–64. See also Frank Dikötter, *The Discourse of Race in Modern China* (Oxford: Oxford University Press, 2015).

29. See Jonathan Z. Smith, *Imagining Religion: From Babylon to Jonestown* (Chicago: University of Chicago Press, 1982), especially chap. 4.

30. David Chidester, *Wild Religion: Tracking the Sacred in South Africa* (Berkeley: University of California Press, 2012), 8.

31. See, for example, John Lagerwey, *China: A Religious State* (Hong Kong: Hong Kong University Press, 2010), 1–17. Lagerwey's book title is enticing given the topic of this study. However, he means religion in a more traditional sense. Specifically, he looks at local customs and the role of Daoism in god production and worship and examines the way the elite combined Buddhism, Daoism, and Confucianism to form a state orthodoxy based on ritual. I am in complete agreement with Lagerwey in that those social formations we might wish to designate as "religious" had a profound influence on imperial politics.

32. These terms are discussed further in the coming chapters, and especially in chapter 1 on territory.

33. See, for example, James A. Millward, *Eurasian Crossroads: A History of Xinjiang* (New York: Columbia University Press, 2007), 95. For more on Qianlong, see Mark C. Elliott, *Emperor Qianlong: Son of Heaven, Man of the World* (London: Pearson, 2009).

34. Odd Arne Westad, *Restless Empire: China and the World Since 1750* (New York: Basic Books, 2012), 2.

35. I use the term "internal colonization" not without some trepidation. Dibyesh Anand has made the compelling argument that by using the term "internal" we thereby accept China's claim that it legitimately rules these "minorities." He writes: "So, why use the term 'internal colonialism' or 'internal orientalism'? What does the qualifier 'internal' signify? It illustrates the hold of normative nation-statism as we take for granted what the state claims and what the international system of sovereign states dictates and allows." See Dibyesh Anand, "Colonization with Chinese Characteristics: Politics of (In)Security in Xinjiang and Tibet," *Central Asian Survey*, November 2018, 6, https://doi.org/10.1080/02634 937.2018.1534801.

36. Peter van der Veer, *Imperial Encounters: Religion and Modernity in India and Britain* (Princeton, N.J.: Princeton University Press, 2001), 54.

37. An example of this prioritization of Han identity can be found in early twentieth-century textbooks. One case study that Robert Culp presents is that of Lü Simian, who wrote in his textbook how the Han were the

core (*zhongxin*) of China. As Culp explains: "Lü attempted to account for the encompassment of other peoples and to acknowledge the contributions they might have made to Chinese culture while crafting an image of a unified ethno-cultural subject that remained historically constant and was rooted in the past." Culp, *Articulating Citizenship*, 63. We saw a culmination of this "unified ethno-cultural subject" during the opening ceremony of the 2008 Olympics. It's an old idea that while China might encounter other cultural groups, at the end of the day, those groups would assimilate and become "Sinicized."

38. Wang, *China from Empire to Nation-State*, 1.

39. Many related ideas traversed the globe before the nineteenth century, particularly along the silk roads. But nothing in history comes close to the sustained force of colonial exportations backed by massive military power.

40. Here I mean Benedict Anderson's notion of imagined community, which as he argues, came about in part thanks to capitalism, vernacularism, and the printing press. See Benedict Anderson, *Imagined Communities: Reflections on the Origin and Spread of Nationalism* (New York: Verso, 1998). This plays out differently in China, as Wang Hui has taught us.

41. Here I mean Michel Foucault's use of the term and practice.

42. Here I use the term *religion* in the same manner that Russell McCutcheon does, "as a discursive technique used in specific rhetorical situations, a type of social classification with significant political import." Russell T. McCutcheon, *The Discipline of Religion: Structure, Meaning, Rhetoric* (London: Routledge, 2003), 43.

43. Roland Barthes, *Mythologies*, trans. Annette Lavers (New York: Farrar, Straus & Giroux, 1972), 122.

44. I am all too painfully aware of McCutcheon's brilliant critique of the "Chicago school," which he argues for the most part treats religion as sui generis, and indeed as a category or phenomena supposedly "free of the kinds of social pressures that condition all other historical moments." McCutcheon, *The Discipline of Religion*, ix. Though to be fair, McCutcheon has far less trouble, as do I, with inhabitants of that school such as David Chidester, Jonathan Z. Smith, and Bruce Lincoln.

1. Territory

1. Rupert Wingfield-Hayes, "Flying Close to Beijing's New South China Sea Islands," *BBC News*, December 14, 2015, http://www.bbc.com/news/magazine-35031313. For another perspective, Wingfield-Hayes also tried to visit some of the islands by fishing vessel. As the boat approached one

of the islands, the Chinese garrisoned there began firing flares in warning. See https://www.youtube.com/watch?v=fZgvqE89KvQ.

2. Hannah Beech, "China's Sea Control Is a Done Deal, 'Short of War with the U.S.,'" *New York Times*, September 20, 2018, https://www.nytimes.com/2018/09/20/world/asia/south-china-sea-navy.html.

3. Beech, "China's Sea Control."

4. Thomas Gibbons-Neff and Steven Lee Myers, "China Won't Yield 'Even One Inch' of South China Sea, Xi Tells Mattis," *New York Times*, June 27, 2018, https://www.nytimes.com/2018/06/27/world/asia/mattis-xi-china-sea.html.

5. See "Hague Announces Decision on South China Sea," July 12, 2016, *New York Times*, http://www.nytimes.com/interactive/2016/07/12/world/asia/hague-south-china-sea.html. The "nine-dash" line refers to nine demarcation lines somewhat arbitrarily drawn around the South China Sea.

6. The paper is titled "Position Paper of the Government of the People's Republic of China on the Matter of Jurisdiction in the South China Sea Arbitration Initiated by the Republic of the Philippines." It is available on the website of the Ministry of Foreign Affairs of the People's Republic of China, http://www.fmprc.gov.cn/mfa_eng/zxxx_662805/t1217147.shtml.

7. See Michael J. Walsh, *Sacred Economies: Buddhist Monasticism and Territoriality in Medieval China* (New York: Columbia University Press, 2010).

8. Ministry of Foreign Affairs, Republic of China (Taiwan), "Position Paper on ROC Sovereignty Over the South China Sea Islands and Their Surrounding Waters, and on the South China Sea Peace Initiative, Republic of China (Taiwan)," March 21, 2016, https://www.mofa.gov.tw/Upload/RelFile/643/156142/Position%20Paper%20on%20ROC%20Sovereignty%20over%20the%20South%20China%20Sea%20Islands%20and%20Their%20Surrounding%20Waters,%20and%20on%20the%20South%20China%20Sea%20Peace%20Initiative.pdf.

9. Section 2, article 3, United Nations Convention on the Law of the Sea. Available at http://www.un.org/depts/los/convention_agreements/texts/unclos/unclos_e.pdf.

10. Emily Rauhala, "GOP Debate: Tough Talking Chris Christie Wants to Fly Air Force One Over the South China Sea," *Washington Post*, November 11, 2015, https://www.washingtonpost.com/news/worldviews/wp/2015/11/11/gop-debate-tough-talking-chris-christie-wants-to-fly-air-force-one-over-the-south-china-sea/.

11. Helene Cooper, "Challenging Chinese Claims, U.S. Sends Warship Near Artificial Island Chain," *New York Times*, October 26, 2015, http://www.nytimes.com/2015/10/27/world/asia/challenging-chinese-claims

-us-sends-warship-near-artificial-island-chain.html. Other, similar incidents have occurred. Whenever U.S. military aircraft approach any of these islands, the Chinese tell them to turn around. See https://www .youtube.com/watch?v=OaKbZWopqkM.

12. Henri Lefebvre, *The Production of Space*, trans. Donald Nicholson-Smith (Oxford: Blackwell, 1974), 38–40.

13. See Steven Lee Meyers, "Squeezed by an India-China Standoff, Bhutan Holds Its Breath," *New York Times*, August 15, 2017, https://www .nytimes.com/2017/08/15/world/asia/squeezed-by-an-india-china -standoff-bhutan-holds-its-breath.html.

14. For more on what's at stake, see Steven Lee Meyers, Ellen Barry, and Max Fisher, "How India and China Have Come to the Brink Over a Remote Mountain Pass," *New York Times*, July 26, 2017, https://www .nytimes.com/2017/07/26/world/asia/dolam-plateau-china-india-bhutan .html. The dispute goes back to British India and the Qing dynasty. The road and the disputed area are close to the Siliguri Corridor. India fears that were China to block that off—an entirely feasible feat—doing so would cut off forty-five million Indians who live in the northeastern states, an area the size of the United Kingdom.

15. Nguyen Minh Quang, "The Bitter Legacy of the 1979 China-Vietnam War," *Diplomat*, February 23, 2017, https://thediplomat.com/2017/02/the -bitter-legacy-of-the-1979-china-vietnam-war/. See also Ezra F. Vogel's magisterial work, *Deng Xiaoping and the Transformation of China* (Cambridge, Mass.: Belknap Press of Harvard University Press, 2011), 526–32. Deng authorized these attacks on Vietnam, in part, as an effort to contain Soviet influence in the region, which he saw as an infringement on China's inviolate. Vogel cites estimates that as many as twenty-five thousand PLA soldiers were killed during the attack (531).

16. The PLA anthem proclaims, "Standing on our ancestral land, we carry the hope of the people" (*Jiao tazhe zuguo de dadi, beifuzhe minzu de xiwang*). Likewise, the motto of the PLA is "Serve the people!" (*Wei renmin fuwu*). This is a sleight of hand. The PLA serves the state and protects the ancestors' territory (*zuguo*). For Georges Bataille, "What is sacrificed is *what serves*." Georges Bataille, *Theory of Religion*, trans. Robert Hurley (New York: Zone Books, 1989), 83. The original text of China's constitution can be found at http://www.gov.cn/gongbao/content/2004 /content_62714.htm.

17. See, among others, Marcel Maus, *The Gift: The Form and Reason for Exchange in Archaic Societies*, trans. W. D. Hall (London: Routledge, 1990); René Girard, *Violence and the Sacred*, trans. Patrick Gregory (Baltimore: Johns Hopkins University Press, 1977); and Bataille, *Theory of Religion*.

18. Carl Schmitt, *Political Theology: Four Chapters on the Concept of Sovereignty*, trans. George Schwab (Chicago: University of Chicago Press, 2006), 36. For a study of Schmitt that helps to better understand our own political moment, see Paul W. Kahn, *Political Theology: Four New Chapters on the Concept of Sovereignty* (New York: Columbia University Press, 2011).

19. David Chidester, *Wild Religion: Tracking the Sacred in South Africa* (Berkeley: University of California Press, 2012), 66.

20. Bataille, *Theory of Religion*, 43, 83.

21. Bataille, *Theory of Religion*, 66.

22. Giorgio Agamben, *Profanations*, trans. Jeff Fort (New York: Zone Books, 2007), 73.

23. Bataille, *Theory of Religion*, 52.

24. Leonard Thompson, *A History of South Africa* (New Haven, Conn.: Yale University Press, 2014), 214.

25. See photos documenting apartheid as a "crime against humanity" on the United Nations website at https://www.unmultimedia.org/photo/gallery .jsp?query=subject:Apartheid&startat=54&sf=. For a timeline of UN action against apartheid, see http://www.un.org/en/events/mandeladay /apartheid.shtml.

26. Raids continued well into the late 1980s. A British Commonwealth committee reported that South Africa's actions between 1980 and 1989 led to the deaths of a million people, left more than three million homeless, and caused economic damage in excess of $35 billion. Thompson, *A History of South Africa*, 236.

27. This is sometimes referred to as the South African Border War. For more on this war, see Gary F. Baines, *South Africa's "Border War": Contested Narratives and Conflicting Memories* (London: Bloomsbury Academic, 2014).

28. Charles Long, *Significations, Signs, Symbols, and Images in the Interpretation of Religion* (Aurora, Colo.: Fortress Press, 1986), 109.

29. Gilles Deleuze and Félix Guattari, *A Thousand Plateaus: Capitalism and Schizophrenia*, trans. Brian Massumi (London: Continuum, 1992), 360.

30. See Yi-Zheng Lian's take on this in a recent essay, "Chinese Ways of Empire, Then and Now," *New York Times*, June 30, 2017, https://www .nytimes.com/2017/06/30/opinion/china-hong-kong-xi-jinping.html.

31. As the *Washington Post* dramatically described it at the time: "After the ceremony, which lasted less than an hour, Prince Charles and Chris Patten, the 28th and last British governor of Hong Kong, left the hall and boarded the royal yacht Britannia, moored at Victoria Harbor. The British had arrived by sea and departed by sea, sailing away into history and

opening a new chapter in Hong Kong's turbulent history." Keith B. Rich-
burg, "After 156 Years, It's Hong Kong, China," *Washington Post*, July 1,
1997, https://www.washingtonpost.com/wp-srv/inatl/longterm/china
/stories/hongkong.htm.

32. Long, *Significations*, 109.
33. The full text of the speech is available at the Xinhua news agency website, http://www.xinhuanet.com/english/special/2017-11/03/c_136725942
.htm; and at *China Daily*, http://www.chinadaily.com.cn/china/19thcpc
nationalcongress/2017-11/04/content_34115212.htm.
34. See Richard C. Bush, "8 Key Things to Notice from Xi Jinping's New
Year Speech on Taiwan," Brookings Institution, January 7, 2019, https://
www.brookings.edu/blog/order-from-chaos/2019/01/07/8-key-things
-to-notice-from-xi-jinpings-new-year-speech-on-taiwan/.
35. In this regard, Dibyesh Anand emphatically argues that "China is a colo-
nizing nation-state." Anand, "Colonization with Chinese Characteristics: Politics of (In)Security in Xinjiang and Tibet," *Central Asian Survey*,
November 2018, https://doi.org/10.1080/02634937.2018.1534801.2. Anand
suggests that securitization (and militarization) is the key to understanding China's practices in Tibet and Xinjiang.
36. It's worth noting, not without some irony, that Chen Quanguo's name
includes the characters *quanguo*— "the whole country," or "making the
country whole again."
37. See Adrian Zenz and James Leibold, "Chen Quanguo: The Strongman
Behind Beijing's Securitization Strategy in Tibet and Xinjiang," Jamestown Foundation, September 21, 2017,https://jamestown.org/program
/chen-quanguo-the-strongman-behind-beijings-securitization
-strategy-in-tibet-and-xinjiang/.
38. As examples, see Shohret Hoshur, "Nearly Half of Uyghurs in Xinjiang's
Hotan Targeted for Re-Education Camps," *Radio Free Asia*, October 9,
2017, https://www.rfa.org/english/news/uyghur/camps-10092017164000
.html; and Gerry Shih, "China's Uighur Minority Shackled by Digital
Technology as Thousands Are Detained for 'Vocational Training,'" *Independent*, December 17, 2017, http://www.independent.co.uk/news
/world/asia/thousands-china-xinjiang-uighur-beijing-disappear-fears
-authorities-thought-police-personal-safety-a8115421.html. The 500,000
number is cited by Adrian Zenz, a researcher at the European School of
Culture and Theology. See James A. Millward, "What It's Like to Live
in a Surveillance State," *New York Times*, February 3, 2018, https://www
.nytimes.com/2018/02/03/opinion/sunday/china-surveillance-state
-uighurs.html.

39. See "Xinjiang to Crack Down on 'Three Evil Forces,'" *China Daily*, March 6, 2012, http://www.chinadaily.com.cn/china/2012-03/06/content _14766900.htm.

40. John Lagerway, *China: A Religious State* (Hong Kong: Hong Kong University Press, 2010), 13. The term *shenzhou* was first used in the third century BCE.

41. We shouldn't, however, overplay this distinction. As Nicola Di Cosmo points out in his book *Ancient China and Its Enemies: The Rise of Nomadic Power in East Asian History* (New York: Cambridge University Press, 2004), 314: "The image of a 'civilized' world pitched against a barbaric wilderness is, however, only a partial, and an ideologically loaded, interpretation of the relations between China and the north." By "north," Di Cosmo is referring to such nomadic tribes as the Xiongnu. Another warning comes from historian Michael Nylan, who writes: "The mere use of the word 'barbarian' (or, in the Chinese case, the use of the generic *hu*, or the four-directional Di, Yi, Man, or Rong) need not invariably signify disdain or inferiority, if only because early writers badly needed, in antiquity no less than now, a convention to indicate 'those people over there.'" Michael Nylan, "Talk About 'Barbarians' in Antiquity," *Philosophy East & West* 62, no. 4 (Honolulu: University of Hawaii Press, 2012), 586. Overinterpretation is an ever-present challenge, but regardless, all these terms were in use at one time or another, and some continue to be used today. During the nineteenth century the British took particular umbrage at the use of the term *yi*, so much so that article 51 of the Treaty of Tianjin, signed in June 1858 after the second Opium War, stated: "It is agreed that, henceforward, the character 'I' [barbarian] shall not be applied to the Government or subjects of Her Britannic Majesty in any Chinese official document issued by the Chinese Authorities either in the Capital or in the Provinces."

42. The Great Learning (*daxue*), ostensibly written or edited by Confucius, makes a similar point: "The point where to rest being known, the object of pursuit is then determined; and, that being determined, a calm unperturbedness may be attained to. To that calmness there will succeed a tranquil repose. In that repose there may be careful deliberation, and that deliberation will be followed by the attainment of the desired end." James Legge, *The Four Books: Confucian Analects, the Great Learning, the Doctrine of the Mean, and the Works of Mencius* (Taipei: SMC, 1991), 356–57. (I wonder how many of the CCP leadership have studied these texts? A great many it would seem.)

43. Legge translates Shangdi as "God." Strictly speaking, the term refers to the primordial first deity of Heaven (*tian*) and is seen on scapular

inscriptions from the Shang period (c. 1600–c. 1045 BCE). During the Zhou period, the dynasty that replaced the Shang, Shangdi and Heaven are conflated under the category of *tianming*, the "mandate of Heaven." The Zhou argued that the Shang had lost that mandate. One of the earliest references to *tianming* dates to c. 998 BCE, when King Kang tells one of his ministers that King Yin has lost the mandate because of the poor conduct of his officials. See Lagerway, *China: A Religious State*, 20–21.

44. From James Legge's translation of *The Shoo King or the Book of Historical Documents* (Taipei: SMC, 1991), book 4, ch. 1.2, 79.

45. Legge, *The Books of Xia*, book 5, ch. 3, 3–4, 195.

46. For more on this, see Xu Bin's work, especially *The Politics of Compassion: The Sichuan Earthquake and Civic Engagement in China* (Stanford, Calif.: Stanford University Press, 2017).

47. The text was meant to be consulted for a range of practical purposes and was in widespread use well into the nineteenth century. Richard E. Strassberg, in an elegant translation and commentary on the *Shanhai jing*, identifies the following in the text: more than 500 animate creatures, 550 mountains, 300 rivers, 95 foreign lands and tribes, 130 kinds of pharmaceuticals (to prevent 70 illnesses), 435 plants, 90 metals and minerals, and forms of sacrifice to be done in a meticulous manner (*relegere*) to all the mountain gods. See Richard E. Strassberg, trans., *A Chinese Bestiary: Strange Creatures from the Guideways Through Mountains and Seas* (Berkeley: University of California Press, 2002), 3.

48. Heaven and Shangdi, incidentally, also show up in this text. The nine regions earlier fashioned by Yu are said to be administered by the god Luwu, who assists Shangdi on Mt. Kunlun, the earthly capital of Di. See Strassberg, *A Chinese Bestiary*, 30, 107.

49. Lagerway, *China: A Religious State*, 13–17.

50. Strassberg, *A Chinese Bestiary*, 32, presents a diagram of the Five Dependencies attributed to Yu the Great.

51. Lagerway, *China: A Religious State*, 15. Lagerway explains *xue* as a geomantic concept, "where telluric energies come to the surface and where, therefore, human beings can tap into the flow of energies hidden deep within the earth." Ancestor halls and temples were always built on such points. Rituals are performed to settle the dragons. As Lagerway points out, ancestors and gods "anchor" local society (also one of the concentric circles), whereas mountains anchor all of China. All these spaces are sacred territory.

52. Strassberg, *A Chinese Bestiary*, 30.

53. As Strassberg explains, "Cosmographies project the possibilities of a totalizing perspective by seamlessly mapping the near and the distant,

the known and the unknown, the visible and the hidden, the verifiable and the imaginary." Strassberg, *A Chinese Bestiary*, 9.

54. For more on this, see Walsh, *Sacred Economies*, chap. 2.

55. Richard Wilhelm, trans., *The I Ching or Book of Changes*, English trans. Cary F. Baynes, 3rd ed. (Princeton, N.J.: Princeton University Press, 1967), 320. (Comes from *The Great Treatise* [*Dazhuan*], book 2, ch. 11, verse 8.)

56. The *Shanhai jing* depicts the world under Heaven constructed by Emperor Yu as sets of mountains in all four directions—north, west, south, and east—with a set at the center bringing the sum of all directions to five, a fantastically important number in Chinese cosmology, second only to nine. Five mountains were identified in ancient times and recognized by emperors who made sacrifices at them. They remain in place today. Called *wuyue*—the "five sacred mountains," or the "five marchmounts," they are Hengshan in the North (Shanxi province), Huashan in the West (Shaanxi province), Hengshan in the South (Hunan province), Taishan in the East (Shandong province), and Songshan in the center (Henan province). These in turn correspond with the "five elements" (*wuxing*) and their attributes of color, direction, element, deity, and so forth.

57. This understanding is then brought explicitly into the classroom, both historically and now, where young Chinese are being molded into citizens. As Robert Culp explains, during the 1930s "textbooks reinforced the perception of a nation that was both bounded and coherent by using images and shapes that separated the national territory from surrounding areas to which it was connected and made it seem like a thing in itself." Culp, *Articulating Citizenship*, 78.

58. A rough breakdown of these four ideographs is as follows: (1) *Shen* can refer to a deity, a spirit, the supernatural, or the numinous in an abstract way; it comprises two parts, one a phonetic graph also meaning "to manifest," and the other component meaning to explain, or to report to a superior. It is also the ninth terrestrial or earth branch in Chinese cosmology. In the *Shanhai jing*, *shen* appear as earthly, mountain gods (in juxtaposition to the Supreme God Di, whom we first meet in the Shang dynasty, c. 1600–c. 1045 BCE). For instance, one group lives among the sixteen mountains. The *shen* all have horse bodies and dragon heads. The correct sacrifice to them is a buried rooster. In the second guideway through the western mountains, *shen*, are seventeen mountain gods; ten have human faces and horse bodies; seven have human faces and ox bodies with four hooves (Strassberg, *A Chinese Bestiary*, 155 and 103, respectively). (2) *Sheng* can refer to a sage, sometimes to an emperor, but as an adjective is usually translated as "sacred." (3) *Ling* can mean a collar, or

even a neck, but as a verb it most often means "to lead." (4) *Tu* means earth or land. Together *shen* and *sheng* are typically translated as sacred, while *ling* and *tu* usually refers to territory, hence "sacred territory."

59. The first was published in 1993; the second, in 2000. The official English translations are available at http://www.gov.cn/english/official/2005-08 /17/content_24165.htm.

60. See, for example, Sebo Koh, "Taiwan Has Never Been China's," *Taipei Times*, March 2, 2018, http://www.taipeitimes.com/News/editorials /archives/2018/03/02/2003688509.

61. President Xi never misses an opportunity to remind the world of Taiwan's eventual reunification with China, the ancestral motherland.

62. Taiwan's constitution, or, more specifically, the Republic of China's constitution, has 175 articles and was adopted in 1947, two years before the founding of the People's Republic of China. The English translation is available at http://law.moj.gov.tw/Eng/LawClass/LawAll.aspx?PCode =A0000001. It has gone through a few amendments, notably in 1992, when it was established that the president could be directly elected by the people.

63. China's foreign investments in other countries grew almost tenfold from 2005 to 2013. The scope of its involvement in other nation-states is impressive. See Gregor Aisch, Josh Keller, and K. K. Rebecca Lai, "The World According to China," *New York Times*, July 24, 2015, https://www .nytimes.com/interactive/2015/07/24/business/international/the-world -according-to-china-investment-maps.html.

64. Arjun Appadurai, *Modernity at Large: Cultural Dimensions of Globalization* (Minneapolis: University of Minnesota Press, 1996), 39.

65. One example can be seen at http://www.travelchinaguide.com/attraction /guizhou/kaili/langde.htm. Another is from a news report by Katie Hunt, "Human Zoos and Disappearing Languages: The Plight of China's Minorities," *CNN*, November 4, 2013, http://www.cnn.com/2013/10/28 /world/asia/china-rural-minorities/. Also see a report by China's *People's Daily* newspaper about how a thousand minority villages will be protected and "improved" (*Xinhua*, December 11, 2012, http://english.people daily.com.cn/90882/8053639.html). Yet the Uighurs and Tibetans garner far more global attention than any of the remaining fifty-three minority groups.

66. Donald Preziosi and Claire Farago point out that there may be upward of a hundred thousand museums in the world today, and that "virtually anything may be made to serve *as* a museum. It may be more useful, today, to ask not '*What* is a museum?,' but rather '*When* is a museum?'" See Donald Preziosi and Claire Farago, eds., *Grasping the World: The Idea*

of the Museum (Aldershot, U.K.: Ashgate, 2004), 3. Scholarship on museum studies and museology is extensive. For excellent suggestions for further reading, see *Grasping the World*, xxi–xxiv. Also see Donald Preziosi, *Brain of the Earth's Body: Art, Museums, and the Phantasms of Modernity* (Minneapolis: University of Minnesota Press, 2003).

67. See James Hevia, *English Lessons: The Pedagogy of Imperialism in Nineteenth-Century China* (Durham, N.C.: Duke University Press, 2003).

68. One need only recall President Trump's slogan "Make America great again"—a cheap throwback to a nostalgicized and mythologized, racist past.

69. A map circulated in textbooks of the 1920s and 1930s was titled "Map of China's National Humiliation" (*Zhongguo guochi ditu*). The map shows the Qing period boundaries along with shaded in territories that were "lost" to imperialists during the nineteenth century. Maps like these were proof to the Chinese people that China's twentieth- and twenty-first-century claims to a range of territory ostensibly ceded during the nineteenth century were in fact founded. Culp, *Articulating Citizenship*, 81.

70. See "How Leaders Are Made," https://www.youtube.com/watch?v=M7340_17H_A.

71. A propaganda video with Xi Jinping explaining this initiative is available at https://www.youtube.com/watch?v=hNKTbMx8PFk.

72. See "A New Platform for Cross-region Cooperation," http://www.belt androad.gov.hk/overview.html. The video can be seen at http://www.beltandroad.gov.hk/videos.html. In it China describes itself as "the super-connector," in a generic American accent, as always. The video itself comes from a Hong Kong site where the reference to Beijing's promotion of "one country, two systems" is touted as a major advantage, though no details are given. It is Hong Kong being drawn tightly into Beijing's vision.

73. Indrani Bagchi, "India Slams China's One Belt One Road Initiative, Says It Violates Sovereignty," *Times of India*, May 14, 2017, https://timesofindia.indiatimes.com/india/china-road-initiative-is-like-a-colonial-enterprise-india/articleshow/58664098.cms.

74. See Mareike Ohlberg and Bertram Lang, "How to Counter China's Global Propaganda Offensive," *New York Times*, September 21, 2016, https://www.nytimes.com/2016/09/22/opinion/how-to-counter-chinas-global-propaganda-offensive.html.

75. See Jason Horowitz and Liz Alderman, "Chastised by E.U., a Resentful Greece Embraces China's Cash and Interests," *New York Times*,

August 26, 2017, https://www.nytimes.com/2017/08/26/world/europe/greece-china-piraeus-alexis-tsipras.html.

76. See, for example, David Barboza, "A Chinese Giant Is on a Global Buying Spree. Who's Behind It?," *New York Times*, May 9, 2017, https://www.nytimes.com/2017/05/09/business/hna-group-hainan-airlines-china-deals.html. See also "HNA Group, Secretive Chinese Conglomerate, Takes Top Stake in Deutsche Bank," *New York Times*, May 3, 2017, https://www.nytimes.com/2017/05/03/business/dealbook/china-hna-group.html.

77. For more on his story and China's global reach, see, Rob Schmitz and Julia Simon, "The Belt, The Road, and the Money," NPR, *Planet Money* podcast no. 837, April 20, 2018, https://www.npr.org/templates/transcript/transcript.php?storyId=604462996. One conservative research group puts China's overseas investments at almost 1.8 trillion dollars. See the American Enterprise Institute's "China Global Investment Tracker," http://www.aei.org/china-global-investment-tracker/. Examples include South Africa at $12.44 billion, the United States at $172.72 billion, Brazil at $61.19 billion, Nigeria at $44.78 billion, and so on. A slightly out-of-date (2013) but fascinating map of China's global investments is "China's Global Reach," *New York Times*, June 1, 2013, http://www.nytimes.com/interactive/2013/06/02/sunday-review/chinas-global-reach.html.

78. See Scott Cendrowski, "The Unusual Journey of China's Newest Oil Baron," *Fortune*, September 28, 2016, http://fortune.com/2016/09/28/cefc-ye-jianming-40-under-40/. CEFC's website can be accessed at http://en.cefc.co/category/wmdzghx.

79. See Eric Ng and Xie Yu, "China Detains CEFC's Founder Ye Jianming, Wiping Out US$153 Million in Value Off Stocks," *South China Morning Post*, March 1, 2018, http://www.scmp.com/business/companies/article/2135238/china-detain-cefc-founder-ye-jianming-stocks.

80. We have to be careful lest we overstate this "third choice." Yes, China is beginning to be a counterbalance to liberal, democratic nation-states, but it is also because of the "old" world order that China can achieve this. As Ho-fung Hung argues, "In the end, China is far from becoming a subversive power that will transform the existing global neoliberal order because China itself is one of the beneficiaries of this order." See Ho-fung Hung, *The China Boom: Why China Will Not Rule the World* (New York: Columbia University Press, 2016), 180. In contradistinction to this argument, see Martin Jacques's *New York Times* bestseller, *When China Rules the World: The End of the Western World and the Birth of a New Global Order* (New York: Penguin Books, 2009.). The subtitle of the former and

the title of the latter are self-explanatory. On the other hand, this "third choice" is still viable, I believe. While Russia continues to destabilize democracies around the globe, China offers the world stability. I don't quite buy it, but there it is on the global table.

81. Appadurai, *Modernity at Large*, 15.
82. Appadurai, *Modernity at Large*, 5.
83. Appadurai, *Modernity at Large*, 9.

2. Constitution

1. On October 18, 1961, South Africa held elections, after which, for the first time, no representation for black South Africans was allowed in Parliament, effectively stripping away the rights of all "nonwhite" South Africans. The year 1994 was a sea change.
2. The languages are Sepedi, Sesotho, Setswana, siSwati, Tshivenda, Xitsonga, Afrikaans, English, isiNdebele, isiXhosa, and isiZulu.
3. The official version of South Africa's constitution is available at http://www.justice.gov.za/legislation/constitution/SAConstitution-web-eng.pdf.
4. Umberto Eco made this startling statement in an interview with *Der Spiegel* while he was opening an exhibition at the Louvre. See Susanne Beyer and Lothar Gorris, "We Like Lists Because We Don't Want to Die," *Der Spiegel*, November 11, 2009, http://www.spiegel.de/international/zeitgeist/spiegel-interview-with-umberto-eco-we-like-lists-because-we-don-t-want-to-die-a-659577.html. See also Eco's own website, http://www.umbertoeco.com/en/umberto-eco-on-lists.html; and Umberto Eco, *The Infinity of Lists: An Illustrated Essay* (New York: Rizzoli, 2009).
5. For a compelling study of how myth, ritual, and classification shape societal discourse, see a study by historian of religion Bruce Lincoln, *Discourse and the Construction of Society: Comparative Studies of Myth, Ritual, and Classification* (Oxford: Oxford University Press, 1989).
6. Prasenjit Duara writes convincingly of a bifurcated conception of history, a blurring of the linear, and the way in which the present in a specific, national moment shapes the past. He writes that a "national history secures for the contested and contingent nation the false unity of a selfsame, national subject evolving through time." Prasenjit Duara, *Rescuing History from the Nation: Questioning Narratives of Modern China* (Chicago: University of Chicago Press, 1997), 4, 233.
7. Roland Barthes, *Mythologies*, trans. Annette Lavers (New York: Farrar, Straus & Giroux, 1972), 117.

8. As Neil Diamant stresses, looking at the constitution and its origins is "a way to peer into a society to get a rough fix on values, normative ideas, and general orientation towards the world." Neil J. Diamant, "What the (Expletive) Is a 'Constitution'?! Ordinary Cadres Confront the 1954 PRC Draft Constitution," *Journal of Chinese History* 2, no. 1 (January 2018): 172. Diamant goes on to point out that unlike many Western constitutions, China's covers far more political geography, "including ideology, economy, rights, obligations, the structure of the state, and national symbols." Furthermore, this was a document that saw wide circulation (in the millions) during the mid-1950s. Diamant says that by the end of 1954, the *People's Daily* reported that 12.5 million copies had been printed. For a deeper understanding of how officials understood constitutionalism during the early 1900s, see Peter Zarrow, "Constitutionalism and the Imagination of the State: Official Views of Political Reform in the Late Qing," in *Creating Chinese Modernity: Knowledge and Everyday Life, 1900–1940*, ed. Peter Zarrow (New York: Peter Lang, 2006), 51–82.

9. Barthes, *Mythologies*, 129. Barthes also argues that there is a type of language that is not mythological, that is, "the language of man as producer," the speech of labor and revolution. I concede that China's constitution is in part that, but because of its ahistorical characteristics and the way in which the language is politicized, I still maintain that it is a mythological narrative. Further, like all myths, it is a creation myth, a narrative of how the state came to be.

10. The original text of the constitution is available at http://www.gov.cn /gongbao/content/2004/content_62714.htm. It was adopted on December 4, 1982.

11. Diamant writes that in doing research in China, he repeatedly encounters skepticism when he tells scholars about his work on constitutionalism. He says he often hears the term "useless" when it comes to China's constitution. Diamant, "What the (Expletive) Is a 'Constitution'?!," 170.

12. For a historical overview of China's constitution, see Qianfan Zhang, *The Constitution of China: A Contextual Analysis* (Oxford: Hart, 2012). For a study of the 1954 constitution, see Han Dayuan, *1954 nian xianfa yu xin Zhongguo xianzheng 1954* (Changsha: Hunan renmin chubanshe, 2004). As to how cadres and citizens reacted to the 1954 working draft of the constitution, see Diamant, "What the (Expletive) Is a 'Constitution'?!" Or, as Diamant puts it: "How did the powerful think about their power?" (170). This quandary comes a mere five years after the Revolution of 1949.

13. Other leading officials pushing for constitutionalism included Yuan Shikai, Sun Baoqi, and Zhang Zhidong.

14. For more on the critical period between 1895 and 1911, see Ya-Pei Kuo, "Redeploying Confucius: The Imperial State Dreams of the Nation, 1902–1911," in *Chinese Religiosities: Afflictions of Modernity and State Formation*, ed. Mayfair Mei-hui Yang (Berkeley: University of California Press, 2008), 65–84.

15. Kang also understood that the imperial tribute system that had sustained dynasties for millennia was failing under the growing intrusion of European imperialism.

16. Though radical in approach, the reforms still could not be broached explicitly. As Peter Zarrow explains, "Constitutionalism was a marginal notion in the 1880s, became a focus of radical attention in the 1890s, and finally turned mainstream . . . beginning in 1902." Zarrow, *Creating Chinese Modernity*, 51.

17. The Self-Strengthening movement (*ziqiang yundong*) was a response to defeats by foreign powers. Several institutional reforms were proposed. For more on these historical shifts, see, among others, Philip A. Kuhn, *Origins of the Modern Chinese State* (Stanford, Calif.: Stanford University Press, 2003); David Pong, *Shen Pao-Chen and China's Modernization the Nineteenth Century* (New York: Cambridge University Press, 1994); and the multiple works of Peter Zarrow, Andrew Nathan, Shen Zhihua, and Prasenjit Duara. Many other distinguished historians have also examined these historical shifts, from Jonathan D. Spence to John King Fairbank to Patricia B. Ebrey, not to mention all the publications that have come out of China, Hong Kong, and Taiwan.

18. Kuhn, *Origins of the Modern Chinese State*, 122–23.

19. The term *guo* appears during the Warring States (Zhanguo) period (475–221 BCE) and during the later Zhou (1046–256 BCE) in the phrase *zhongguo*. For more on the history of this category, see Wang Ermin, "'Zhongguo' mingcheng suyuan jiqi jindai quanshi" (On the origins of the term "zhongguo" and its modern interpretations), *Zhongguo jindai sixiang shi lun* (Discussions of modern Chinese history) (Taipei: n.p., 1977).

20. Coupled with *zhong*, it is the name for China. ("China" comes from a Wade-Giles transliteration of the Ch'in—in pinyin, Qin. Over time the apostrophe was dropped and an "a" put in place.) The name is old, going back to the Yin-Shang period (c. 1600–c. 1045 BCE), where we see it on scapular inscriptions, the first time we discover the ideographs that came to form the Chinese script. One scholar argues that over time the term developed three overlapping meanings: geographic China, political China, and cultural China. For more on the history of the term, see Chun-Chieh Huang, "The Idea of 'Zhongguo' and Its Transformation in Early Modern Japan and Contemporary Taiwan," *Nihon Kan bungaku*

kenkyū (Japan-Han literary research), Nishogakusha University, no. 2 (March 2007): 398–408.

21. Kuo, "Redeploying Confucius," 69.

22. Liang Qichao, in an essay written in 1901, had argued for constitutional monarchy. See https://zh.wikisource.org/zh-hant/立憲法議.

23. Zhang, *The Constitution of China*, 14.

24. Zhang Qianfan makes an obvious but important point when he writes that today "what is missing, however, is a critical link—a way for the people's voices to be effectively translated into policymaking." Zhang, *Constitution of China*, 262.

25. Lincoln, *Discourse and the Construction of Society*, 24.

26. Wendy Doniger, *The Implied Spider: Politics and Theology in Myth* (New York: Columbia University Press, 1999), 2.

27. Russell T. McCutcheon, *The Discipline of Religion: Structure, Meaning, Rhetoric* (London: Routledge, 2003), 153.

28. For dramatic images of housing disparity, see Johnny Miller, "Divided Cities: South Africa's Apartheid Legacy Photographed by Drone," *Guardian*, June 23, 2016,https://www.theguardian.com/cities/gallery/2016/jun/23/south-africa-divided-cities-apartheid-photographed-drone.

29. Doniger, *The Implied Spider*, 2.

30. The full text can be accessed at https://www.gov.za/documents/constitution/republic-south-africa-constitution-act-110-1983.

31. These are not random choices but instead reflect my own personal interest in these countries. At first glance this might appear to be cherry-picking the data; however, constitutional language regarding religion and belief is remarkably consistent in all the documents I have read. Where possible, and this is in most cases, I use the official English translation provided by each government's website. In some (China, the Netherlands, South Africa), I also rely on my own translations, especially if there are disparities between the official translation and my own.

32. For Taiwan's constitution, see http://law.moj.gov.tw/Eng/LawClass/LawAll_print.aspx?PCode=A0000001. See also http://english.president.gov.tw/Default.aspx?tabid=1107.

33. For the South African constitution, see https://www.gov.za/sites/default/files/images/a108-96.pdf.

34. This is the First Amendment to the U.S. Constitution, ratified on December 15, 1791. An official version of the constitution is available at https://www.archives.gov/founding-docs/constitution-transcript.

35. For the Turkish constitution, see https://global.tbmm.gov.tr/docs/constitution_en.pdf.

36. For the Japanese constitution, see https://japan.kantei.go.jp/constitu tion_and_government_of_japan/constitution_e.html.
37. For the Australian constitution, see http://www.aph.gov.au/About_Par liament/Senate/Powers_practice_n_procedures/Constitution.
38. For Canada's Constitution Act of 1982, see http://laws.justice.gc.ca/PDF /CONST_E.pdf.
39. For the Constitution of the Kingdom of the Netherlands, see http:// www.government.nl/documents-and-publications/regulations/2012/10 /18/the-constitution-of-the-kingdom-of-the-netherlands-2008.html.
40. For the Mexican constitution, see http://www.oas.org/juridico/mla/en /mex/en_mex-int-text-const.pdf. There is more on religion, but the material quoted is enough to show the complexity of this constitution. All in all, the terms "religion" or "religious" are used twenty-six times.
41. For the Chilean constitution, see http://confinder.richmond.edu/admin /docs/Chile.pdf.
42. For the Lebanese constitution, see http://www.lebanon-elections.org /Modules/Document/UploadFile/3368_15,04,YYConstitution%20-%20 English.pdf.
43. For India's constitution, see http://lawmin.nic.in/olwing/coi/coi-english /coi-indexenglish.htm.
44. Excerpts from the Meiji Constitution are at http://afe.easia.columbia.edu /ps/japan/meiji_constitution.pdf.
45. What backs up article 36 and, one could even say, puts careful restrictions on the rights it purports is a decree (no. 426) of the State Council that lays out the Regulations on Religious Affairs. The State Council adopted these regulations, forty-eight articles in all, on July 7, 2004. They went into full effect on March 1, 2005. Decree no. 426 is discussed further in chapter 3. A more in-depth discussion of article 36 is in chapter 4.
46. Jeremy T. Gunn, "The Complexity of Religion and the Definition of 'Religion' in International Law," *Harvard Human Rights Journal* 16 (Spring): 190, 195.
47. *Oxford English Dictionary*, http://www.oed.com/.
48. The sacrality of the emperor renders him inviolate. In Giorgio Agam-ben's language, the emperor as sovereign, as sacred and therefore invio-late, can be killed but not sacrificed. Agamben points out that traces of this unsacrificeability can still be seen today in modern constitutions. He writes: "The unsacrificeability of the sovereign's life still survives in the principle according to which the head of state cannot be submitted to an ordinary legal trial. In the American Constitution, for example, impeachment requires a special session of the Senate presided over by the chief justice, which can be convened only for "high crimes and

misdemeanors," and whose consequence can never be a legal sentence but only dismissal from office." Giorgio Agamben, *Homo Sacer: Sovereign Power and Bare Life*, trans. Daniel Heller-Roazen (Stanford, Calif.: Stanford University Press, 1998), 103. In China's constitution, article 74 stipulates that "no deputy to the National People's Congress may be arrested or placed on criminal trial without the consent of the Presidium of the current session of the National People's Congress or, when the National People's Congress is not in session, without the consent of its Standing Committee." It is a self-protective and self-perpetuating system. The Presidium is a 178-member body that presides over sessions of the National People's Congress, with its 2,924 members.

49. The inviolateness of home is in place, but only until the law allows for the home to be searched (in the case of Chile, for example). The inviolableness holds until the state decides it does not. This is Agamben's state of exception. Your home is inviolable until we decide it is not.

50. This is one of the oldest forms of the inviolate. We see it as article 17 of the Declaration of the Rights of Man (1789): "Since property is an inviolable and sacred right, no one shall be deprived thereof except where public necessity, legally determined, shall clearly demand it, and then only on condition that the owner shall have been previously and equitably indemnified." A copy of the declaration is available at the Yale Law School archive, http://avalon.law.yale.edu/18th_century/rightsof.asp.

51. The "Nineteen Articles" mentioned above also stipulate that the emperor is sacred and inviolable (*huangdi shensheng buke qinfan*). Another way to translate this might be "The emperor's sacrality cannot be infringed upon." In other words, he is the inviolate.

3. Religion

1. Many scholars over the past fifteen years have critically rethought the category. See, for example, works by Timothy Fitzgerald, Russell T. McCutcheon, and Tomoko Masuzawa.

2. Just because a term for something does not exist does not mean that a social formation or human activity, one that we might wish to designate as "religious, does not exist.

3. Some time ago the late, great scholar of comparative religion Wilfred Cantwell Smith remarked that "human history might prove more intelligible if we learned to think of religion and the religions as adjectives rather than as nouns—that is, as secondary to persons or things rather than as things in themselves." Wilfred Cantwell Smith, *The Meaning and End of Religion* (New York: Macmillan, 1962), 20.

4. Often in classes I teach at the introductory level, I ask my students to create a list of terms that they think best describe religion. The lists are almost identical each year—deities, texts, rituals, rules, sacred space, music, icons, food, devotees, etc. I then talk to the students about Babe Ruth, Yankee Stadium, and baseball fans. All the terms match up. It's a cheap trick but always worth doing. For more on baseball and religion, see David Chidester, "The Church of Baseball, the Fetish of Coca-Cola, and the Potlatch of Rock 'n' Roll: Theoretical Models for the Study of Religion in American Popular Culture," *Journal of the American Academy of Religion* 64, no. 4 (Winter 1996): 743–65.

5. See Talal Asad, *Genealogies of Religion: Discipline and Reasons of Power in Christianity and Islam* (Baltimore: Johns Hopkins University Press, 1993), especially chap. 1. Asad argues that the idea of religion is a Western invention, and that Euroamerican nation-states reified a separate sphere for "religion." This sphere is then exported to the rest of the world. Thus religion becomes a critical component of modern nation-state building.

6. See Jonathan Z. Smith, https://www.youtube.com/watch?v=iTVeX 4Jp418. See also Fairfield University's Digital Commons, http://digital commons.fairfield.edu/asrvideos/193/, which has several documented interviews with Smith, arguably one of the foremost scholars of religion in the world today.

7. See Jonathan Z. Smith's and David Chidester's work in this regard. As Chidester points out, "during the nineteenth century, European social scientists developed different terms—*fetishism, totemism,* and *animism*—for the original religion of humanity." But these terms did not designate religion in the true Christian sense. Primitives, or usually savages, as they were called, lacked real religion, hence the terms above. David Chidester, *Religion: Material Dynamics* (Oakland: University of California Press, 2019), 24.

8. One of the first times we see the term *shūkyō* is when it is used to translate the English term "religion" in a letter of protest against the treatment of Christians in Japan. See Jason Ananda Josephson, *The Invention of Religion in Japan* (Chicago: University of Chicago Press, 2012), 189. See also Thomas David DuBois, *Religion and the Making of Modern East Asia* (Cambridge: Cambridge University Press, 2011); and Anthony C. Yu, *State and Religion in China* (Chicago: Open Court, 2005). Yu contends that Japan used *shūkyō* to translate the German word *Religionsübung* (9).

9. See Helen Hardacre, *Shinto and the State: 1868–1988* (Princeton, N.J.: Princeton University Press, 1991); much of Allan Grapard's work; and, importantly, Josephson, *The Invention of Religion in Japan.* See also Thomas David DuBois, "Hegemony, Imperialism, and the Construction

of Religion in East and Southeast Asia," *History and Theory*, theme issue 44 (December 2005): 113–31.

10. Josephson, *The Invention of Religion in Japan*, 21.

11. Josephson, *The Invention of Religion in Japan*, 256.

12. Guangxu's reign lasted from 1875 to 1908. After him came Puyi, the final emperor of the Qing dynasty, whose reign ended in 1912, effectively marking the end of the Qing Empire.

13. For more on the Hundred Days' reform, a time of existential crisis for China, see Jonathan D. Spence, *The Search for Modern China* (New York: Norton, 1990), 224–30.

14. See Vincent Goossaert, "Republican Church Engineering: The National Religious Associations in 1912 China," in *Chinese Religiosities: Afflictions of Modernity and State Formation*, ed. Mayfair Mei-hui Yang (Berkeley: University of California Press, 2008), 211.

15. See Vincent Goossaert and David A. Palmer, *The Religious Question in Modern China* (Chicago: University of Chicago Press, 2011), 50. See also Vincent Goossaert, "1898: The Beginning of the End for Chinese Religion," *Journal of Asian Studies* 65, no. 2 (2006): 307–36; David A. Palmer, "Heretical Doctrines, Reactionary Secret Societies, Evil Cults: Labeling Heterodoxy in Twentieth-Century China," in Yang, *Chinese Religiosities*, 113–34; and Rebecca Nedostup, *Superstitious Regimes: Religion and the Politics of Chinese Modernity* (Cambridge, Mass.: Harvard University Press, 2009).

16. Nedostup, *Superstitious Regimes*, 2.

17. See Yang's "Introduction" in *Chinese Religiosities*, 12.

18. Timothy Fitzgerald, *Discourse on Civility and Barbarity: A Critical History of Religion and Related Categories* (New York: Oxford University Press, 2007), 52. A crucial aspect of Fitzgerald's project is to investigate how religion operates in relation to other categories (see 44–45).

19. Mary Douglas, *How Institutions Think* (Syracuse, N.Y.: Syracuse University Press, 1986), 36.

20. Here we can recall the Parliament of World Religions conference held in Chicago in 1893. For more on this, see Tomoko Masuzawa, *The Invention of World Religions: Or, How European Universalism Was Preserved in the Language of Pluralism* (Chicago: University of Chicago Press, 2005). The conferences continue, with the most recent one held in Toronto in November 2018.

21. The museum was founded by the Buddhist monk Hsin Tao in 2001 and officially opened with a dedication in late 2002.

22. Giorgio Agamben, *Profanations*, trans. Jeff Fort (New York: Zone Books, 2007), 84.

23. As Donald Preziosi and Claire Farago put it: "Any museological collection is, by definition, only made possible by dismembering another context and reassembling a new museological whole." Preziosi and Farago, eds., *Grasping the World: The Idea of the Museum* (Aldershot, U.K.: Ashgate, 2004), 5.

24. I wish to thank a former student of mine, Lisa Nakashima, for bringing this group to my attention. Its website is https://www.uscirf.gov/about -uscirf.

25. The State Department also has a division called the Bureau of Democracy, Human Rights, and Labor that monitors "religious freedom" around the globe and produces an annual report. It operates under the International Religious Freedom Act of 1998. Its archived website (for materials prior to 2017) is https://2009-2017.state.gov/j/drl/index.htm, and its current site (since 2017) is https://www.state.gov/bureaus-offices /under-secretary-for-civilian-security-democracy-and-human-rights /bureau-of-democracy-human-rights-and-labor/. In its 2016 report, the bureau points to some infractions and hate crimes in South Africa, mostly against Jews and Muslims. For China, the bureau notes that the country has been on the Country of Particular Concern (CPC) list since 1999. Most of the data on China appears to come from China's State Administration for Religious Affairs.

26. United States Commission on International Religious Freedom, http:// www.uscirf.gov/about-uscirf.html. Of note is that in some years there has not been a single scholar of religious studies on the commission.

27. Annual reports are available at http://www.uscirf.gov/reports-briefs.

28. Religion shows up only in the First Amendment, lumped together with freedom of the press and freedom of expression. Ratified on December 15, 1791, the amendment reads as follows: "Congress shall make no law respecting an establishment of religion, or prohibiting the free exercise thereof; or abridging the freedom of speech, or of the press; or the right of the people peaceably to assemble, and to petition the Government for a redress of grievances." Also see Philip Hamburger, *Separation of Church and State* (Cambridge, Mass.: Harvard University Press, 2004).

29. For instance, we might think of President George W. Bush's response to 9/11, or stereotypes of the Muslim world and the violence of Islam. Or, given the now over one hundred self-immolations by Tibetan monks and nuns since 2009, the Chinese government's violent response (rebuke?) against Tibetan Buddhists. See William Cavanaugh, *The Myth of Religious Violence: Secular Ideology and the Roots of Modern Conflict* (New York: Oxford University Press, 2009). Cavanaugh accurately points out

that what counts as religious or secular is entirely dependent on the contextual power configurations.

30. The State Department operates the Office of International Religious Freedom; the USCIRF operates independently of the State Department and evaluates the efficacy of the department's efforts to promote religious freedom.

31. Stephen Hopgood, "Human Rights: Past Their Sell-by Date," *Open Democracy*, June 18, 2013, http://www.opendemocracy.net/openglobal rights/stephen-hopgood/human-rights-past-their-sell-by-date.

32. Lynn Hunt, *Inventing Human Rights* (New York: Norton, 2007), 19.

33. Stephen Hopgood, *The Endtimes of Human Rights* (Ithaca, N.Y.: Cornell University Press, 2013), xiii.

34. Hopgood, *The Endtimes of Human Rights*, x–xi.

35. Agamben, *Homo Sacer*, 127.

36. Giorgio Agamben, "Beyond Human Rights," *Open*, no. 15 (2008), *Social Engineering*: 90–95.

37. Agamben, "Beyond Human Rights," 91.

38. We saw the stripping of citizenship and the rights pertaining to such during the two world wars. In the first, many Hungarian, Russian, and Armenian refugees were denationalized by new Turkish and Soviet governments. Agamben, "Beyond Human Rights," 91. In World War II, during the "Final Solution" in Germany, Jews were systematically stripped of their citizenship before being sent to the death camps. And more recently, in Britain, forty-two people have been stripped of their citizenship since 2006. This was typically done when individuals were said to allegedly have ties to terrorist groups. For example, in 2010 Mohamed Sakr was stripped of his citizenship when the state claimed he had ties to Al Qaeda. Less than two years later Sakr was killed in a drone strike. Katrin Benhold, "Britain Increasingly Invokes Power to Disown Its Citizens," *New York Times*, April 9, 2014, http://www.nytimes .com/2014/04/10/world/europe/britains-power-to-disown-its-citizens -raises-questions.html?_r=0.

39. Hannah Arendt wrote about this more than half a century ago in *The Origins of Totalitarianism* (New York: Harcourt Brace, 1951), chap. 5.

40. On the debates surrounding the notion of religious freedom, see Winnifred Fallers Sullivan et al., eds., *Politics of Religious Freedom* (Chicago: University of Chicago Press, 2015). See also Elizabeth Shakman Hurd, *Beyond Religious Freedom: The New Global Politics of Religion* (Princeton, N.J.: Princeton University Press, 2017). Hurd asks many provocative and crucial questions, among them: "What are the consequences when the category of religion becomes an object of international law

and international public policy?" (2). Hurd, like Fitzgerald, finds the term "religion" to be inherently unstable. She concludes that "while religious practices are an important dimension of human life, the category of religion is too complex and unstable to serve as a platform from which to pursue these political ends." By "political ends," Hurd is referring to the new political reality of singling out religion "as a basis to conduct foreign policy, write laws and constitutions, and pursue rights advocacy" (111).

41. Michel Foucault, *The Order of Things: An Archaeology of the Human Sciences* (New York: Random House, 1970), xix.

42. Wilfred Cantwell Smith struggled with the category decades ago. The most compelling essay I have read on how the category might be used, specifically in China, is by Robert Ford Campany, "On the Very Idea of Religions (in the Modern West and in Early Medieval China)," *History of Religions* 42, no. 4 (May 2003): 287–319. Campany suggests that we think of religions as imagined communities that include practices, texts, persons, and ideas as "repertoires of resources" (317). One advantage of this is that, "if we imagine religions and cultures as repertoires, then everyone—not merely those who study religions but also those who participate in them—is potentially in the position of bricoleur, syncretist, and comparativist" (319).

43. Document 19 is available on the State Administration for Religious Affairs website, http://www.sara.gov.cn/gb/zcfg/zc/75352506-2bd0-11da -8858-93180af1bb1a.html. A decent English translation is in Donald E. MacInnis, *Religion in China Today: Policy and Practice* (New York: Orbis Books, 1989), as well in a report by Mickey Spiegel for Human Rights Watch/Asia 1997, https://www.hrw.org/reports/1997/china1/. A PDF version can be found at https://www.purdue.edu/crcs/wp-content/up loads/2014/08/Document_no._19_1982.pdf.

44. This bureau later becomes the State Administration for Religious Affairs (Guojia zongjiao shiwuju, SARA).

45. See, for example, James W. Tong, *Revenge of the Forbidden City: The Suppression of the Falungong in China, 1999–2005* (Oxford: Oxford University Press, 2009). For an extensive history of Falungong as understood within China's history of religiosities, see David Ownby, *Falun Gong and the Future of China* (New York: Oxford University Press, 2008). Ownby struggles with the category of religion in China vis-à-vis Falungong as a suppressed religious group.

46. SARA's reach is far and wide. It gets to decide what counts as a religion (as opposed to "superstition," *mixin*), who can become a monk, nun, or

imam, which curriculum is taught, and what version of history is presented. It's an extraordinarily powerful institution.

47. See http://www.china.org.cn/english/features/state_structure/64784.htm.

48. The Ministry of Public Security (Gong'an bu) is responsible for internal security in China.

49. China comprises twenty-two provinces, four municipalities (Beijing, Shanghai, Tianjin, and Chongqing), and five autonomous regions (Guangxi, Inner Mongolia, Ningxia, Xinjiang, and Tibet). Each of these is further divided into cities, municipal districts/prefecture districts, counties, townships, and villages. At every level in most settings there is a religious affairs bureau that reports to the local PSB and to SARA. Given that provinces, municipalities, and their respective subdivisions have considerable autonomy in how they conduct their affairs, one can only imagine how varied the interpretation of laws and regulations regarding religion must be.

50. The original Chinese version is available at http://www.gov.cn/zhengce /content/2017-09/07/content_5223282.htm. An English translation is at https://www.refworld.org/docid/474150382.html.

51. The issues and problems surrounding the term "belief" will be discussed further in the next chapter.

52. Religious citizens and nonreligious citizens should mutually respect one another other and coexist in harmony.

53. The oversight organizations are the Buddhist Association of China, Chinese Daoist Association, Islamic Association of China, Three-Self Patriotic Movement (represents Protestantism), and Chinese Patriotic Catholic Association.

54. See Sarah Cook and Leeshai Lemish, "The 610 Office: Policing the Chinese Spirit," *China Brief* 11, no. 17, https://jamestown.org/program/the -610-office-policing-the-chinese-spirit/. See also Flora Sapio, *Sovereign Power and the Law in China* (Leiden: Brill, 2010), 62–70.

55. In his speech Ye Xiaowen said that China is "ready to join the international community in safeguarding the religion-related human rights." Ye Xiaowen, "China's Religions: Retrospect and Prospect," http://www .china.org.cn/english/features/45466.htm. Ye was director of the Bureau of Religious Affairs from 1995 until 1998. The name was then changed to the State Administration for Religious Affairs, and Ye served as director-general until 2009.

56. I see no problem in historicizing a process of policy making, in other words, Ye reifying document 19 (albeit a biased assessment); where the crux of the problem lies is the use of *guochi* (national humiliation) as a

tool to explicate the central government's position on religion as a social phenomenon that must be carefully controlled.

57. Winnifred Fallers Sullivan, *The Impossibility of Religious Freedom* (Princeton, N.J.: Princeton University Press, 2007), 3.

58. The term *tulku* derives from the Tibetan *sprulku*, used to refer to incarnate lamas, or living buddhas, the most famous being the Dalai lamas. *Sprul sku* is a translation of the Sanskrit *nirmanakaya*, the third emanation body of a buddha, which has direct control over its rebirth. There are about three thousand lines of incarnation in Tibet. For more, see Robert E. Buswell, Jr., and Donald S. Lopez, Jr., eds., *The Princeton Dictionary of Buddhism* (Princeton, N.J.: Princeton University Press, 2014), 847. The term used in Chinese for mature *tulkus* is *huofo*, which translates as "living Buddha." This is a misnomer, as most *tulkus* are understood to be bodhisattvas. See John Powers, *The Buddha Party: How the People's Republic of China Works to Define and Control Tibetan Buddhism* (New York: Oxford University Press, 2017), 106.

4. Reincarnation

1. State permission is obtained via a complicated application process. Order no. 5 is available at http://www.gov.cn/gongbao/content/2008/content _923053.htm.

2. See José Ignacio Cabezón, "State Control of Tibetan Buddhist Monasticism in the People's Republic of China," in *Chinese Religiosities: Afflictions of Modernity and State Formation*, ed. Mayfair Mei-hui Yang (Berkeley: University of California Press, 2008), 261–91. Cabezón focuses on a state-published booklet, *Book No. 4*, used for the "patriotic education" of monks and nuns. He explains that *Book No. 4* makes the case that religion must contribute to the goal of economic and material success. "The fundamental duty of religious work," *Book No. 4* tells us, "is to build modernity and bring about the sacrosanct progress of Chinese minorities" (268). As I will suggest later with regard to order no. 5, this type of statement in *Book No. 4* is what I call a theojuridical or theopolitical statement. The state is claiming to know what truly constitutes "religious work."

3. John Powers rightly points out that the Chinese translation contradicts a basic Buddhist tenet that there is no such thing as a "soul." See Powers, *The Buddha Party: How the People's Republic of China Works to Define and Control Tibetan Buddhism* (New York: Oxford University Press, 2017), especially chap. 3. The idea of no fixed self/soul (Sk. *anatman*) is one of the earliest teachings by the Buddha.

4. Gyaincain Norbu is the son of Communist Party cadres. Powers, *The Buddha Party*, 121.

5. See Elliot Sperling, "Reincarnation and the Golden Urn in the 19th Century: The Recognition of the 8th Panchen Lama," in *Studies on the History and Literature of Tibet and the Himalaya*, ed. Roberto Vitali (Kathmandu: Vajra Publications, 2012), 97. Sperling also explains how the golden urn came to be used as a divinational tool during the Qing dynasty. Powers also discusses the use of the golden urn in *The Buddha Party*, chap. 3.

6. The China Buddhist Association website is http://www.chinabuddhism .com.cn.

7. Elliot Sperling, "Awe and Submission: A Tibetan Aristocrat at the Court of Qianlong," *International History Review* 20, no. 2 (June 1998): 325.

8. Elliot Sperling, "Don't Know Much About Tibetan History," *New York Times*, April 13, 2008, http://www.nytimes.com/2008/04/13/opinion/13 sperling.html.

9. See Pankaj Mishra, "The Last Dalai Lama," *New York Times* magazine, December 1, 2015, https://www.nytimes.com/2015/12/06/magazine/the -last-dalai-lama.html.

10. As reported by Reuters (and many other news organizations). See Roberta Rampton and Sui-Lee Wee, "Obama Meets with the Dalai Lama Despite China Warnings," *Reuters*, February 20, 2015, http://www .reuters.com/article/2014/02/21/us-usa-china-tibet-idUSBREA1K01 P20140221. The *People's Daily* also cites the same official. See Zhou Yan, "China Voice: Obama-Dalai Lama Meeting a Lose-Lose Deal," *People's Daily*, February 21, 2014, http://en.people.cn/90883/8543194.html.

11. Obama White House archives, https://obamawhitehouse.archives.gov /the-press-office/2014/02/21/press-briefing-press-secretary-jay-carney -2212014, and https://obamawhitehouse.archives.gov/the-press-office /2016/06/15/readout-presidents-meeting-his-holiness-xiv-dalai-lama.

12. More often than not, the term "religion," or here, "religious," obfuscates more than clarifies.

13. One of the primary arguments made by Timothy Fitzgerald in his recent book *Discourse on Civility and Barbarity* is that the category of religion for the most part naturalizes Euroamerican secular rationality. If this is indeed the case, then we face the task of unraveling the usage of "religion" in non-Euroamerican contexts, part of what I'm trying to do in this book. Scholar of Chinese religions Paul Katz has also begun this unraveling process in his book *Religion in China and Its Modern Fate* (Lebanon, N.H.: Brandeis University Press, 2014). He writes: "In short, the modern Chinese state's mission of governing based on Western ideas

of secularization impelled Chinese religious groups to redefine themselves in ways that the authorities could accept and attempt to regulate,
because any separation of 'church and state' could only prove viable if
'religion' were to be accepted as a legitimate category distinct from other
political and social entities" (11–12). Katz then quotes another scholar of
Chinese religions, Robert Weller: "Secularization as a state project thus
requires religionization" (12).

14. Saba Mahmood has made a convincing argument that in postcolonial
Egypt secular governance has in fact exacerbated religious tensions. This
is, in part, because the state tries to control religious differences. Mahmood rightly points out that, even though "secular political rationality"
espouses religious neutrality, "the modern state has become involved in
the regulation and management of religious life to an unprecedented
degree." Saba Mahmood, *Religious Difference in a Secular Age: A Minority Report* (Princeton, N.J.: Princeton University Press, 2015), 2. The same
holds true for China. Differences, for instance, between Tibetan Buddhism and traditional Chinese Buddhism are regulated by the state,
hence the ability of the state to control who can or cannot reincarnate.

15. See "Rule on Living Buddhas Aids Religious Freedom," *China Daily*,
December 27, 2007, http://www.chinadaily.com.cn/china/2007-12/27
/content_6351750.htm.

16. The official Chinese government version in English is at http://www.gov
.cn/english/2005-08/05/content_20813.htm. The Chinese version is available at http://www.gov.cn/gongbao/content/2004/content_62714.htm.

17. For example, see this in an otherwise fine study, Shuk-wah Poon, *Negotiating Religion in Modern China: State and Common People in Guangzhou,
1900–1937* (Hong Kong: Chinese University Press, 2011), 2. Poon is not
the only author to make such a statement; many others do so as well.

18. Yoshiko Ashiwa and David L. Wank, *Making Religion, Making the
State: The Politics of Religion in Modern China* (Stanford, Calif.: Stanford
University Press, 2009), 1. The figure quoted is from the many white
papers issued by the Chinese government, all available online. For
example, it is reported in "The Present Conditions of Religion in China,"
http://english.gov.cn/official/2005-08/17/content_24165.htm, a white
paper link from the central government's website to China's official
online news service, http://www.china.org.cn/e-white/Freedom/f-1.htm.
At a panel discussion at the Brookings Institution in April 2009, the
moderator, Dennis Wilder, cited a study from Huadong Teachers University that put the number of "believers" at 300 million. Dennis Wilder,
"China's Religions (Re)Awakening and the Impact of Religion on Chinese Society," *Brookings Institution*, April 6, 2009, https://www.brook

ings.edu/wp-content/uploads/2012/04/20090406_china.pdf. The category of "belief" will be examined later in this chapter.

19. Peter van der Veer, *Imperial Encounters: Religion and Modernity in India and Britain* (Princeton, N.J.: Princeton University Press, 2001), 16.

20. Timothy Fitzgerald, "Encompassing Religion, Privatized Religions, and the Invention of Modern Politics," in *Religion and the Secular: Historical and Colonial Formations*, ed. Timothy Fitzgerald (London: Routledge Taylor and Francis Group, 2007), 234.

21. Talal Asad, *Formations of the Secular: Christianity, Islam, Modernity* (Stanford, Calif.: Stanford University Press, 2003), 1–2, 182.

22. Ian Buruma makes an important point when he writes, "Religion is not a rational enterprise. Its metaphysical claims cannot be proven; either one believes them or one does not." See Ian Buruma, *Taming the Gods: Religion and Democracy on Three Continents* (Princeton, N.J.: Princeton University Press, 2010), 9. Buruma, of course, reifies the term, and one has to wonder what religion in this instance refers to. He goes on to say that "when reflecting on the problems of religion and democracy, the main issue is how to stop irrational passions from turning violent" (9–10). This connects to Mahmood's argument about the ostensible religious neutrality of the secular state. The state is essentially trying to make religion, what for Buruma is an irrational phenomenon, into a rational enterprise.

23. See Charles Taylor, *A Secular Age* (Boston: Belknap Press of Harvard University Press, 2007).

24. José Casanova, *Public Religions in the Modern World* (Chicago: University of Chicago Press, 1994). This is also cited in Asad, *Formations of the Secular*, 181.

25. Prasenjit Duara righty argues that "religion and secularism were formed by two types of circulations: by global and regional circulations, and by circulation between the constantly reconstituting spheres of religion and the secular themselves." Prasenjit Duara, "Religion and Citizenship in China and the Diaspora," in *Chinese Religiosities: Afflictions of Modernity and State Formation*, ed. Mayfair Mei-hui Yang, 43–64 (Berkeley: University of California Press, , 2008), 46.

26. Rebecca Nedostup, *Superstitious Regimes: Religion and the Politics of Chinese Modernity* (Cambridge, Mass.: Harvard University Press, 2009), 1–4. Nedostup convincingly refers to two "superstitious regimes." The first is the realm of superstition, an unseen realm that breeds irrational behavior and thus is anathema to Nationalist leaders; and, the second is the desire to have the state and all its nationalist sensibilities replace the ties that previous religiosities had established over centuries. The Japan model, with its impressive and oppressive result, state Shinto, would not

work in China, where an emperor was never again to be had, and in which the Nationalists faced a serious challenge in, as Nedostup puts it, being stuck between "total iconoclasm and cultural restorationism" (5). See also Rebecca Nedostup, "Ritual Competition and the Modernizing Nation-State," in *Chinese Religiosities: Afflictions of Modernity and State Formation*, ed. Mayfair Mei-hui Yang (Berkeley: University of California Press, 2008), 87–112.

27. Fitzgerald, "Encompassing Religion," 220.

28. The official government English translation of China's constitution does indeed use the phrase "freedom of religious belief." The characters being translated are *zongjiao xinyang ziyou*. We have already discussed the neologism China uses to translate "religion," namely, *zongjiao*. The characters *xinyang* literally mean "to put one's trust in," what government officials are translating as "belief." The final set of characters, *ziyou*, is typically translated as "freedom." So another translation might be "religious freedom to put one's trust in," not elegant by any stretch. The first four characters, *zongjiao xinyang*, could just be translated as "religion," as in "trust in a particular religion. Then you would have: freedom to have trust in religion." Or the entire phrase could simply be translated as "religious freedom." The point is the translation could be challenged, but the government goes with "freedom of religious belief," thereby making belief the cornerstone of the sentence, especially given that the second sentence of article 36 in China's constitution uses the term "believe" four times.

29. To add to the above, and to further break down the term into its constituent components, *xin* translates more as "trust," whereas *yang* might be translated as "rely on." Together we have *xinyang*, to trust and rely on. "Belief" seems an inadequate translation.

30. Donald S. Lopez, Jr., "Belief," in *Critical Terms for Religious Studies*, ed. Mark C. Taylor (Chicago: Chicago University Press, 1998), 21.

31. See Tomoko Masuzawa, *The Invention of World Religions: Or, How European Universalism Was Preserved in the Language of Pluralism* (Chicago: University of Chicago Press, 2005).

32. An excellent example of this can be found in David Chidester's book *Savage Systems: Colonialism and Comparative Religion in Southern Africa* (Charlottesville: University of Virginia Press, 1996). See also Jonathan Z. Smith, "Religion, Religions, Religious" in *Critical Terms for Religious Studies*, ed. Mark C. Taylor (Chicago: University of Chicago Press, 1998), 269–84.

33. For instance, France's constitution refers to a "respect for all beliefs." South Africa's constitution: "Everyone has the right to . . . religion."

The U.S. Constitution refers to the "free exercise" of religion. The UN charter refers to, among other freedoms, the "freedom of religion."

34. For more on what Vincent Goossaert and David Palmer call the "Christian-secular" mode, see their *The Religious Question in Modern China* (Chicago: University of Chicago Press, 2011), chap. 3.

35. We saw this play out in the Chinese context with the crackdown on Falungong in 1999. To have thousands of Falungong practitioners suddenly amass in Zhongnanhai in Beijing, the central headquarters of the Communist Party and the State Council, was too much for Beijing to accept. Organized opposition, ostensibly a religious intrusion into public space, would not be tolerated by the state. The persecution continues to this day.

36. Qianfang Zhang, *The Constitution of China: A Contextual Analysis* (Oxford: Hart, 2012), 241.

37. The official English version on the Chinese government website uses the word "enjoy," though that is not what the original Chinese says.

38. Asad, *Formations of the Secular*, 186, points this out, not in China per se, but I think it is applicable here.

39. Lydia Liu discusses the beginnings of rights in China, specifically in the Chinese translation of Henry Wheaton's highly influential book, *Elements of International* Law (Oxford, 1936; orig. ed. 1836), when the term *quan* is used as an equivalent for the "right." See Lydia H. Liu, *The Clash of Empires: The Invention of China in Modern World Making* (Cambridge, Mass.: Harvard University Press, 2004), 131 and indeed all of chapter 4.

40. As pointed out in the previous chapter, it was Liang Qichao who first systematically sought to define *mixin* in opposition to religion (*zongjiao*). See Goossaert and Palmer, *The Religious Question in Modern China*, 50–55. The term "superstition" was used frequently in medieval Europe, where it was most often employed to describe the activities of pagans and heathens. Mayfair Yang describes how once when interviewing an official at the Religious Affairs Bureau she inquired about ancestor rituals, ghost festivals, deity temples, and divinational practices such as *fengshui*. She was promptly told that the bureau only dealt with the five officially sanctioned religions—Buddhism, Daoism, Protestantism, Islam, and Catholicism—and not with superstitions. For those she would have to talk with the Ministry of Civil Affairs or the Ministry of Public Security. Mayfair Mei-hua Yang, ed., *Chinese Religiosities: Afflictions of Modernity and State Formation* (Berkeley: University of California Press, 2008), 18. In effect, *mixin* came to replace the oft-used category *yinsi* (illicit cult) in imperial China. David Palmer argues that since 1999 and the banning of Falungong the term *xiejiao* (evil cults), once used in imperial times,

has been "rediscovered" (though he also points out that since 2007 he has seen a decline in its usage.) David A. Palmer, "Heretical Doctrines, Reactionary Secret Societies, Evil Cults: Labeling Heterodoxy in Twentieth-Century China," in Yang, *Chinese Religiosities*, 113 and 133, respectively. Palmer concludes that the contemporary use of *xiejiao* is a category that borrows from imperial Chinese ideology traditional notions of the state as stabilizer and protector of social harmony. It also borrows from a universalistic Western approach that defines religion and order in the broadest of terms (if it defines them at all) (133–34).

41. Goossaert and Palmer, *The Religious Question in Modern China*, 50.

42. Goossaert and Palmer, *The Religious Question in Modern China*, 46, 53.

43. See Thomas David DuBois, *Religion and the Making of Modern East Asia* (Cambridge: Cambridge University Press, 2011), 173.

44. Goossaert and Palmer discuss this text briefly in *The Religious Question in Modern China*, chap. 2, especially 62. For a rich and nuanced account of the Republican period attitudes, strategies, and struggles with religion, see Nedostup's superb study, *Superstitious Regimes*. Also see Poon, *Negotiating Religion in Modern China*, especially chap. 5.

45. Vincent Goossaert, "The Destruction of Immoral Temples in Qing China," *Journal of Chinese Studies*, ICS Visiting Professor Lecture Series no. 2 (2009): 2, 5, 7.

46. What Giorgio Agamben essentially means when he uses the phrase a "state of exception" is a social space where there is no recourse to legal determinations and with no distinction between public and private. This is therefore necessarily a space of violence. A sovereign power can suspend the rule of law and initiate a state of exception.

47. It was on April 25, 1999, when upwards of ten thousand Falungong practitioners showed up at the Communist Party headquarters at Zhongnanhai to protest the persecution of their practices and the arrest of several dozen of their members a few days before in the city of Tianjin. This mass action startled the state, which then began a mass persecution of the group.

48. Fitzgerald, "Encompassing Religion," 212–13.

49. Pitman B. Potter, "Belief in Control: Regulation of Religion in China," in *Religion in China Today*, ed. Daniel L. Overmyer (Cambridge: Cambridge University Press, 2003), 11.

50. While national identity and nationalism did not yet exist in the nineteenth century, I would still argue that there are nationalistic forms and specters in any time period, including the nineteenth century. The love of emperor, the land on which you live and die, the stories your family tells you, origin stories, and the language you speak all existed in imperial China as they did in other parts of the world. I agree with Gayatri

Chakravorty Spivak when she says that the ingredients from nationalism are to be found in what she calls "reproductive heteronormativity."
Gayatri Chakravorty Spivak, *Nationalism and the Imagination* (London:
Seagull Books, 2010), 12. These ingredients include the context within
which you are born, the migratory patterns that are your life, your mother
tongue, and your connections to the land and to ancient narratives.

51. Zheng Wang, *Never Forget National Humiliation: Historical Memory in
Chinese Politics and Foreign Relations* (New York: Columbia University
Press, 2012), 21. Wang discusses these and other phrases in chapter 2. The
real danger with this incendiary and pervasive nationalism is when, as
Spivak argues, citizens lack the cognitive faculty to really know nationalism and this in turn messes with our imagination and limits it. Spivak, *Nationalism and the Imagination*, 47. I see this so clearly in China.
The onslaught of state nationalism relentlessly fed to the public stunts
the imagination and therefore our ability to imagine an otherwise future.
I say "our ability" because we all succumb to this on a regular basis. China
is just an exemplum. The trick is to turn the equation around and imagine beyond the nation, and also to see what Michael Taussig, in a talk
he gave at the University of California, Santa Barbara, in the early 1990s,
called "the reality of the really made up."

52. James Hevia, *English Lessons: The Pedagogy of Imperialism in Nineteenth-
Century China* (Durham, N.C.: Duke University Press, 2003), 348.

53. For more on Catholicism in China, see much of Richard Madsen's
work, specifically *China's Catholics: Tragedy and Hope in an Emerging
Civil Society* (Berkeley: University of California Press, 1998). Also see
Daniel H. Bays, *A New History of Christianity in China* (Chichester,
U.K.: Wiley-Blackwell, 2012). Discussions between Beijing and the
Vatican have been fraught for at least seventy years. The Vatican then
formally recognized the so-called legitimacy of seven CCP-approved
bishops. See Francis X. Rocca and Eva Dou, "Pope Francis to Bow to
China with Concessions on Bishops," *Wall Street Journal*, February 1, 2018,
https://www.wsj.com/articles/pope-francis-to-bow-to-china-with-con
cession-on-bishops-1517507751. See also Bethany Allen-Ebrahimian,
"Pope Francis Is Giving in to the Chinese Communist Party," *Washington Post*, February 2, 2018, https://www.washingtonpost.com/news/demo
cracy-post/wp/2018/02/02/pope-francis-is-giving-in-to-the-chinese
-communist-party.

5. Contact

1. Emperor Puyi then appropriately goes on to ask if the tutor considers
himself to be a gentleman. The reply: "I try to be."

2. Historian James Hevia writes: "One common thread running from Macartney to Wade [Sir Thomas Francis Wade, the nineteenth-century British sinologist and diplomat] . . . involved the notion that the Qing court did not have a clear understanding of the true character of Englishmen." James Hevia, *English Lessons: The Pedagogy of Imperialism in Nineteenth-Century China* (Durham, N.C.: Duke University Press, 2003), 145.

3. Rev. William C. Milne, *Life in China* (London: Routledge, 1857), 112, 113. Milne, a Protestant missionary, was the son of William Milne (1785–1822), considered to be the second Protestant missionary sent to China after Robert Morrison (1782–1834). Missionaries such as Milne and Morrison of the London Missionary Society and James Hudson Taylor (1832–1905) of the China Inland Mission played an outsized role in shaping the effect of colonial contact. William C. Milne lived in China from 1830 to 1854. Initially restricted primarily to China's coastal cities, missionaries began rapidly expanding into the interior following the signing of the Treaty of Tianjin by Lord Elgin in 1858.

4. William Dean, *The China Mission* (New York: Sheldon, 1859), 7, 11–13.

5. Eric Reinders, *Borrowed Gods and Foreign Bodies: Christian Missionaries Imagine Chinese Religion* (Berkeley: University of California Press, 2004), 40, 41, 90.

6. W. E. Soothill, *A Mission in China* (Edinburgh: Oliphant, Anderson & Ferrier, 1907), 15.

7. Hevia, *English Lessons*, 3.

8. As Lydia Liu points out, these traits continue to this day in postcolonial international politics. See Lydia Liu, *The Clash of Empires: The Invention of China in Modern World Making* (Cambridge, Mass.: Harvard University Press, 2004), 27.

9. Charles Long, *Significations, Signs, Symbols, and Images in the Interpretation of Religion* (Aurora, Colo.: Fortress Press, 1986), 109.

10. An important book exploring this time period is James Hevia's *Cherishing Men from Afar: Qing Guest Ritual and the Macartney Embassy of 1793* (Durham, N.C., Duke University Press, 1995). Hevia makes the convincing argument that all Qing dynastic foreign policy making was structured through ritual. As such, the emperor "cherished those who travelled great distances to come to his court" (*huairou yuanren*, "cherishing men from afar") (xi). As the mediator between the heavens and earth, the emperor had the responsibility to set order to all things. Hevia also argues that the British relied completely on ritual and "cosmological content" (God and Nature). For more on the importance of court ritual (*li*), see, among others, Angela Zito, *Of Body and Brush: Grand Sacrifice as*

Text/Performance in Eighteenth-Century China (Chicago: University of Chicago Press, 1997). Beyond China, see also Catherine Bell, *Ritual Theory, Ritual Practice* (New York: Oxford University Press, 1992), and *Ritual: Perspectives and Dimensions* (New York: Oxford University Press, 1997). There is a revised 2009 edition of the latter as well. For Bell, ritual is the production and negotiation of power relations.

11. John Barrow, *Travels in China* (London: Cadell and Davies, 1847), 53.

12. The ritual-cosmological structures of these two empires were incompatible from the get-go. When Macartney had his audience with the emperor on September 14, 1793, he bowed on one knee as opposed to what was expected when one met the Son of Heaven, a full-body "kowtow" (*ketou*) done three times; each time one's forehead had to touch the ground.

13. Hui Wang, *China from Empire to Nation-State* (Cambridge, Mass.: Harvard University Press, 2014), 35. The practice of *wanghua* in theory prioritized "culture" (a complicated term in classical Chinese) over military conquest; however, as Wang wryly asks: "Where, after all, in the histories of the Qin, Han, Sui, Tang, Song, Yuan, Ming, and Qing dynasties do we see a lack of historical records of military conquest?" (36).

14. J. M. Coetzee, *Dusklands* (New York: Penguin Books, 1985).

15. Coetzee, *Dusklands*, 57, 58.

16. Coetzee, *Dusklands*, 106, 97, 116

17. Aimé Césaire, *Discourse on Colonialism*, trans. Joan Pinkham (New York: Monthly Review Press, 1972), 42.

18. Part of article 3 of the treaty stipulates that "the Ambassador, Minister, or other Diplomatic Agent, so appointed by Her Majesty the Queen of Great Britain . . . shall not be called upon to perform any ceremony derogatory to him as representing the Sovereign of an independent nation, on a footing of equality with that of China."

19. Liu, *The Clash of Empires*, 31, 32, 72, 62.

20. For more on some of these complexities, see David Chidester, *Savage Systems: Colonialism and Comparative Religion in Southern Africa* (Charlottesville: University of Virginia Press, 1996), and *Empire of Religion: Imperialism and Comparative Religion* (Chicago: University of Chicago Press, 2014). Barrow's book that followed his time spent in South Africa is titled *An Account of Travels Into the Interior of Southern Africa, in the Years 1797 and 1798* (London: Cadell and Davies, 1801). During those two years, Barrow held the post of auditor-general of public accounts at the Cape of Good Hope. He begins his narrative by praising Britain and its capture of the colony at Cape Town, as well as its many other colonies around the globe. By the "power of arms," he dramatically writes, "the

British language is now heard at the southern extremities of the four great continents or quarters of the globe" (1).

21. Barrow, *An Account of Travels*, 214.

22. Aside from Hevia's work, more examples of cultural and linguistic misunderstandings can be read in Julia Lovell's *The Opium War: Drugs, Dreams, and the Making of Modern China* (New York: Overlook Press, 2014).

23. For an excellent study of how the British imagined Chinese religions, see Eric Reinders, *Borrowed Gods and Foreign Bodies*. As for trade, opium was always the mainstay of British exchange with China. See Lovell, *The Opium War*. When Commissioner Lin Zexu, sent by the Daoguang emperor to put an end to the opium trade, destroyed almost three million pounds of raw opium, the stage was set for confrontation. Tensions had been building ever since Lord Napier's arrival in Guangzhou in 1834 to take up his post as the British government's first superintendent of trade in China. But Lin's act in May 1839 was only partially the trigger. Historian Jonathan Spence, gives three interconnected reasons in his overview of the first Opium War in *The Search for Modern China* (New York: Norton, 1990), 153.

24. The "great game," for the most part, was a series of diplomatic confrontations that took place between the British and Russian Empires as they vied for access and control over Central Asia. China was dragged into conflicts from time to time. I would argue that part of the great game involved trade access to China via the eastern seaports, but also through Central Asia. This played out with repeated attempts by all parties to gain control over the silk roads. See, for instance, Peter Hopkirk, *Foreign Devils on the Silk Road: The Search for the Lost Treasures of Central Asia* (London: John Murry, 1980); Hopkirk, *The Great Game: The Struggle for Empire in Central Asia* (Tokyo: Kodansha, 1992); Xinru Liu, *The Silk Road in World History* (London: Oxford University Press, 2010); Christopher Beckwith, *Empires of the Silk Road: A History of Central Eurasia from the Bronze Age to the Present* (Princeton, N.J.: Princeton University Press, 2009); and Valerie Hansen, *The Silk Road: A New History* (New York: Oxford University Press, 2012).

25. Bruno Latour, *We Have Never Been Modern*, trans. Catherine Porter (Cambridge, MA: Harvard University Press, 1993); and Bruno Latour, "Visualization and Cognition: Drawing Things Together," in *Knowledge and Society Studies in the Sociology of Culture Past and Present*, ed. H. Kuklick, vol. 6 (Greenwich, Conn.: Jai Press, 1986), 1–40.

26. Liu, *The Clash of Empires*, 113.

27. Wang, *China from Empire to Nation-State*, 127.
28. Tani Barlow, ed. *Formations of Colonial Modernity* (Durham, N.C.: Duke University Press, 1997).
29. Peter Zarrow, *China in War and Revolution, 1895–1949* (London: Routledge, 2005), 3.
30. In the early nineteenth century most missionaries were male. This began to shift toward the end of the century. See Jane Hunt, *The Gospel of Gentility: American Women Missionaries in Turn-of-the-Century China* (Yale, Conn.: Yale University Press, 1989).
31. Milne, *Life in China*, 1–16.
32. Milne, *Life in China*, 251.
33. See Rudolf Otto, *The Idea of the Holy: An Inquiry Into the Non-Rational Factor in the Idea of the Divine and Its Relation to the Rational* (London: Oxford University Press, 1936).
34. Milne, *Life in China*, 254.
35. This is part of the reason that Confucianism is not listed as one of the five legal religions in China today.
36. *Church Missionary Gleaner*, November 1876, 126. A copy of this text is at https://babel.hathitrust.org/cgi/pt?id=coo.31924071164747;view=1up;seq=151.
37. *Church Missionary Gleaner*, February 1863, 14. A copy of this text is at https://babel.hathitrust.org/cgi/pt?id=hvd.ah6j3z;view=1up;seq=176.
38. For more on the Victorian construction of Buddhism, see Philip C. Almond, *The British Discovery of Buddhism* (Cambridge: Cambridge University Press, 1988). As Almond puts it, the "imaginative creation of Buddhism in the first half of the nineteenth century, whereby the construction and interpretation of Buddhism reveals much about nineteenth-century concerns in Victorian England" (6). Almond demonstrates a range of Victorian attributes placed on the creation of Buddhism: infantile, docile, dangerously similar to Catholicism, and idolatrous. Buddhism became a taxonomic object, one that existed only in texts and manuscripts, a creature of the library, so to speak.
39. Harlan P. Beach, *Dawn on the Hills of T'ang; or, Missions in China* (New York: Student Volunteer Movement for Foreign Missions, c. 1898), 56. 56, 71, 91. Beach was a missionary in China from 1883 to 1890.
40. Dean, *The China Mission*, 53, 59, 61, 65, 66.
41. Soothill, *A Mission in China*, 271, 272. The "Light of Asia" refers to the narrative poem composed by Sir Edwin Arnold, published in London in 1879. In it Arnold tries to describe the life of Siddhartha Gautama, the Buddha.

42. Winterbotham, *An Historical, Geographical, and Philosophical View of the Chinese Empire* (London: Ridgway & Button, 1795), 65, 68.

43. Winterbotham, *An Historical, Geographical, and Philosophical View*, 92.

44. See Leigh Eric Schmidt, *Hearing Things: Religion, Illusion, and the American Enlightenment* (Cambridge, Mass.: Harvard University Press, 2000). Schmidt writes: "With its clear-eyed pursuit of detached observation, imperial sweep, and visual instrumentation, the Enlightenment was the keystone in the arch of the eye's ascendancy" (16). See also Martin Jay, *Downcast Eyes: The Denigration of Vision in Twentieth-Century French Thought* (Berkeley: University of California Press, 1993).

45. A Spanish edition came out in Mexico in 1854, an Italian edition in 1860, and a Japanese edition in 1876, ushering in, as Liu points out, a wave of discussions centered around the notion of "international law" and dramatically influencing Japanese imperialism. Liu, *The Clash of Empires*, 108–9.

46. Spence, *The Search for Modern China*, 201–2.

47. Henry Wheaton, *Elements of International Law* (1836; reprint Oxford, 1936), 19.

48. See, for instance, Richard Madsen, *China's Catholics: Tragedy and Hope in an Emerging Civil Society* (Berkeley: University of California Press, 1998); and Vincent Goossaert and David A. Palmer, *The Religious Question in Modern China* (Chicago: University of Chicago Press, 2011), 382. As an example of Beijing's containment tactics, see Ian Johnson, "China Moves to Sideline Underground Bishop, His Colleagues Say," *New York Times*, March 28, 2018, https://www.nytimes.com/2018/03/28/world/asia/catholic-bishop-detained-china.html. Johnson tellingly concludes his article as follows: "In recent years, the party has signaled that its main concern is foreign involvement in religious issues. This culminated in new regulations that took effect on Feb. 1 calling on all religions in China to 'Sinicize'—to become Chinese: In other words, to come under closer government control."

49. China's modernity, to be sure, was in many ways a response to external pressures in the form of other nation-states with armies and navies and technological superiority. But it was not only that: internal pressures about how to be a human in a cosmological and sociopolitical space have long been the mainstay of Chinese identity struggles.

50. Lovell, *The Opium War*, 80

51. Zarrow, *Creating Chinese Modernity*, 3.

52. Zarrow, *Creating Chinese Modernity*, 9.

53. Philip A. Kuhn, *Origins of the Modern Chinese State* (Stanford, Calif.: Stanford University Press, 2003), 1.

54. Edward Wong, "A Chinese Empire Reborn," *New York Times*, January 5, 2018, https://www.nytimes.com/2018/01/05/sunday-review/china-military -economic-power.html.

55. This was clearly demonstrated during a massive military parade in 2015 when thirty world leaders paid their respects to President Xi Jinping before watching thousands of troops (a not so subtle signifier of China's military power), tanks, and missile carriers make their way through the streets of Beijing. See Edward Wong, Jane Perlez, and Chris Buckley, "China Announces Cuts of 300,000 Troops at Military Parade Show- ing Its Might," *New York Times*, September 2, 2015. https://www.nytimes .com/2015/09/03/world/asia/beijing-turns-into-ghost-town-as-it-gears -up-for-military-parade.html?_r=0. Furthermore, the new empire has a new emperor. With the recent abolishment of presidential term lim- its, Xi could go on to rule China indefinitely.

6. Nativity

1. Michel Foucault, "The Subject and Power," *Critical Inquiry* 8, no. 4 (1982): 783.

2. Foucault calls it "royal power" in a lecture at the Collége de France on January 14, 1976. See Michael Foucault, *"Society Must Be Defended"" Lec- tures at the College de France, 1975–76*, trans. David Macey (New York: Picador, 2003), 25. The rights to be found here are the king's rights, not those of his subjects. Furthermore, royal power "demands a sacrifice from its subjects to save the throne." See Foucault, "The Subject and Power," 783.

3. He also likes to be portrayed as a paternal, modern-day Confucius, and indeed he often quotes Confucius. See, for instance, Jeremy Page, "Why China Is Turning Back to Confucius," *Wall Street Journal*, Sep- tember 20, 2015, https://www.wsj.com/articles/why-china-is-turning -back-to-confucius-1442754000.

4. Foucault, "The Subject and Power," 785.

5. Judith Butler and Gayatri Chakravorty Spivak ask a provocative ques- tion based on Arendt: "Are there modes of belonging that can be rigor- ously non-nationalist?" (I wish Presidents Trump and Xi would pose this question.) Butler and Spivak, *Who Sings the Nation-State: Language, Poli- tics, Belonging* (Kolkata: Seagull Books, 2011), 49.

6. Foucault, *"Society Must Be Defended,"* 36.

7. We don't need to go into Marx's explanation of the exploitation of the working class, but all irony aside when it comes to Chinese Marxism, the exploitation of the worker, as a body, was paramount.

202 ■ 6. Nativity

8. Nation-states are, by definition, systemic. There is a paradox at stake: discrete nation-states with their territoriality versus the apparent globalization of everything we know. Borders cannot contain effectively. As Wendy Brown puts it: "What we have come to call a globalized world harbors fundamental tensions between opening and barricading, fusion and partition, erasure and reinscription." Wendy Brown, *Walled States, Waning Sovereignty* (New York: Zone Books, 2010), 7.

9. Judith Butler asks the right question about the hyphen that separates nation and state: "Does it suggest a fallibility at the heart of the relation?" To which I would respond with a resounding "Yes!" Butler and Spivak, *Who Sings the Nation-State*, 2.

10. There are too many first-rate (and mediocre) studies of this time period to list here. As good a place as any to start is Ernest Gellner, *Nations and Nationalism* (Ithaca, N.Y.: Cornell University Press, 1983).

11. Hannah Arendt, *The Human Condition* (Chicago: University of Chicago Press, 1958), 256.

12. Giorgio Agamben, *Homo Sacer: Sovereign Power and Bare Life*, trans. Daniel Heller-Roazen (Stanford, Calif.: Stanford University Press, 1998), 129, 128, 85.

13. A copy of the declaration is available at https://www.archives.gov /founding-docs/declaration-transcript.

14. A copy of this declaration is available at http://avalon.law.yale.edu/18th_ century/rightsof.asp.

15. Butler and Spivak, *Who Sings the Nation-State*, 3. For what I call "making citizens," Peter Zarrow uses the phrase "citizenizing the masses." Peter Zarrow, ed., *Creating Chinese Modernity: Knowledge and Everyday Life, 1900–1940* (New York: Peter Lang, 2006), 55. The classic on European citizenry is T. H. Marshall, *Citizenship and Social Class* (Cambridge: Cambridge University Press, 1950). For discussions specifically about China, see, for example, Merle Goldman and Elizabeth J. Perry, eds., *Changing Meanings of Citizenship in Modern China* (Cambridge, Mass.: Harvard University Press, 2002).

16. During the twentieth century the term *guomin* became regularly used to denote a new conceptualization of citizenry, "nation-state people," though not many Chinese would have understood the ramifications of the term vis-à-vis the international pressure put on China to operate more like other nation-states. The roots of the term, however, go back more than two thousand years to pre-Qin times, where we see it used to label inhabitants of rival states. See Goldman and Perry, *Changing Meanings of Citizenship in Modern China*, 4. When Japan began its experiment with nation-statism, this was the term used for its citizenry. Like

many other terms, it was borrowed back again by China, specifically by Liang Qichao, who was searching for what Goldman and Perry call a "state-conferred membership" (4). Race and culture, for Liang, seemed inadequate alone to unify a new nation. (Race, *zhongzu*, for Liang was nevertheless essential to a reformed Han identity.) By 1911 *guomin* began to be used in state-sponsored textbooks, widely distributed around China. See Leo Ou-fan Lee, *Shanghai Modern: The Flowering of a New Urban Culture in China* (Cambridge, Mass.: Harvard University Press, 1999), 52–53, as cited in Goldman and Perry.

17. The idea of a citizen and what it meant was debated fiercely and widely after the first constitution of 1954. As Neil Diamant points out: "Officials as well as ordinary citizens could not differentiate between a 'national' (*guomin*), 'the people' (*renmin*), or a 'citizen' (*gongmin*)." Neil Diamant, "What the (Expletive) Is a 'Constitution'?! Ordinary Cadres Confront the 1954 PRC Draft Constitution," *Journal of Chinese History* 2, no. 1 (January 2018): 180. See also Prasenjit Duara, "Religion and Citizenship in China and the Diaspora," in *Chinese Religiosities: Afflictions of Modernity and State Formation*, ed. Mayfair Mei-hui Yang (Berkeley: University of California Press, 2008), 43–64. The term *guomin*, a neologism from the Japanese *kokumin*, became prevalent in the early 1900s when scholar-officials like Zhang Zhidong and Yuan Shikai advocated for educational reform.

18. This is the amended version of article 28, approved on March 15, 1999. The original version referred to counterrevolutionaries.

19. Both Hannah Arendt and later Agamben make this compelling argument. See Hannah Arendt, *The Origins of Totalitarianism* (New York: Harcourt Brace Jovanovich, 1979), and Agamben, *Homo Sacer*, 126.

20. Stripping an individual's citizenship is a way, though not always practical, for the state to expel individuals. In the United States, for instance, stripping citizenship usually involves an act of treason. See U.S. Code, title 8, Legal Information Institute, Cornell Law School, https://www .law.cornell.edu/uscode/text/8/1481.

21. The issuance of passports and the visa system are good examples of this. Citizens or individuals cannot just move around the globe willy-nilly. Extensive documentation is required that must clearly demonstrate which state you belong to and the reasons you are exiting that state and why you would wish to enter another state. John Torpey refers to this as the state's monopolization of the legitimate means of movement. See his fascinating book *The Invention of the Passport: Surveillance, Citizenship and the State* (Cambridge: Cambridge University Press, 2000). It wasn't until recently that the average Chinese citizen could apply for and acquire

a passport. There is also ample evidence to suggest that the government uses the issuance or denial of passports as a political means of control. An ethnic Han citizen can easily apply for one; a Tibetan, not so much the case. For more on this, see Andrew Jacobs, "No Exit: China Uses Passports as Political Cudgel," *New York Times*, February 22, 2013, http://www.nytimes.com/2013/02/23/world/asia/chinese-passports-seen-as -political-statement.html.

22. See, for example, Saskia Sassen, *Territory-Authority-Rights: From Medieval to Global Assemblages* (Princeton, N.J.: Princeton University Press, 2006), especially chaps. 6 and 7. Also see Linda Bosniak's work, such as "Citizenship Denationalized Symposium: The State of Citizenship," *Indian Journal of Global Legal Studies* 7, no. 2 (2000): 447–510, and "Universal Citizenship and the Problem of Alienage," *Northwestern University Law Review* 94, no. 3 (2000): 963–84. In the latter Bosniak explores the perception that rights and status-based paths to citizenship are obsolete. This perception is based in part on the idea (a false one, I would argue) that the basic rights of citizenship are universal. Bosniak counters this by contrasting alienage (noncitizens, or, as the nation-state prefers to say, "aliens") with this perceived universality.

23. See, for example, Jonathan Kaiman, "Razing History: The Tragic Story of a Beijing Neighborhood's Destruction," *Atlantic*, February 9, 2012, https://www.theatlantic.com/international/archive/2012/02/razing -history-the-tragic-story-of-a-beijing-neighborhoods-destruction /252760/.

24. The last sentence about human rights was only added in an amendment approved on March 14, 2004, no doubt to appease the United Nations.

25. Paul Kahn points out that Carl Schmitt believed that a world order in which potential enemies are feared cannot lend itself to transnational law. Paul Kahn, *Political Theology: Four New Chapters on the Concept of Sovereignty* (New York: Columbia University Press, 2011), 11. This is the reason that in the European Union no state within the union can see any of the other states as a potential enemy. This is the foundation of European citizenship. Today in Europe this is further complicated by the rise of far-right nationalism bordering on fascism.

26. Agamben, *Homo Sacer*, 170, 175.

27. Bruce Lincoln, *Holy Terrors: Thinking About Religion After September 11* (Chicago: University of Chicago Press, 2003), 67.

28. Ho-fung Hung makes the convincing argument that in our postcolonial world, China's investments in Africa amount to a form of neocolonialism. Ho-fung Hung, *The China Boom: Why China Will Not Rule the World* (New York: Columbia University Press, 2016), chap. 5. Other

scholars, like Ching Kwan Lee, push back on the term "neocolonialism," saying that it distracts from an empirical reality of China embarking on risky financial investments. See Ching Kwan Lee, *The Specter of Global China: Politics, Labor, and Foreign Investment in Africa* (Chicago: University of Chicago Press, 2018).

29. Basil Davidson, *The Black Man's Burden: Africa and the Curse of the Nation-State* (New York: Random House, 2002), 10.

30. See Leonard Thompson, *A History of South Africa* (New Haven, Conn.: Yale University Press, 2014), 210.

31. Article 80 of China's constitution stipulates: "The President of the People's Republic of China proclaims entering of the state of emergency." This can be done throughout the country or just in specific regions. It is the suspension of all regular laws as the state bends both the political and public sphere to its bidding. Paul Kahn challenges us, referring to the ability of the president of the United States to launch nuclear weapons at any time with legal review: "When we try to bring the reality of a president's world-destroying power under a theory of constitutional allocation of power, we are falling exactly within a puzzle that Schmitt raises: Is the exception a concept within or without the order of the law? Can a norm define the exception, or is it the other way round? How exactly is a decision that places itself outside of law nevertheless bound to law?" Kahn, *Political Theology*, 15. He goes on to say that if we make the exception an instance of the norm, we then lose the concept.

32. Working off Agamben, Flora Sapio argues that bare life "denotes a condition in which a person is totally at the mercy of raw power, as he has been made unable to enjoy the protection human rights could afford." Flora Sapio, *Sovereign Power and the Law in China* (Leiden: Brill, 2010), 18.

33. As Sapio rightly states: "Once the state of exception slowly becomes a steady condition of politics, all life potentially becomes bare life. The condition of bare life does not depend, then, on the existence of any given political system, but on the inherent capacity to be killed or abused." Sapio, *Sovereign Power and the Law in China*, 250.

34. Talal Asad, *On Suicide Bombing* (New York: Columbia University Press, 2007), 60.

35. Agamben, *Homo Sacer*, 142.

36. Agamben, in thinking through Walter Benjamin, writes:

> The violence exercised in the state of exception clearly neither preserves nor simply posits law, but rather conserves it in suspending it and posits it in excepting itself from it. . . . Sovereign violence

opens a zone of indistinction between law and nature, outside and inside, violence and law. And yet the sovereign is precisely the one who maintains the possibility of deciding on the two to the very degree that he renders them indistinguishable from each other. As long as the state of exception is distinguished from the normal case, the dialectic between the violence that posits law and the violence that preserves it is not truly broken, and the sovereign decision even appears simply as the medium in which the passage from the one to the other takes place.

The law is then suspended. Agamben, *Homo Sacer*, 64.

37. Arjun Appadurai, *Modernity at Large: Cultural Dimensions of Globalization* (Minneapolis: University of Minnesota Press, 1996), 31.

38. See much of Pierre Bourdieu's work. For example, in *Practical Reason: On the Theory of Action*, trans. Randall Johnson (Stanford, Calif.: Stanford University Press, 1998), Bourdieu writes of the social positions between agents (6) as being a relational concept, subject to their *habitus* (tastes and distinctions) and their location in what he calls the "field of power," defined "as the space of play within which the holders of capital (of different species) struggle in particular for power over the state, that is, over the statist capital granting power over the different species of capital and over their reproduction (particularly through the school system)" (42). For Bourdieu, the "field of power" is not the same as the political field. (The latter will have different but often overlapping networks of relations that express to some extent Foucault's notion of governmentality.) The field of power is about the different kinds of capital held by agents as they attempt to dominate a corresponding field. As for the school system mentioned above, Bourdieu has on several occasions cited Thomas Bernhard: "School is the state school where young people are turned into state persons and thus into nothing other than henchmen of the state" (34). A bit blunt, but we might wish to think about the Chinese educational system in this regard, along with article 19 of the constitution.

39. Agamben will ask a different question, one beyond the scope of our study: "Why does power need glory?" See Giorgio Agamben, *The Kingdom and the Glory*, trans. Lorenzo Chiesa with Matteo Mandarini (Stanford, Calif.: Stanford University Press, 2011). Agamben will juxtapose power as government and effective management up against power as ceremonial and liturgical regality. Here, too, we will find *relegere*, the meticulousness of state ritual. The negligence that Agamben speaks of is critical. Negligence leads to an undoing of the national fabric and an

undermining of state power that cannot go unchecked. To prevent that negligence, states tend to watch their citizens closely. Think of the National Security Agency scandal of the United States government spying on its own citizens in 2014. The steady gaze of the state ensures a link between its territorialization and the process of sacralizing all in its territory. It is through the watching and the tactical deployment of state police to quell its citizenry—representatives of the sanctity of the state—that disputed territory can be immediately and violently reclaimed if need be and thus be maintained. Following the 2008 Lhasa riots, thousands of cameras were installed in monasteries, mosques, hotels, and public sites. By the next year China's camera surveillance market was estimated to be over $1.4 billion, with an expected annual growth of 20 percent or more. Michael Wines, "In Restive Chinese Area, Cameras Keep Watch," *New York Times*, August 2, 2010, http://www.nytimes.com/2010/08/03/world/asia/03china.html. In Urumqi, Xinjiang province, China's periphery and home to most Uighurs, 47,000 cameras keep an eye on the citizenry. In Beijing, 470,000 cameras and counting operate around the clock. Yet these numbers pale in comparison to the United States and especially Britain. See, for instance, Vicki Haddock, "Public Eye / Hundreds of Thousands of Surveillance Cameras Across America Track Our Behavior Every Day," *SFGATE*, October 17, 2004, http://articles.sfgate.com/2004-10-17/opinion/17450294_1_surveillance-cameras-panopticon-cell-phones. In the United Kingdom, surveillance cameras number approximately 4.2 million, or about one for every fourteen people. "Britain Is "Surveillance Society,'" *BBC News*, November 2, 2006, http://news.bbc.co.uk/2/hi/uk_news/6108496.stm. See also Anna Mitchell and Larry Diamond, "China's Surveillance State Should Scare Everyone," *Atlantic*, February 2, 2018, https://www.theatlantic.com/international/archive/2018/02/china-surveillance/552203/. Paul Mozur suggests that China is attempting to ultimately monitor all 1.4 billion of its citizens. Technology is not the great "democratizer" but really about control of the citizenry. See "Inside China's Dystopian Dreams," *New York Times*, July 8, 2018, https://www.nytimes.com/2018/07/08/business/china-surveillance-technology.html.

40. Butler and Spivak, *Who Sings the Nation-State*, 5.
41. Butler and Spivak, *Who Sings the Nation-State*, 18.
42. Anthony C. Yu, *State and Religion in China* (Chicago: Open Court, 2005), 146.
43. Here I am tempted to quote Karl Marx, but Agamben already did that during an interview: "The hopeless conditions of the society in which I live fill me with hope."

44. I am intrigued by Spivak's utopian quest, which is to see regionalism as a way to push back from the inevitability of the nation-state. (Africa could use this.)

45. Ian Buruma, *Taming the Gods: Religion and Democracy on Three Continents* (Princeton, N.J.: Princeton University Press, 2010), 46.

Bibliography

Agamben, Giorgio. "Beyond Human Rights." *Open*, no. 15 (2008), *Social Engineering*.
——. *Homo Sacer: Sovereign Power and Bare Life*. Trans. Daniel Heller-Roazen. Stanford, Calif.: Stanford University Press, 1998.
——. *The Kingdom and the Glory*. Trans. Lorenzo Chiesa with Matteo Mandarini. Stanford, Calif.: Stanford University Press, 2011.
——. *Profanations*. Trans. Jeff Fort. New York: Zone Books, 2007.
Almond, Philip C. *The British Discovery of Buddhism*. Cambridge: Cambridge University Press, 1988.
Anand, Dibyesh. "Colonization with Chinese Characteristics: Politics of (In) Security in Xinjiang and Tibet." *Central Asian Survey*, November 2018. https://doi.org/10.1080/02634937.2018.1534801.
Anderson, Benedict. *Imagined Communities: Reflections on the Origin and Spread of Nationalism*. New York: Verso, 1998.
Appadurai, Arjun. *Modernity at Large: Cultural Dimensions of Globalization*. Minneapolis: University of Minnesota Press, 1996.
Arendt, Hannah. *The Human Condition*. Chicago: University of Chicago Press, 1958.
——. *The Origins of Totalitarianism*. New York: Harcourt Brace, 1951.
Asad, Talal. *Formations of the Secular: Christianity, Islam, Modernity*. Stanford, Calif.: Stanford University Press, 2003.
——. *Genealogies of Religion: Discipline and Reasons of Power in Christianity and Islam*. Baltimore: Johns Hopkins University Press, 1993.
——. *On Suicide Bombing*. New York: Columbia University Press, 2007.
Ashiwa, Yoshiko, and David L. Wank. *Making Religion, Making the State: The Politics of Religion in Modern China*. Stanford, Calif.: Stanford University Press, 2009.

Baines, Gary F. *South Africa's 'Border War:' Contested Narratives and Conflicting Memories*. London: Bloomsbury Academic, 2014.

Barlow, Tani, ed. *Formations of Colonial Modernity*. Durham, N.C.: Duke University Press, 1997.

Barrow, John. *An Account of Travels Into the Interior of Southern Africa, in the Years 1797 and 1798*. London: Cadell and Davies, 1801.

———. *Travels in China*. 1804. Reprint, London: Cadell and Davies, 1847.

Barthes, Roland. *Mythologies*. Trans. Annette Lavers. New York: Farrar, Straus & Giroux, 1972.

Bataille, Georges. *Theory of Religion*. Trans. Robert Hurley. New York: Zone Books, 1989.

Bays, Daniel H. *A New History of Christianity in China*. Chichester, U.K.: Wiley-Blackwell, 2012.

Beach, Harlan P. *Dawn on the Hills of T'ang; or, Missions in China*. New York: Student Volunteer Movement for Foreign Missions, c. 1898.

Beckwith, Christopher. *Empires of the Silk Road: A History of Central Eurasia from the Bronze Age to the Present*. Princeton, N.J.: Princeton University Press, 2009.

Bell, Catherine. *Ritual: Perspectives and Dimensions*. New York: Oxford University Press, 1997.

———. *Ritual Theory, Ritual Practice*. New York: Oxford University Press, 1992.

Bin, Xu. *The Politics of Compassion: The Sichuan Earthquake and Civic Engagement in China*. Stanford, Calif.: Stanford University Press, 2017.

Bosniak, Linda. "Citizenship Denationalized Symposium: The State of Citizenship." *Indian Journal of Global Legal Studies* 7, no. 2 (2000): 447–510.

———. "Universal Citizenship and the Problem of Alienage." *Northwestern University Law Review* 94, no. 3 (2000): 963–84.

Bourdieu, Pierre. *Practical Reason: On the Theory of Action*. Trans. Randall Johnson. Stanford, Calif.: Stanford University Press, 1998.

Brown, Wendy. *Walled States, Waning Sovereignty*. New York: Zone Books, 2010.

Buruma, Ian. *Taming the Gods: Religion and Democracy on Three Continents*. Princeton, N.J.: Princeton University Press, 2010.

Bush, Richard C. "8 Key Things to Notice from Xi Jinping's New Year Speech on Taiwan." Brookings Institution, January 7, 2019. https://www.brookings .edu/blog/order-from-chaos/2019/01/07/8-key-things-to-notice-from-xi -jinpings-new-year-speech-on-taiwan/.

Buswell, Robert E., Jr., and Donald S. Lopez, Jr., eds. *The Princeton Dictionary of Buddhism*. Princeton, N.J.: Princeton University Press, 2014.

Butler, Judith, and Gayatri Chakravorty Spivak. *Who Sings the Nation-State: Language, Politics, Belonging*. Kolkata: Seagull Books, 2011.

Cabezón, José Ignacio. "State Control of Tibetan Buddhist Monasticism in the People's Republic of China." In *Chinese Religiosities: Afflictions of Modernity and State Formation*, ed. Mayfair Mei-hui Yang. Berkeley: University of California Press, 2008.

Campany, Robert Ford. "On the Very Idea of Religions (in the Modern West and in Early Medieval China)." *History of Religions* 42, no. 4 (May 2003): 287–319.

Casanova, José. *Public Religions in the Modern World*. Chicago: University of Chicago Press, 1994.

Cavanaugh, William. *The Myth of Religious Violence: Secular Ideology and the Roots of Modern Conflict*. New York: Oxford University Press, 2009.

Cendrowski, Scott. "The Unusual Journey of China's Newest Oil Baron." *Fortune*, September 28, 2016. http://fortune.com/2016/09/28/cefc-ye-jianming -40-under-40/.

Césaire, Aimé. *Discourse on Colonialism*. Trans. Joan Pinkham. New York: Monthly Review Press, 1972.

Chidester, David. "The Church of Baseball, the Fetish of Coca-Cola, and the Potlatch of Rock 'n' Roll: Theoretical Models for the Study of Religion in American Popular Culture." *Journal of the American Academy of Religion* 64, no. 4 (Winter 1996): 743–65.

——. *Empire of Religion: Imperialism and Comparative Religion*. Chicago: University of Chicago Press, 2014.

——. *Religion: Material Dynamics*. Oakland: University of California Press, 2019.

——. *Savage Systems: Colonialism and Comparative Religion in Southern Africa*. Charlottesville: University of Virginia Press, 1996.

——. *Shots in the Streets: Violence and Religion in South Africa*. Boston: Beacon Press, 1991.

——. *Wild Religion: Tracking the Sacred in South Africa*. Berkeley: University of California Press, 2012.

"China Global Investment Tracker." American Enterprise Institute. http:// www.aei.org/china-global-investment-tracker/.

Coetzee, J. M. *Dusklands*. New York: Penguin Books, 1985.

Constitution Acts of Canada. http://laws.justice.gc.ca/PDF/CONST_E.pdf.

Constitution of Australia. http://www.aph.gov.au/About_Parliament/Senate /Powers_practice_n_procedures/Constitution.

Constitution of Japan. https://japan.kantei.go.jp/constitution_and_govern ment_of_japan/constitution_e.html.

Constitution of the Kingdom of the Netherlands. http://www.government.nl /documents-and-publications/regulations/2012/10/18/the-constitution-of -the-kingdom-of-the-netherlands-2008.html.

Constitution of Lebanon. http://www.lebanon-elections.org/Modules/Docu
  ment/UploadFile/3368_15,04,YYConstitution%20-%20English.pdf.
Constitution of Mexico. http://www.oas.org/juridico/mla/en/mex/en_mex-int
  -text-const.pdf.
Constitution of the People's Republic of China (Chinese). http://www.gov.cn
  /gongbao/content/2004/content_62714.htm.
Constitution of the People's Republic of China (English). http://www.gov.cn
  /english/2005-08/05/content_20813.htm.
Constitution of the Republic of Chile. http://confinder.richmond.edu/admin
  /docs/Chile.pdf.
Constitution of the Republic of China. http://law.moj.gov.tw/Eng/LawClass
  /LawAll.aspx?PCode=A0000001.
Constitution of the Republic of South Africa. http://www.justice.gov.za
  /legislation/constitution/SAConstitution-web-eng.pdf.
Constitution of the Republic of Turkey. https://global.tbmm.gov.tr/docs
  /constitution_en.pdf.
Constitution of the United States of America. https://www.archives.gov
  /founding-docs/constitution-transcript.
Cook, Sarah, and Leeshai Lemish. "The 610 Office: Policing the Chinese
  Spirit." *China Brief* 11, no. 17 (September 16, 2011). https://jamestown.org
  /program/the-610-office-policing-the-chinese-spirit/.
Culp, Robert. *Articulating Citizenship: Civic Education and Student Politics in
  Southeastern China, 1912–1940*. Cambridge, Mass.: Harvard University
  Press, 2007.
Dauphinee, Elizabeth. *The Politics of Exile*. New York: Routledge, 2013.
Davidson, Basil. *The Black Man's Burden: Africa and the Curse of the Nation-
  State*. New York: Random House, 2002.
Dean, William. *The China Mission*. New York: Sheldon, 1859.
Declaration of Independence. https://www.archives.gov/founding-docs
  /declaration-transcript.
Declaration of the Rights of Man. http://avalon.law.yale.edu/18th_century
  /rightsof.asp.
Deleuze, Gilles, and Félix Guattari. *A Thousand Plateaus: Capitalism and
  Schizophrenia*. Trans. Brian Massumi. London: Continuum, 1992.
Diamant, Neil J. "What the (Expletive) Is a 'Constitution'?! Ordinary Cadres
  Confront the 1954 PRC Draft Constitution." *Journal of Chinese History* 2,
  no. 1 (January 2018): 169–90.
Di Cosmo, Nicola. *Ancient China and Its Enemies: The Rise of Nomadic Power
  in East Asian History*. New York: Cambridge University Press, 2004.
Dikötter, Frank. *The Discourse of Race in Modern China*. Oxford: Oxford Uni-
  versity Press, 2015.

Doniger, Wendy. *The Implied Spider: Politics and Theology in Myth*. New York: Columbia University Press, 1999.

Douglas, Mary. *How Institutions Think*. Syracuse, N.Y.: Syracuse University Press, 1986.

Duara, Prasenjit. "Religion and Citizenship in China and the Diaspora." In *Chinese Religiosities: Afflictions of Modernity and State Formation*, ed. Mayfair Mei-hui Yang, 43–64. Berkeley: University of California Press, 2008.

——. *Rescuing History from the Nation: Questioning Narratives of Modern China*. Chicago: University of Chicago Press, 1997.

DuBois, Thomas David. "Hegemony, Imperialism, and the Construction of Religion in East and Southeast Asia." *History and Theory* 44 (December 2005).

——. *Religion and the Making of Modern East Asia*. Cambridge: Cambridge University Press, 2011.

Durkheim, Émile. *The Elementary Form of Religious Life*. Trans. Carol Cosman. New York: Oxford University Press, 2001.

Eco, Umberto. *The Infinity of Lists: An Illustrated Essay*. New York: Rizzoli, 2009.

Elliott, Mark C. *Emperor Qianlong: Son of Heaven, Man of the World*. London: Pearson, 2009.

Fitzgerald, Timothy. *Discourse on Civility and Barbarity: A Critical History of Religion and Related Categories*. New York: Oxford University Press, 2007.

——. "Encompassing Religion, Privatized Religions, and the Invention of Modern Politics." In *Religion and the Secular: Historical and Colonial Formations*, ed. Timothy Fitzgerald. London: Routledge Taylor and Francis Group, 2007.

Fogel, Joshua A., and Peter G. Zarrow. *Imagining the People: Chinese Intellectuals and the Concept of Citizenship, 1890–1920*. Armonk, N.Y.: M. E. Sharpe, 1997.

Foucault, Michel. *The Order of Things: An Archaeology of the Human Sciences*. New York: Random House, 1970.

——. *"Society Must Be Defended": Lectures at the College de France, 1975–76*. Trans. David Macey. New York: Picador, 2003.

——. "The Subject and Power." *Critical Inquiry* 8, no. 4 (1982).

"Full Text of Xi Jinping's Report at 19th CPC National Congress." *Xinhua News Agency*, October 18, 2017. http://www.xinhuanet.com/english/special /2017-11/03/c_136725942.htm.

Gellner, Ernest. *Nations and Nationalism*. Ithaca, N.Y.: Cornell University Press, 1983.

Girard, René. *Violence and the Sacred*. Trans. Patrick Gregory. Baltimore: Johns Hopkins University Press, 1977.

Goldman, Merle, and Elizabeth J. Perry, eds. *Changing Meanings of Citizenship in Modern China*. Cambridge, Mass.: Harvard University Press, 2002.

Goossaert, Vincent. "The Destruction of Immoral Temples in Qing China." *Journal of Chinese Studies*, ICS Visiting Professor Lecture Series no. 2 (2009).

———. "1898: The Beginning of the End for Chinese Religion." *Journal of Asian Studies* 65, no. 2 (2006): 307–36.

———. "Republican Church Engineering: The National Religious Associations in 1912 China." In *Chinese Religiosities: Afflictions of Modernity and State Formation*, ed. Mayfair Mei-hui Yang. Berkeley: University of California Press, 2008.

Goossaert, Vincent, and David A. Palmer. *The Religious Question in Modern China*. Chicago: University of Chicago Press, 2011.

Gunn, Jeremy T. "The Complexity of Religion and the Definition of 'Religion' in International Law." *Harvard Human Rights Journal* 16 (Spring).

Hamburger, Philip. *Separation of Church and State*. Cambridge, Mass.: Harvard University Press, 2004.

Han, Dayuan. *1954 nian xianfa yu xin Zhongguo xianzheng* 1954 年宪法与新中国宪政 (The 1954 constitution and the new constitution of China). Changsha: Hunan renmin chubanshe, 2004.

Hansen, Valerie. *The Silk Road: A New History*. New York: Oxford University Press, 2012.

Hardacre, Helen. *Shinto and the State: 1868–1988*. Princeton, N.J.: Princeton University Press, 1991.

Harrison, Henrietta. *The Making of the Republican Citizen: Political Ceremonies and Symbols in China, 1911–1929*. New York: Oxford University Press, 1999.

Hegel, Georg W. F. *The Philosophy of History*. Trans. J. Sibree. Minneapolis: University of Minnesota Press, 1996.

Hevia, James. *Cherishing Men from Afar: Qing Guest Ritual and the Macartney Embassy of 1793*. Durham, N.C.: Duke University Press, 1995.

———. *English Lessons: The Pedagogy of Imperialism in Nineteenth-Century China*. Durham, N.C.: Duke University Press, 2003.

Hopgood, Stephen. *The Endtimes of Human Rights*. Ithaca, N.Y.: Cornell University Press, 2013.

———. "Human Rights: Past Their Sell-by Date." *Open Democracy*, June 18, 2013. http://www.opendemocracy.net/openglobalrights/stephen-hopgood/human-rights-past-their-sell-by-date.

Hopkirk, Peter. *Foreign Devils on the Silk Road: The Search for the Lost Treasures of Central Asia*. London: John Murray, 1980.

——. *The Great Game: The Struggle for Empire in Central Asia*. Tokyo: Kodansha, 1992.

"How Leaders Are Made." *YouTube*, October 15, 2013. https://www.youtube .com/watch?v=M7340_17H_A.

Huang, Chun-Chieh. "The Idea of 'Zhongguo' and Its Transformation in Early Modern Japan and Contemporary Taiwan." *Nihon Kan bungaku kenkyū* (Japan-Han literary research), no. 2 (March 2007): 398–408.

Hung, Ho-fung. *The China Boom: Why China Will Not Rule the World*. New York: Columbia University Press, 2016.

Hunt, Jane. *The Gospel of Gentility: American Women Missionaries in Turn-of-the-Century China*. New Haven, Conn.: Yale University Press, 1989.

Hunt, Lynn. *Inventing Human Rights*. New York: Norton, 2007.

Hurd, Elizabeth Shakman. *Beyond Religious Freedom: The New Global Politics of Religion*. Princeton, N.J.: Princeton University Press, 2017.

Jacques, Martin. *When China Rules the World: The End of the Western World and the Birth of a New Global Order*. New York: Penguin Books, 2009.

Jay, Martin. *Downcast Eyes: The Denigration of Vision in Twentieth-Century French Thought*. Berkeley: University of California Press, 1993.

Josephson, Jason Ananda. *The Invention of Religion in Japan*. Chicago: University of Chicago Press, 2012.

Kahn, Paul W. *Political Theology: Four New Chapters on the Concept of Sovereignty*. New York: Columbia University Press, 2011.

Kaiman, Jonathan. "Razing History: The Tragic Story of a Beijing Neighborhood's Destruction." *Atlantic*, February 9, 2012. https://www.theatlantic .com/international/archive/2012/02/razing-history-the-tragic-story-of-a -beijing-neighborhoods-destruction/252760/.

Katz, Paul. *Religion in China and Its Modern Fate*. Lebanon, N.H.: Brandeis University Press, 2014.

Kuhn, Philip A. *Origins of the Modern Chinese State*. Stanford, Calif.: Stanford University Press, 2003.

Kuo, Ya-Pei. "Redeploying Confucius: The Imperial State Dreams of the Nation, 1902–1911." In *Chinese Religiosities: Afflictions of Modernity and State Formation*, ed. Mayfair Mei-hui Yang. Berkeley: University of California Press, 2008.

Lagerwey, John. *China: A Religious State*. Hong Kong: Hong Kong University Press, 2010.

Latour, Bruno. "Visualization and Cognition: Drawing Things Together." In *Knowledge and Society: Studies in the Sociology of Culture Past and Present*, ed. H. Kuklick and Elizabeth Long. Vol. 6. Greenwich, Conn.: JAI Press, 1986, 1–40. http://www.bruno-latour.fr/sites/default/files/21-DRAWING -THINGS-TOGETHER-GB.pdf.

———. *We Have Never Been Modern.* Trans. Catherine Porter. Cambridge, Mass.: Harvard University Press, 1993.

Lee, Ching Kwan. *The Specter of Global China: Politics, Labor, and Foreign Investment in Africa.* Chicago: University of Chicago Press, 2018.

Lee, Leo Ou-fan. *Shanghai Modern: The Flowering of a New Urban Culture in China.* Cambridge, Mass.: Harvard University Press, 1999.

Lefebvre, Henri. *The Production of Space.* Trans. Donald Nicholson-Smith. Oxford: Blackwell, 1974.

Legge, James. *The Four Books: Confucian Analects, the Great Learning, the Doctrine of the Mean, and the Works of Mencius.* Taipei: SMC, 1991.

———. *The Shoo King or the Book of Historical Documents.* Taipei: SMC, 1991.

Liang, Qichao. "Li xianfa yi 立憲法議 (Discussing constitutionalism). https://zh.wikisource.org/zh-hant/立憲法議.

Lincoln, Bruce. *Discourse and the Construction of Society: Comparative Studies of Myth, Ritual, and Classification.* Oxford: Oxford University Press 1989.

———. *Holy Terrors: Thinking About Religion After September 11.* Chicago: University of Chicago Press, 2003.

Liu, Lydia H. *The Clash of Empires: The Invention of China in Modern World Making.* Cambridge, Mass.: Harvard University Press, 2004.

Liu, Xinru. *The Silk Road in World History.* Oxford: Oxford University Press, 2010.

Long, Charles. *Significations, Signs, Symbols, and Images in the Interpretation of Religion.* Aurora, Colo.: Fortress Press, 1986.

Lopez, Jr., Donald S. "Belief." In *Critical Terms for Religious Studies,* ed. Mark C. Taylor. Chicago: Chicago University Press, 1998.

Lovell, Julia. *The Opium War: Drugs, Dreams, and the Making of Modern China.* New York: Overlook Press, 2014.

MacInnis, Donald E. *Religion in China Today: Policy and Practice.* New York: Orbis Books, 1989.

Madsen, Richard. *China's Catholics: Tragedy and Hope in an Emerging Civil Society.* Berkeley: University of California Press, 1998.

Mahmood, Saba. *Religious Difference in a Secular Age: A Minority Report.* Princeton, N.J.: Princeton University Press, 2015.

Marshall, T. H. *Citizenship and Social Class.* Cambridge: Cambridge University Press, 1950.

Masuzawa, Tomoko. *The Invention of World Religions: Or, How European Universalism Was Preserved in the Language of Pluralism.* Chicago: University of Chicago Press, 2005.

Maus, Marcel. *The Gift: The Form and Reason for Exchange in Archaic Societies.* Trans. W. D. Hall. London: Routledge, 1990.

McCutcheon, Russell T. *The Discipline of Religion: Structure, Meaning, Rhetoric.* London: Routledge, 2003.

Millward, James A. *Eurasian Crossroads: A History of Xinjiang.* New York: Columbia University Press, 2007.

Milne, William C. *Life in China.* London: Routledge, 1857.

Ministry of Foreign Affairs, People's Republic of China. "Position Paper of the Government of the People's Republic of China on the Matter of Jurisdiction in the South China Sea Arbitration Initiated by the Republic of the Philippines." December 7, 2014. http://www.fmprc.gov.cn/mfa_eng /zxxx_662805/t1217147.shtml.

Ministry of Foreign Affairs, Republic of China (Taiwan). "Position Paper on ROC Sovereignty Over the South China Sea Islands and Their Surrounding Waters, and on the South China Sea Peace Initiative, Republic of China (Taiwan)." March 21, 2016. https://www.mofa.gov.tw/Upload /RelFile/643/156142/Position%20Paper%20on%20ROC%20Sovereignty %20over%20the%20South%20China%20Sea%20Islands%20and%20Their %20Surrounding%20Waters,%20and%20on%20the%20South%20China %20Sea%20Peace%20Initiative.pdf.

Mishra, Pankaj. "The Last Dalai Lama." *New York Times* magazine, December 1, 2015. https://www.nytimes.com/2015/12/06/magazine/the-last-dalai -lama.html.

——. *Temptations of the West: How to Be Modern in India, Pakistan, Tibet, and Beyond.* New York: Picador, 2006.

Mitchell, Anna, and Larry Diamond. "China's Surveillance State Should Scare Everyone." *Atlantic*, February 2, 2018. https://www.theatlantic.com /international/archive/2018/02/china-surveillance/552203/.

Nedostup, Rebecca. "Ritual Competition and the Modernizing Nation-State." In *Chinese Religiosities: Afflictions of Modernity and State Formation*, ed. Mayfair Mei-hui Yang. Berkeley: University of California Press, 2008.

——. *Superstitious Regimes: Religion and the Politics of Chinese Modernity.* Cambridge, Mass.: Harvard University Press, 2009.

"A New Platform for Cross-Region Cooperation." *Belt and Road Initiative.* 2017. http://www.beltandroad.gov.hk/overview.html.

Nylan, Michael. "Talk About 'Barbarians' in Antiquity." *Philosophy East & West* 62, no. 4 (2012).

Otto, Rudolf. *The Idea of the Holy: An Inquiry Into the Non-Rational Factor in the Idea of the Divine and Its Relation to the Rational.* London: Oxford University Press, 1936.

Ownby, David. *Falun Gong and the Future of China.* New York: Oxford University Press, 2008.

Palmer, David A. "Heretical Doctrines, Reactionary Secret Societies, Evil Cults: Labeling Heterodoxy in Twentieth-Century China." In *Chinese Religiosities: Afflictions of Modernity and State Formation*, ed. Mayfair Mei-hui Yang. Berkeley: University of California Press, 2008.

Pong, David. *Shen Pao-Chen and China's Modernization in the Nineteenth Century*. New York: Cambridge University Press, 1994.

Poon, Shuk-wa. *Negotiating Religion in Modern China: State and Common People in Guangzhou, 1900–1937*. Hong Kong: Chinese University Press, 2011.

Potter, Pitman B. "Belief in Control: Regulation of Religion in China." In *Religion in China Today*, ed. Daniel L. Overmyer. Cambridge: Cambridge University Press, 2003.

Powers, John. *The Buddha Party: How the People's Republic of China Works to Define and Control Tibetan Buddhism*. New York: Oxford University Press, 2017.

"The Present Conditions of Religion in China." *Chinese Government White Paper*. http://www.china.org.cn/e-white/Freedom/f-1.htm.

"President Xi Jinping: Why I Proposed the Belt and Road." *YouTube*, May 12, 2017. https://www.youtube.com/watch?v=hNKTbMx8PFk.

Preziosi, Donald. *Brain of the Earth's Body: Art, Museums, and the Phantasms of Modernity*. Minneapolis: University of Minnesota Press, 2003.

Preziosi, Donald, and Claire Farago, eds. *Grasping the World: The Idea of the Museum*. Aldershot, U.K.: Ashgate, 2004.

Quang, Nguyen, Minh. "The Bitter Legacy of the 1979 China-Vietnam War." *Diplomat*, February 23, 2017. https://thediplomat.com/2017/02/the-bitter-legacy-of-the-1979-china-vietnam-war/.

Redden, Elizabeth. "New Scrutiny for Confucius Institutes." *Inside Higher Ed*, April 26, 2017. https://www.insidehighered.com/news/2017/04/26/report-confucius-institutes-finds-no-smoking-guns-enough-concerns-recommend-closure.

Reinders, Eric. *Borrowed Gods and Foreign Bodies: Christian Missionaries Imagine Chinese Religion*. Berkeley: University of California Press, 2004.

Sapio, Flora. *Sovereign Power and the Law in China*. Leiden: Brill, 2010.

Sassen, Saskia. *Territory-Authority-Rights: From Medieval to Global Assemblages*. Princeton, N.J.: Princeton University Press, 2006.

Schmidt, Leigh Eric. *Hearing Things: Religion, Illusion, and the American Enlightenment*. Cambridge, Mass.: Harvard University Press, 2000.

Schmitt, Carl. *Political Theology: Four Chapters on the Concept of Sovereignty*. Trans. George Schwab. Chicago: University of Chicago Press, 2006.

Schmitz, Rob, and Julia Simon. "The Belt, The Road, and the Money." *NPR, Planet Money* podcast, no. 837, April 20, 2018. https://www.npr.org/templates/transcript/transcript.php?storyId=604462996.

Smith, Jonathan Z. *Imagining Religion: From Babylon to Jonestown.* Chicago: University of Chicago Press, 1982.

——. "Religion, Religions, Religious." In *Critical Terms for Religious Studies,* ed. Mark C. Taylor. Chicago: University of Chicago Press, 1998.

Smith, Wilfred Cantwell. *The Meaning and End of Religion.* New York: Macmillan, 1962.

Soothill, W. E. *A Mission in China.* Edinburgh: Oliphant, Anderson & Ferrier, 1907.

Spence, Jonathan D. *The Search for Modern China.* New York: Norton, 1990.

Sperling, Elliot. "Awe and Submission: A Tibetan Aristocrat at the Court of Qianlong." *International History Review* 20, no. 2 (June 1998).

——. "Reincarnation and the Golden Urn in the 19th Century: The Recognition of the 8th Panchen Lama." In *Studies on the History and Literature of Tibet and the Himalaya,* ed. Roberto Vitali. Kathmandu, Nepal: Vajra, 2012.

Spivak, Gayatri Chakravorty. *Nationalism and the Imagination.* London: Seagull Books, 2010.

Strassberg, Richard E. *A Chinese Bestiary: Strange Creatures from the Guideways Through Mountains and Seas.* Berkeley: University of California Press, 2002.

Sullivan, Winnifred Fallers. *The Impossibility of Religious Freedom.* Princeton, N.J.: Princeton University Press, 2007.

Sullivan, Winnifred Fallers, Elizabeth Shakman Hurd, Saba Mahmood, and Peter G. Danchin, eds. *Politics of Religious Freedom.* Chicago: University of Chicago Press, 2015.

Taylor, Charles. *A Secular Age.* Cambridge, Mass.: Belknap Press of Harvard University Press, 2007.

Thompson, Leonard. *A History of South Africa.* New Haven, Conn.: Yale University Press, 2014.

Tong, James W. *Revenge of the Forbidden City: The Suppression of the Falungong in China, 1999–2005.* Oxford: Oxford University Press, 2009.

Torpey, John. *The Invention of the Passport: Surveillance, Citizenship and the State.* Cambridge: Cambridge University Press, 2000.

United Nations. Convention on the Law of the Sea. http://www.un.org/depts /los/convention_agreements/texts/unclos/unclos_e.pdf.

Van der Veer, Peter. *Imperial Encounters: Religion and Modernity in India and Britain.* Princeton, N.J.: Princeton University Press, 2001.

Vogel, Ezra F. *Deng Xiaoping and the Transformation of China.* Cambridge, Mass.: Belknap Press of Harvard University Press, 2011.

Walsh, Michael J. *Sacred Economies: Buddhist Monasticism and Territoriality in Medieval China.* New York: Columbia University Press, 2010.

———. "States of Exception: The Violence of Territoriality, Sacrality, and Religion in China-Tibet Relations." *Journal of Religion and Violence* 1, no.1 (Spring 2013): 60–82.

Wang, Ermin 王爾敏. "'Zhongguo' mingcheng suyuan jiqi jindai quanshi" 中國'名稱溯源及其 近代詮釋 (On the origins of the term "Zhongguo" and its modern interpretations). In *Zhongguo jindai sixiang shi lun* 中國近代思想史論 (Discussions of modern Chinese history). Taipei: n.p., 1977.

Wang, Hui. *China from Empire to Nation-State*. Cambridge, Mass.: Harvard University Press, 2014.

———. *Xiandai Zhongguo sixiang de xingqi* 现代中国思想的兴起 (The rise of modern Chinese thought). Beijing: Shenghuo dushu xinzhi sanlian shudian, 2004.

Wang, Zheng. *Never Forget National Humiliation: Historical Memory in Chinese Politics and Foreign Relations*. New York: Columbia University Press, 2012.

Weber, Max. "Politics as a Vocation." In *The Vocation Lectures*, ed. David Owen and Tracy B. Strong, trans. Rodney Livingstone. Indianapolis: Hackett, 2004.

Westad, Odd Arne. *Restless Empire: China and the World Since 1750*. New York: Basic Books, 2012.

Wheaton, Henry. *Elements of International Law*. 1836. Reprint Oxford, 1936.

Wilder, Dennis. "China's Religions (Re)Awakening and the Impact of Religion on Chinese Society." *Brookings Institution*, April 6, 2009. https://www.brookings.edu/wp-content/uploads/2012/04/20090406_china.pdf.

Wilhelm, Richard, trans. *The I Ching or Book of Changes*. Translated into English by Cary F. Baynes. 3rd ed. Princeton, N.J.: Princeton University Press, 1967.

Winterbotham, William. *An Historical, Geographical, and Philosophical View of the Chinese Empire*. London: Ridgway & Button, 1795.

Wydra, Harald. *Politics and the Sacred*. Cambridge: Cambridge University Press, 2015.

Ye, Xiaowen. "China's Religions: Retrospect and Prospect." Address at Chung Chi College of Chinese University of Hong Kong, February 19, 2001. http://www.china.org.cn/english/features/45466.htm.

Yu, Anthony C. *State and Religion in China*. Chicago: Open Court, 2005.

Yu Hua. *China in Ten Words*. Trans. Allan H. Barr. New York: Anchor Books, 2011.

Zarrow, Peter. *China in War and Revolution, 1895–1949*. London: Routledge, 2005.

———. "Constitutionalism and the Imagination of the State: Official Views of Political Reform in the Late Qing," in *Creating Chinese Modernity:*

Knowledge and Everyday Life, 1900–1940, ed. Peter Zarrow. New York: Peter Lang, 2006.

——. "Liang Qichao and the Conceptualization of 'Race' in Late Qing China." *Bulletin of the Institute of Modern History*, Academia Sinica 52 (June 2006): 113–64.

Zenz, Adrian, and James Leibold. "Chen Quanguo: The Strongman Behind Beijing's Securitization Strategy in Tibet and Xinjiang." Jamestown Foundation, September 21, 2017. https://jamestown.org/program/chen-quang uo-the-strongman-behind-beijings-securitization-strategy-in-tibet-and -xinjiang/.

Zhang, Qianfan. *The Constitution of China: A Contextual Analysis*. Oxford: Hart, 2012.

Zito, Angela. *Of Body and Brush: Grand Sacrifice as Text/Performance in Eighteenth-Century China*. Chicago: University of Chicago Press, 1997.

Index

International Religious Freedom
Act (IRFA) (1998), 70, 184*n*25
inviolate: citizenship and, 139;
constitutions as expression of,
42; definitions of, 56; property
as, 59, 181*n*50; ritual purification
and, xviii; ruler as, 59, 181*n*51;
sacralization and, xvii, xix, xx,
22, 152; sovereignty and, xxi; in
worldwide constitutions, 56–59,
181*nn*49–51. *See also* sacred state
territory
Islam, 85, 96, 128, 145, 184*n*29,
185*n*38

Jacques, Martin, 175–76*n*80
Japan: Christians in, 182*n*8;
constitution (current), 48, 58;
guomin term and, 202*n*16;
imperialism, 3, 38, 39, 62–63;
Meiji constitution, 38, 39, 46, 54;
South China Sea sovereignty
claims, 4; state Shinto, 63–64,
191–92*n*26
Johnson, Ian, 200*n*48
Josephson, Jason Ananda, 63
Judaism, 67–68, 185*n*38

Kahn, Paul, 204*n*25
Kangxi emperor, 118
Kang Youwei, 38, 39–40, 64, 103,
178*n*15
Kant, Immanuel, 134, 151
Katz, Paul, 189–90*n*13
Kuhn, Philip, 39, 129–30, 205*n*31
Kuo, Ya-pei, 40

Lagerwey, John, 15, 18, 164*n*31,
171*n*51
Lao Jun, 67
Last Emperor, The, 109, 115, 195*n*1

Latour, Bruno, 117
Lebanon, 52–53
Lee, Ching Kwan, 205*n*28
Lee Teng-hui, 22
Lefebvre, Henri, 6
Legge, James, 170*n*43
Leviathan (Hobbes), 136
Lhasa riots (2008), 207*n*39
Liang Qichao, 38–39, 40, 64, 163*n*28,
179*n*22, 193*n*40, 203*n*16
Li Keqiang, 83
Lincoln, Bruce, 43, 146–47
Lin Zexu, 198*n*23
Liu, Lydia, 115–16, 196*n*8
Locke, John, 101–2
Long, Charles, 12, 13, 109, 112
Lopez, Donald, 98
Lovell, Julia, 129
Lü Simian, 164–65*n*37

Macao, 9
Macartney, George, 112–13, 115,
123–24, 128–29, 197*n*12
McCutcheon, Russell, 43, 165*nn*42,
44
Mahmood, Saba, 190*n*14, 191*n*22
Malaysia, 4
Mandela, Nelson, ix, 21, 34, 147–48
Mao Zedong, 17, 33, 36, 91
Martin, W. A. P., 117–18, 126
Marx, Karl, 207*n*43
May Fourth period (1919), xiii
Meiji Constitution (Japan), 38, 39,
46, 54, 58, 180*n*48
Mexico, constitution, 50–52, 57
Milne, William C., 110, 118–19, 120,
196*n*3
Ming dynasty, 91
Ministry of Public Security (China),
82, 187*n*48
Mishra, Pankaj, 161*n*15